THE
DARING
DOZEN

OSPREY
PUBLISHING

12 SPECIAL
FORCES
LEGENDS OF
WORLD WAR II

THE
DARING
DOZEN

Gavin Mortimer

First published in Great Britain in 2012 by Osprey Publishing
Midland House, West Way, Botley, Oxford, OX2 0PH
44-02 23rd Street, Suite 219, Long Island City, NY, 11101, USA

E-mail; info@ospreypublishing.com

Osprey Publishing is part of the Osprey Group

A CIP catalogue record for this book is available from the British Library

ISBN: 978 1 84908 842 8
PDF e-book ISBN: 978 1 78096 454 6
e-pub ISBN: 978 1 78096 455 3

Page layout by Ken Vail Graphic Design, UK
Index by Sandra Shotter
Printed in China through Worldprint Ltd

12 13 14 15 16   10 9 8 7 6 5 4 3 2 1

Osprey Publishing is supporting the Woodland Trust, the UK's leading
woodland conservation charity, by funding the dedication of trees.

WWW.OSPREYPUBLISHING.COM

CONTENTS

INTRODUCTION

World War II was the first conflict of the modern age. While the Great War of 1914–18 had much in common with the American Civil War of the 1860s and the 1870 Franco-Prussian War, World War II benefited from the rapid technological advances of the 20th century. There were modern aircraft (even jet aircraft by the end of the war), powerful radio communications, light and rapid motorized transport, mobile armoured vehicles and new and destructive weapons, from Germany's flying bombs to sub-machine guns such as the Sten and the Schmeisser MP40.

Unfortunately many senior officers, irrespective of nationality, failed to grasp the potential of the innovations, or how soldiering might change in this new world. For them, war was still fought along the lines of the massed infantry attacks of World War I.

The man who did much to alter this moribund mindset, certainly on the Allies' side, was British Prime Minister Winston Churchill. After German paratroopers had jumped into the Low Countries in May 1940 with such devastating effect, Churchill knew the British must produce their own Special Forces to counter them and to inspire fear among the enemy. On 5 June 1940 he ordered his Chiefs of Staff to 'propose me measures for a vigorous, enterprising and ceaseless offensive'. What sprang from the memo was the first Commando unit.

Yet despite the enthusiastic endorsement of the Prime Minister, the formation of these special units was viewed with distaste by many senior officers within the British Army and, later, in the American high command. This cabal of Luddites considered Commando units as 'irregular' or 'renegades', an affront to civilized soldiering.

Fortunately there were enough younger officers with sufficient boldness and determination to pursue their vision of what modern warfare should entail. One of the most famous was a 25-year-old Scottish lieutenant called David Stirling, the founder of the Special Air Service; he called the superannuated staff officers 'freemasons of mediocrity'.[1]

In North Africa, in 1941, Stirling saw that the Desert War was ripe for irregular warfare; the vast, uninhabited regions of the Libyan Desert could be exploited by small units of highly trained, motivated and well-equipped men. It was a theatre made for hit-and-run raids, as was the war in the Pacific, the fighting in Burma and much of the conflict in Western Europe. And it wasn't just on land that the nature of warfare had irrevocable changed. At sea the mechanical and technological progress of the 20th century had opened up new opportunities for destruction. One of the first to recognize this was the brilliant Italian naval commander Junio Valerio Borghese, whose human torpedo unit caused grave trouble for the Royal Navy in 1941–42. The following year the British Special Boat Squadron wreaked havoc of its own kind on Axis forces using lightweight kayaks and small but powerful explosives.

The men featured in this book fully deserve to be called 'daring'. But there was more to the Daring Dozen – arguably the 12 most important British, American, German and Italian Special Forces leaders of the war – than just personal audacity. Between them, these men pioneered the concept of Special Forces, often struggling to establish and maintain their special units against opponents within their own armed forces. They were determined enough to press on despite what Stirling called the 'fossilized shits' among the top brass who stood in their way. They were courageous enough to put their theories into practice against the enemy, but above all they had the self-belief to persevere when – as in the early days they often did – their plans went awry.

They had something else in common, too. They shared a common attitude, a creed best encapsulated by one of World War II's finest guerrilla fighters, 'Mad Mike' Calvert:

> If we have got to fight in this world we prefer to fight where any skill or initiative counts a lot, and where even on the smallest scale it is possible to practice the art of war against a personal opponent rather than just being pawns in a very large operation.[2]

ANDERS LASSEN
SPECIAL BOAT SQUADRON

Lake Comacchio has been likened in terrain to the Fens, that marshy land leaking out from the Wash on England's east coast. Situated between Rimini to the south and Venice to the north on Italy's Adriatic coast, the shallow and fetid waters of Lake Comacchio are a haven to the myriad breeds of fish as well as a million and more mosquitoes. A thin strip of sand, known as 'the spit', separates the eastern edge of the lake from the Adriatic Sea and several small islands are dotted across the lake, which stretches for five miles at its widest point and 20 at its longest.

In the spring of 1945, as the Allies swept north through Italy, Lake Comacchio was still in the hands of the Germans, whose seasoned troops under the command of General Heinrich von Vietinghoff were well dug in among the reeds and alongside the causeways of the lake's shores. The eastern side was defended by the 162nd Turkoman Division with dozens of mines sewn into the thin strip of sand.

The lake posed a problem for the Allies, blocking as it did the progress north of Lieutenant-General Mark Clark's V Corps and of the British Eighth Army as they sought to overrun the retreating Germans. The solution was Operation *Grapeshot*. On 6 April a southern promontory was seized by the British 56th Division and 700 enemy soldiers fell into Allied hands as the first stage of the operation was accomplished successfully. Now Clark was nearly ready to launch the next stage of his assault on Comacchio, sending 2 Commando and 9 Commando to secure a bridgehead on the northern shore of the lake preparatory to the main attack.

Appreciating the hazardous nature of his task, the brigadier of the Commandos, Ronnie Tod, instructed the Special Boat Squadron (SBS) to create a diversionary raid on the German positions on the eastern shore in the hope of fooling the Germans into deploying troops from the north shore to repel the assault.

The man chosen to lead the diversionary raid was Major Anders Frederik Emil Victor Schau Lassen, or as he preferred to be called, 'Andy'. The 25-year-old Dane was a holder of a Military Cross and two Bars, and a reputation as the finest fighter in the Special Boat Squadron. His commanding officer, George Jellicoe, considered Lassen to have 'all the qualities of the buccaneering Viking – extraordinary courage, physical endurance, devil-may-care and keenness'.

In the wake of the raid on Comacchio Lassen would have something else – a Victoria Cross, the first for a member of the British Special Forces, but it would come at a terrible price.

✦ ✦ ✦ ✦

Lassen was born on 22 September 1920 to Emil, a captain in the Danish Lifeguards, and his wife, Suzanne, a writer whose children's books had earned her fame and fortune throughout Scandinavia. Lassen was born in the family home, a mansion near Mern in South Zealand that boasted nearly as many rooms as it did acres, an ideal stamping ground for a young boy to grow up in.

As boys Lassen and his younger brother Frants spent hours roaming the woods that encircled the family home, exploring as far as the coastline that lay two miles from the house, and learning how to fire a rifle and use a bow and arrow. Their parents did little to check their behaviour and Anders developed a reputation as a wild boy at school, charming but occasionally cruel in his humour. He felt imprisoned by the classroom, lessons bored him – except nature studies – and he resented having to wear a school uniform. One female childhood acquaintance of Lassen's described him thus many years later: 'I remember very clearly his incredible beauty, the looks of the perfect hero – but I was repelled by his aggressive, macho behaviour.'

Tall, athletic, blond and blue-eyed, Lassen conformed to the Danish stereotype, but there was far more to him than beauty. Though he had not done particularly well at school, Lassen was intelligent and forceful, and imbued with the self-confidence of the privileged. To no one's great surprise, Lassen declared peremptorily at the start of 1939 that he was going to sea to discover the world. He sailed from Denmark in June that year aboard the *Elenora Maersk*, a merchant tanker skippered by Captain P.V.J. Pedersen. Lassen was just 18, but a few months later he was the ringleader of a mutiny.

On 9 April 1940 the 16,500-ton *Elenora Maersk* was en route towards the Persian Gulf when news reached them of the German invasion of Denmark. Captain Pedersen said there was nothing they could do and ordered the oil tanker to continue on its way. But Lassen demanded they hold a council of

13

war among the ship's company, the outcome of which that the vessel sailed out of neutral waters to British-held Bahrain. 'Mutinied in the Persian Gulf,' wrote Lassen in his diary.

It took Lassen a further eight months to negotiate his passage to Britain, but on Christmas Eve 1940 he stepped ashore at Oban on the west coast of Scotland. From there he travelled to Newcastle, then on to London where, on 25 January 1941, he became one of the 467 Danes who would enlist in the British armed forces during the war. On joining the Free Danes, as they were then known, Lassen swore an oath of allegiance to King Christian X and also vowed 'to serve loyally whatever authority is working against the enemy that occupied my Fatherland'.

If Lassen had been expecting imminent action he was sadly disabused. The war in early 1941 was not going well for Britain, which stood alone against Nazi Germany in Europe and against Italy in Africa. The only glimpse of an enemy that Lassen saw in those first, dragging months were the Luftwaffe bombers overhead, targeting Britain's cities and docks.

Instead of seeing action, Lassen was ordered to Scotland to undergo weeks of training at Arisaig, a remote spot on the west coast of Scotland just south of the Isle of Skye. Lassen and 16 other Danes were put through a series of demanding physical and mental tests as their British instructors assessed their suitability for Special Operations Executive (SOE). One of the assessors was Brook Richards, a former naval commander who had joined the organization a few weeks earlier. He described Lassen as 'a remarkable young Dane' and remembered in particular his unshakeable conviction as to the outcome of the war. 'He started telling everybody how important it was for Denmark's future that Denmark should be fighting [for] the Allied cause because the Allies were going to win,' reflected Richards. 'For a 19-year-old (he was actually 20 at this time) this is really rather a remarkable vision.'[1]

However, for Lassen's fellow Danes, it was not his self-belief that most impressed them on Arisaig but rather his skill as a hunter. One of them recalled how they were on a map-reading exercise when Lassen spotted among the gorse two red deer 50 yards away. 'We knew he was a hunter and, seeing one animal move off, we left him to it,' one of the Danes later told Lassen's mother. 'He ran round the bushes, got up close and stabbed it with his knife.'[2]

Richards said that Lassen's SOE instructors were as 'astonished' as everyone else by his stealth and ruthlessness. The SOE knew they had someone special in their midst, but a man whose temperament was perhaps more suited to combat than espionage. In the late spring of 1941 Lassen and two other Danes were posted south, to Poole Harbour, where they were met by Major Gus March-Phillips and Captain Geoffrey Appleyard.

Lassen at once felt at home in the company of the pair, both of whom were inclined to care less about the finer points of army etiquette, while placing great emphasis on a man's self-discipline and initiative. There wasn't an HQ as such in Poole; instead March-Phillips based himself in the *Maid Honor*, a 70ft ketch that had been converted from a cup-winning racing yacht into a mini-warship with a 2-pounder cannon concealed beneath a dummy deckhouse and two heavy machine guns with a field of fire through the scuppers.

Lassen initially assumed the objective of *Maid Honor* Force, as the unit was known, would be to attack enemy shipping in the English Channel but March-Phillips soon explained the real nature of their role. Disguised as a fishing boat they were to sail 3,000 miles south and wage a war of piracy in the seas off West Africa.

Lassen was among the five men selected by March-Phillips for the mission. The commander had already confided to Appleyard his belief about Lassen, saying 'unless I'm very wrong that young man will go far', while Appleyard had described the Dane in a letter home as 'a splendid seaman and a crackshot with any kind of weapon ... he's good-hearted and good at everything – even [if] he does dislike discipline'.[3]

The *Maid Honor* left England on 12 August 1941 with March-Phillips at the helm and Lassen the only Dane on board. They arrived at Freetown after 41 days at sea, and after a refit and rest they departed on 10 October having loaded their vessel with four depth charges in case they should spot a German submarine.

For weeks the *Maid Honor* patrolled fruitlessly along the coasts of Sierra Leone and Portuguese Guinea before, on 15 January 1942, March-Phillips decided to attack a German tanker and an Italian liner at anchor on the Spanish colonial island of Fernando Po. The mission was a success with Lassen, as 'lithe as a cat', and his fellow raiders (reinforced by the crews of two British tugboats) capturing the two vessels without any bloodshed. The prizes were sailed to Lagos with the raiders feted upon their arrival. Congratulatory telegrams were sent from London and March-Phillips rewarded Lassen with a commission and a promise that there would be more adventure to come in 1942.

Upon their return to Britain the men of *Maid Honor* Force were renamed by SOE as the 'Small Scale Raiding Force' (SSRF) and based at Anderson Manor, a Jacobean house on the banks of the river Winterborne in Dorset. From the original nine men the SSRF grew to a strength of 55, and the new recruits underwent a punishing training regime similar to that which Lassen had experienced in Scotland a year earlier. They trained at sea, on Exmoor and on the firing ranges set up around the manor. Soon the men were all proficient with explosives, grenades and small arms, but Lassen believed the SSRF should also revive a weapon from Britain's martial past. Writing to the War Office, he stated: 'I have considerable experience in hunting with bow and arrow. I have shot everything from sparrows to stags, and although I have never attempted to shoot a man yet it is my opinion that the result would turn out just as well.'[4] Lassen added that such was his skill with a bow he could fire 15 arrows in a minute. The War Office rejected the idea, describing the weapon as 'inhuman'.[5]

It wasn't all work and no play, however, for the SSRF in Dorset. The nearby village of Winterborne Kingston boasted a fine country pub and in addition there was a plentiful supply of energetic Land Army girls working the surrounding fields. Lassen, often with Appleyard in tow, ploughed a rich furrow through their ranks. 'Apple and Andy were both good-looking, and Andy's broken English charmed the girls,' remembered Ian Warren, one of the SSRF. 'Whenever they turned up at a dance ... the rest of us knew we'd probably be going home by bus because Apple and Andy would walk off with the best girls.'[6]

One woman who was off-limits, however, even for Lassen, was the new wife of Gus March-Phillips, who was a frequent visitor at Anderson Manor in the early summer of 1942. She remembered Lassen as having 'straight yellow hair, a high complexion that was also sunburned, and a rather gappy grin because a lot of front teeth had been bashed out'. Majorie March-Phillips was able to spot that even among a force of young, aggressive and highly trained men Lassen stood out: 'Andy behaved impeccably while I was there but you could see he was pretty wild,' she said. 'One of the wildest of the lot.'

The SSRF was blooded in August 1942 when they launched a night raid on the Cotentin Peninsula, killing three German soldiers they found patrolling the coastline. In material terms the raid achieved little, but psychologically it reminded the Germans of Winston Churchill's taunt a few months earlier: 'there comes out of the sea from time to time a hand of steel which plucks the German sentries from their posts.'

The SSRF next struck at the Les Casquets lighthouse, eight miles north-west of Alderney, scaling an 80ft cliff and capturing the seven Germans in the lighthouse without a shot being fired. Lassen led a reconnaissance raid on the Channel Island of Burhou in early September and was then sent on leave while March-Phillips took a party to Normandy to test the enemy defences.

It was a good raid to miss. When Lassen returned from leave he was to learn that none of the 11-strong party had returned. Word later reached the SSRF that the men had had the misfortune to come ashore just as a German patrol was passing. Three men – including March-Phillips – were killed in the initial exchange of fire and the rest were all rounded up in the days and weeks that followed. One of the men, Graham Hayes, who had sailed with Lassen to West Africa, got as far as the France–Spain border, before being betrayed and subsequently executed by the Gestapo.

Hayes was a victim of Adolf Hitler's infamous Commando Order, issued in October 1942, that instructed that all captured Allied Commandos be treated as terrorists and shot. The Order was in retaliation for two incidents that had occurred earlier in the year. The first came after the failed raid on Dieppe in August 1942, when German troops learned of an Allied order to 'bind prisoners' captured on the raid. The second incident concerned a commando attack on the Channel Island of Sark on the night of 4 October – a raid in which Lassen was instrumental in incurring Hitler's wrath.

The Channel Islands had been in German hands for 16 months when Lassen, Appleyard and a combined 14-strong team from SSRF and 62 Commando landed on Sark with the intention of snaring several prisoners. With Appleyard leading the way – he had holidayed on the island pre-war – the raiders soon had five German engineers in their possession, while Lassen had disposed of the solitary sentry with his knife. None of the captives were manacled but their thumbs were tied together with cord and the string on their pyjama bottoms cut, so the prisoners had their hands occupied if they wished to protect their modesty. But on their way down to the beach the Germans made a bolt for freedom and four of the five were shot. The Germans were outraged when they found the four bodies at dawn and their Supreme Command declared that following the incident, 'all territorial and sabotage parties of the British and their confederates, who do not act like soldiers but like bandits, will be treated by the German troops as such and wherever they are encountered they will be ruthlessly wiped out in action.'[7]

This statement formed the basis for Hitler's subsequent Commando Order, though with once crucial difference – the Führer demanded the liquidation of all commandos, whether in action or once they were captured.

Lassen evidently had no remorse about what had happened on Sark. Once the remaining German prisoner had been turned over to the authorities, the raiding party returned to Anderson Manor and Ian Warren recalled being woken by an excited Lassen. 'He held his unwiped knife under my nose and said, "look, blood".' The Dane's conduct in the Channel Island raids resulted in a Military Cross, the citation praising Lassen's 'dash and reliability'.

By the end of 1942 the SSRF had served its purpose. Defences on the Channel Islands had been bolstered in light of the earlier raids (13,000 more mines were planted in the Sark beaches) and there seemed little point in raiding the French coast for the sake of a handful of prisoners. In addition, the war in the Mediterranean was reaching a critical stage and it was decided that a man of Lassen's ability should be sent somewhere where he could help inflict far greater damage on the enemy.

Lassen arrived in Cairo in February 1943, and was sent on a ski course at the British Army ski school at the Cedars of Lebanon. From there he went to Beirut, giving a lift to a young Special Air Service (SAS) officer called Stephen Hastings. Hastings had spent weeks operating deep in the desert behind German lines, but for the first time he felt real fear as Lassen negotiated the precipitous track that led down from the ski school. 'I have never been more terrified and well understood later how Andy got so many medals,' reflected Hastings. 'We hurtled down to sea level on two wheels. Fear was simply left out of his disposition.'[8]

Lassen had arrived in Egypt just as the SAS was being re-formed. The regiment's founder, David Stirling, had been captured in January 1943 just as the Desert War was reaching its successful denouement. There was no longer a role for the SAS in North Africa and so the regiment was split in two, with half forming the Special Raiding Squadron (SRS) under Major Blair 'Paddy' Mayne, and the other half designated the Special Boat Squadron with Captain the Rt Hon George, Earl Jellicoe as their CO.

Jellicoe was the son of the famous admiral who had led the British fleet at the battle of Jutland in 1916, but his own speciality lay in guerrilla warfare. Throughout 1942 Jellicoe had led a series of audacious raids against Axis targets in both Libya and Crete under the auspices of the Special Boat Section. This had in fact been the seaborne wing of the SAS but in 1943 they were reconstituted as the Special Boat Squadron (SBS) and their 55-strong ranks swelled to include the 250 officers and men from the SAS.

Their base was at Athlit and the training was ferocious. One recruit, R.A.C. Summers, recalled that their PT instructors were a 'mad sadistic bunch' who took them out on night marches carrying packs that became progressively heavier as the weeks went by. Captain David Sutherland recalled that 'Lassen out marched us all, he had a quite extraordinary capacity for marching ... it so happened that he was far better than all of us at all the martial arts – shooting, thinking tactically, physical endurance, bravery. He really outdid everyone.'[9]

The only aspect of the SBS training that troubled Lassen was the parachute jump. He had first learned how to parachute as part of his SSRF training in England and the experience left him unsettled; on the ground Lassen felt in control of his own fate but in the air, jumping from an aircraft or a tethered balloon, he was at the mercy of a silk canopy.

As the men trained Jellicoe, organized the SBS into three detachments, each one comprised of 70 men and seven officers. L Detachment was put under the command of Captain Tommy Langton, while Fitzroy Maclean took charge of M Detachment (though Ian Lapraik assumed command when Maclean was recalled to London), and Sutherland was given command of S Squadron with Lassen as one of his officers.

The culmination of the SBS training coincided with the next stage of the war in the Mediterranean – the invasion of Sicily and Italy, what Churchill described as the 'soft underbelly of Europe'. Before the main invasion could take place the SBS was tasked with carrying out a series of reconnaissance raids on Crete, Sardinia and Sicily. S Squadron was ordered to Crete on the night of 22 June to attack the airfields of Heraklion, Kastelli and Tymbaki and destroy as many enemy aircraft as possible.

The SBS party came ashore without problem and split up, but the two sections whose targets were Heraklion and Tymbaki airfields soon discovered that neither was in use. Lassen's patrol, however, was in luck at Kastelli, with a fleet of aircraft on the airfield including eight Stuka dive-bombers and five Ju 88 bombers. Lassen took care of the sentry with his knife while his comrades began planting bombs on the aircraft. But another guard appeared, and Lassen had no choice but to shoot him. The shot brought the airfield's defenders running out of their billet and the SBS melted into the darkness. Half an hour later Lassen returned with Corporal Ray Jones, but as they crept onto the airfield they were spotted. What ensued was described in the citation for Lassen's second Military Cross:

> The enemy then rushed reinforcements from the eastern side of the aerodrome and, forming a semi-circle, drove the two attackers into the middle of an anti-aircraft battery where they were fired upon heavily from three sides. This danger was ignored and bombs were placed on a caterpillar tractor which was destroyed. The increasing numbers of enemy in that area finally forced the party to withdraw.

Despite the faulty intelligence on Crete, Sutherland's men destroyed several aircraft, killed a number of Germans and blew up a 50,000-gallon petrol dump at Peza, and all for the loss of one man. For his part Lassen had shown great courage and boldness in returning to Kastelli for a second crack at the airfield but one of the soldiers on the raid, Les Nicholson, said it was the act of a 'stupidly brave' man.

As was the case with Paddy Mayne, arguably the only other member of the wartime British Special Forces whose martial prowess was equal to the Dane's, Lassen was imbued with exceptional courage. But whereas Mayne was a supremely calculating operator, blessed with the gift of being able to assess a risk to any given action in the blink of an eye, Lassen relied more on luck and his monumental self-confidence to see him through. Arthur Walter, a chaplain to the Parachute Regiment, came to know Lassen later in the war and reflected that: 'Without denigrating his bravery, I think he was one of those people who act without foreseeing the consequences. Something had to be done so they go out and do it.'[10]

There was another marked difference between Paddy Mayne and Anders Lassen, and that concerned appearance. Mayne could be 'regimental' when the mood took him, bawling out a soldier if his beret was half an inch astray. But Lassen rarely cared about his appearance, leading even his mother to describe it as 'haphazard and careless'. Having been awarded a Bar to his Military Cross, Lassen was entitled to wear two small rosettes on his medal ribbon. Instead he cut two circles from a tobacco tin and had a friend sew them to the ribbon. 'Rough and ready, maybe,' said Lassen, 'but according to regulations, properly dressed!'

The month after the raid on Crete, the Allies invaded Sicily and, in September 1943, they crossed the Strait of Messina into Italy. The armistice between Italy and the Allies was announced on 8 September and within days British forces were sweeping through the Aegean, taking possession from the Italians of Dodecanese islands such as Leros, Samos, Kos, Icaria and Simi. A force of SBS landed on the latter on 17 September 1943, Lassen among them, and for three weeks they were left alone to enjoy the sea and sun in the company of the small and nervous Italian garrison. But the German High Command was determined to wrest control of the islands back from the British, and particularly those with airstrips that played an important role in safeguarding German interests in the Balkans. On 7 October a force of 120 Germans landed on Simi.

Lassen was suffering from dysentery and a scalded leg when the Germans came ashore but he rose from his sickbed and joined in the heavy fighting in the ramshackle old town of Simi. For his conduct throughout the fight, Lassen was awarded a second Bar to his Military Cross, the citation describing how:

> The heavy repulse of the Germans from Simi on 7 Oct 1943 was due in no small measure to his inspiration and leadership on the one hand: and the highest personal example on the other. He himself crippled with a badly burned leg and internal trouble, stalked and killed at least three Germans at the closest range. At that time the Italians were wavering and I attribute their recovery as due to the personal example and initiative of this officer ... he himself led the Italian counter attack which finally drove the Germans back to their caiques [fishing boats] with the loss of 16 killed, 35 wounded and 7 prisoners.

In contrast, the SBS lost only one man in fighting off the attempted invasion. The next day the Germans adopted a new tactic – air attack. Wave after wave of Stuka dive-bombers swooped down on the town, sirens shrieking, to drop their bombs from as low as 100ft. It was a terrifying experience for the defenders. 'They Stuka-ed us to bloody death,' recalled Doug Wright, a former Guardsman who had volunteered for the SAS in late 1942. 'The noise they made was horrible, that's what scared you most, and they came in so low we could see the pilots looking at us. It was the only time I ever saw Andy looking a little frightened.'[11]

Miraculously only one SBS soldier was killed during the air assault (in addition to the one fatality from the previous day's street fighting) but on 12 October the SBS withdrew from Simi. Over the course of the next few weeks a similar situation unfolded across the Aegean as the Germans retook the islands one by one: Kos, Leros and then Samos at the end of November – where Lassen and his SBS comrades helped in the evacuation of 5,000 civilians and soldiers. It brought down the curtain on a period of intense frustration for Lassen and the SBS in general. Although trained as guerrilla fighters, in the Dodecanese campaign that autumn the SBS had been serving as glorified garrison troops.

Lassen's health was also troubling him and he spent much of December 1943 in the 8th General hospital in Alexandria recovering from dysentery and his scalded leg. When he was discharged from hospital in January 1944, Lassen, now promoted to captain, rejoined the SBS and sailed on the *Tewfik* to a coastal base in neutral Turkey. The *Tewfik* was a 180-ton caique and the command ship from which small SBS parties embarked to raid German targets in the Aegean throughout the early spring of 1944. One of the men, John Lodwick, described life on board the *Tewfik* in his 1947 book *The Filibusters*:

> Picture the deep, indented Gulf of Cos, with uninhabited shores and sullen, fir-covered mountains rising abruptly from the water's edge … entering this bay you would at first judge it to be empty. Closer inspection would show you a large, squat, ugly schooner lying close to one shore, with her gangplank down and a horde of dories, folboats [collapsible canoes], rubber dinghies and rafts nuzzling one flank like kittens about the teats of their mother … in her vast stern a naked figure is crouching, and whittling at something with a knife. It is Lassen, and he is making a bow with which to shoot pigs. Down below, in the murky cabin at the foot of the steep companionway, David Sutherland, pipe in mouth, is writing an operational order. Beside him are rum bottles, magnums of champagne from Nisiros reserved for special occasions.[12]

Idyllic it might have appeared, but life for the SBS in the Gulf of Kos was punctuated by frequent raids against German-held islands, and none was more violent than that of Lassen's visit to Santorini, the southernmost island of the Cyclades. It became known as 'Lassen's Bloodbath' and a detailed account was written of the raid in its aftermath (according to David Sutherland, although it was signed by Lassen, it was penned by another member of the raiding party).

Lassen split his force into two patrols, 'P' and 'Z', the former led by himself and comprising nine men in total, and the other consisting of nine men under Lieutenant Keith Balsillie. The two patrols came ashore at Santorini in the early hours of 23 April 1944, and spent the daylight hours lying up in a cave overlooking the inland village of Vourvoulos. At nightfall Lassen ordered everyone to take two Benzedrine pills, known colloquially to British troops as 'stay-awake pills', and shortly before midnight the raiders moved off.

Balsillie's target was the wireless station at Imerovigli, while Lassen and his men headed a mile south to Thira where the main German garrison was billeted on the first floor of a bank. Lassen's information indicated there were 38 Italians and ten Germans in the bank, but this turned out to be false as the operational report noted: 'There were less than 35 men in the billet. We succeeded in getting the main force into the billet unobserved, in spite of barking dogs and sentries. The living quarters comprised twelve rooms.'

Lassen cleared the rooms one by one, Sergeant Jack Nicholson kicking in the door so that the Dane could throw in a pair of grenades. The second after the grenades exploded, the sergeant swept the room with machine-gun fire before Lassen entered the room to dispatch any survivors with his pistol. It was a bloody business, and at the end of it more than 30 of the enemy lay dead. 'That was the only time I was in action side-by-side with Lassen and it's one of the reasons why I'm trying to forget the war,' said Nicholson in 1987 when interviewed by Mike Langley for Lassen's biography. 'It's no fun throwing grenades into rooms and shooting sleeping men. That garrison could have been captured.'

But for Lassen the war, and particularly killing Germans, did seem to be fun. Everyone who ever served with him – even experienced soldiers who had accounted for numerous Germans themselves – were struck by the depth of Lassen's hatred for the enemy. 'He was a killer and he really hated Germans,' said Doug Wright, who himself was reputed to have killed nine Germans with his bare hands during the war. 'He liked to kill them most with his knife.'[13]

Wright believed Lassen's attitude to the Germans was directly due to their occupation of Denmark – a view not shared by Porter Jarrell, an American who served with Lassen in the Aegean campaign as a medical orderly. He saw a deterioration in Lassen as the war progressed. 'At the beginning he was not a killer,' said Jarrell, 'but once the action started he was out to kill. Basically he was a sensitive, decent person whom the war made tough.'[14]

Lassen and his men arrived back at the Gulf of Kos on 29 April. Though they had lost two men on the Santorini raid, the SBS had killed more than 40 of the enemy and brought back 19 prisoners (eight of which were taken during Balsillie's successful attack on the wireless station). The result of the raid on Santorini was the arrival in the Aegean of an additional 4,000 German troops to bolster the islands' defences. At a time when the Germans were trying to stem the inexorable advance of the Allies in Italy, these were resources the German High Command could ill afford to spare. But their arrival persuaded the SBS it was time to move on; as Lassen put it: 'You can do some of it, part of the time, for quite a while, but you can't do all of it all the time for very long.'[15]

By the middle of August 1944 the SBS had left the Special Forces role in the Aegean theatre to the Greek Sacred Squadron and were establishing a base in Italy in readiness to attack targets in Yugoslavia. Already in the Balkans was the Long Range Desert Group (LRDG), which was proving as effective a reconnaissance force in the rugged hills of Yugoslavia as they had been in the immense deserts of North Africa. A five-man LRDG patrol had discovered a large railway bridge close to Karasovici and the task of destroying it fell to Lassen. He set out with 41 men on the night of 27 August, and when he returned to the SBS base over a week later he made a verbal report to Jellicoe that purportedly ran: 'We landed, we reached the bridge, we destroyed it.' When Jellicoe asked for a bit more detail, Lassen shrugged and said, 'What else is there to say?'[16]

In fact there was a lot more to say. From the moment the SBS saboteurs landed just north of the Yugoslav–Albanian border, they were in the midst of a heavy enemy presence – not just Germans but also their notoriously savage Croat allies, known as the Ustachi. Tales of their brutality towards captured Allied personnel were legend, but Lassen's men avoided contact with the enemy and at 2300hrs on 30 August two of the bridge's spans were blown. 'The job itself was easy,' remembers Doug Wright. 'There were about 12 of us carrying a hundredweight of explosive each so we had no trouble blowing it. The problem was how to get back to the RV afterwards.'[17]

From the landing point, Lassen and his men headed north up the valley, covering ten miles in the hours before dawn. They made contact with some friendly partisans, remembered Wright, 'and when day broke the partisan girls gave us a good feed, a cauldron of stew, and then we all got our heads down.' The plan was to move off at nightfall, but before they could depart their mountain position was attacked. 'There were hundreds of them,' said

Wright, 'and there was no point in standing and fighting against 400 so we split up into twos and made for the RV. But they were a vicious lot the Ustachi and we heard later that the partisan girls were caught and chopped into bits.'[18]

After operations in Yugoslavia, the SBS was ordered back to Greece in late September, where the German hold was being weakened on an almost daily basis. With Romania and Bulgaria now out of the war, the Third Reich was being squeezed on two fronts and German troops in Greece were being withdrawn to defend the Fatherland. Welcome as the news was in London, Prime Minister Winston Churchill was desperate to keep Greece out of Stalin's hands; on 13 October 1944 Athens was liberated by British troops. Lassen, meanwhile, recently promoted to major and given command of M Squadron, was sailing from Volos in the east to Salonika in the north. His 50-strong force disembarked at the Potidia Canal, 30 miles south of the city, in a region fraught with tension; not only were there still some Germans in the throes of evacuating Salonika, but the Greek People's Liberation Army (ELAS) were claiming the area as their own and starting to prepare for the struggle for power in post-war Greece. None of this, however, concerned Lassen, who made it clear to the ELAS leaders that he would not hesitate to use force if his passage to Salonika was impeded.

With 9,000 British troops steaming towards Salonika, Lassen wanted to be the first Allied soldier to enter the city, even though Greek intelligence warned that the Germans had at least two tanks and some artillery among their defences as Wehrmacht engineers began demolishing the city's breakwater. Commandeering four local fire engines, Lassen ordered his men on board and off they raced towards the city centre. 'It was great,' recalled Doug Wright. 'The welcome we received was unbelievable and there were women everywhere wanting to kiss us!'[19]

The western half of the city was free of Germans, but the Greeks told the SBS that the enemy was still in the eastern side, preparing to withdraw in a large convoy. Lassen ordered his men to dismount from the engines and divided them into two patrols, one under his command and the other led by Lieutenant James Henshaw. 'I was in Henshaw's patrol,' recalled Wright, 'and we took a farm boy with us who knew where the minefields were. We got round the back of them [the Germans] and opened fire. I must have fired a dozen magazines of Bren gun as they were stood there. When they started throwing flares up, we pulled out leaving behind a lot of dead and wounded.'[20]

The surviving Germans hastily fled Salonika and a subsequent British Intelligence report said of the SBS action: 'But for Lassen and his band, Salonika would not have been evacuated as soon as the 30th October 1944. The town would have suffered greater destruction. His solitary jeep and few troops were seen everywhere; behind the enemy's lines, with E.L.A.S. and in the mountains. Their numbers and strength were magnified into many hundreds.'

Lassen next took his men to Athens for a spot of rest and recuperation, where for three weeks they partied hard on drink and women. On one occasion a jealous husband came looking for Lassen with a pistol, but fortunately for the Greek his quarry had already fled from the scene. After Athens Lassen left for Crete as commander of a Special Forces unit tasked to maintain order on the island. As well as the thousands of German prisoners to marshal, there were also rival Greek factions among the islanders whose politics made them mortal enemies. For Lassen it was an opportunity for more carousing and he became a frequent visitor to the island's brothels and taverns. When David Sutherland came to visit Lassen at Christmas he was treated to 'the most extraordinary party ... a lot was drunk. He was a great example of how to live up to the limits in all respects.'

Sutherland had recently assumed command of the SBS following Jellicoe's promotion and appointment to a Staff College in Haifa, but at the start of 1945 he was unsure of the squadron's future role. Some patrols were sent to Yugoslavia to help clear the Croatian coastline of stubborn German outposts, but it wasn't until the early spring that Sutherland received orders to move back into Italy.

Lassen arrived at Lake Comacchio in April 1945, having spent a few days on leave in Rome with a pretty English WAAF girl. Opinions vary on his state of mind. Some comrades said he was his usual self, eager to kill more Germans after several months of inactivity, while others remembered him tired and listless, as if he was reaching the end of his tether after nearly four years of fighting. In addition, his pet dog had not come north with him from their base in Monopoli, and two weeks earlier James Henshaw had been killed while attempting to blow a bridge that linked the islands of Cherso and Lussin. Henshaw was a good friend of Lassen's, and perhaps his death, coming so near the end of the war, made the Dane more aware of his own mortality. His spirits would hardly have been improved by his new posting. The landscape around Comacchio is flat and lifeless, and its waters a putrid haven for mosquitoes.

Lake Comacchio was also shallow, in some places only between 6in and 3ft deep. In order for 9 and 62 Commandos to cross the lake and establish a bridgehead for V Corps, they required a channel deep enough to take their Goatley floats – engineless vessels that could each accommodate ten men and their equipment. The first task for Lassen and his SBS men was to reconnoiter a passage across the lake.

One of the SBS men was Corporal Ken Smith. 'We used to go out each night in our canoes,' he recalled. 'Now on the lake, on the right [eastern shore] was the spit, a narrow neck of land that separated the lake from the sea and that was where the Germans had some machine gun battalions.' It required a steady nerve and a lot of skill with the paddle for a canoeist to negotiate his way unseen across the shallow waters. 'As you were paddling what we had to be careful about was the phosphorous on the paddle,' recalled Smith. 'So we had to make long gliding strokes to make as little noise and phosphorous as possible.'[21]

The SBS patrols searched the lake only at night and at first light they took cover, dismantling their canoes and concealing them among the reeds on the marshes, where they lay waiting for darkness. 'I remember the mossies at dawn would come over and they raised an almighty noise, like bombers going overhead,' said Smith. 'We had mossie cream and at dusk they would come over again and settle on us. At dark we would paddle off again at the north shore.'[22]

When a channel deep enough (2ft) to facilitate a crossing of the lake was found, the SBS were then instructed to launch the diversionary raid against the Germans' positions on the eastern shore, the three-mile-long spit that separated the lake from the Adriatic. Ken Smith recalled the conversation between Brigadier Ronnie Tod of the commandos and Lassen: 'We sat round in a small circle and the brigadier said to Lassen "I want you to spread your chaps out tonight, right along the front, get ashore, and make as much commotion to give an impression of a big landing." Lassen kept interrupting him: "But I can take Comacchio." The brigadier said "I don't want you to, just spread your chaps out."[23]

Lassen's belief that he could take Comacchio with 50 men was either bravado or a sign that he was becoming, in the parlance of the time, 'bomb happy' after four years of almost constant action. Ranged against him were hundreds of Germans, well entrenched in positions affording them an excellent field of fire.

Among the 50 men in Lassen's squadron were several veterans of the Dodecanese campaign. At least one, Freddie Crouch, believed that they were being sacrificed so that the commandos could establish their bridgehead on the north shore. Crouch had a premonition of his own death, and one of his comrades, Les Stephenson, was also uneasy with the plan because there 'had been no proper reconnaissance' on account of the impossibility of getting close enough to scout the enemy positions without being seen.

Lassen split his small force into three patrols. His own patrol would be first onto the spit while a section under the command of Lieutenant Turnbull would then land a little further north. Meanwhile a third patrol led by New Zealand's Lieutenant Dion Stellin, nicknamed 'Stud' on account of his success with the ladies, would discharge numerous thunderflashes and other explosive charges to fool the enemy into believing the main assault was underway.

The SBS had to endure an excruciating delay to their mission as they waited for the commandos to drag their landing craft across the mud to the channels. Everyone was tense. Then, at 0430hrs on 9 April, Lassen and his patrol pushed off in their canoes. Ken Smith followed in Turnbull's patrol a short while later. 'We lined up in our canoes and made for the shore,' remembered Smith. 'Lassen was away to the right and met land before us and he managed to get ashore.'[24]

But already Lassen's patrol had encountered problems in disembarking from their canoes. The mud that bordered the spit was thick, glutinous and treacherous, and Freddie Crouch got stuck as he tried to get ashore. 'He began sinking but would not call for help because that would give away our positions,' remembered Trooper Fred Green, who watched in horror as Crouch vanished beneath the mud.[25]

Already one man down, Lassen told Green to accompany him down the spit while the rest of the patrol followed a few yards behind. Green could speak Italian and Lassen's hope was that the Turkomans would be fooled into thinking they were local fishermen about to embark on a day's work. The plan failed, and a Spandau machine gun began firing from a pillbox. However, the pillboxes housing the defenders were not the imposing hexagonal concrete structures found along the French coast; rather, they were small bunkers made of stone and earth.

Lassen told Green to take cover. Then, removing a grenade from his battledress, Lassen charged the pillbox and destroyed it. A second machine gun opened fire, so Lassen continued down the spit, rallying his men with a cry of: 'Come on! Forward, you bastards. Get on, get forward!'

As Lassen wiped out the second pillbox, his patrol dashed towards him along the spit, but more machine guns began firing and men started to fall. Les Stephenson caught up with Lassen and was ordered by his commander to hand over his grenades. These Lassen used to attack a third pillbox, whereupon a cry was heard of '*Kamerad!*'. Stephenson recalled later: 'He told the rest of us to stay put while he went across in the darkness. As he neared the pillbox there was a burst of machine-gun fire and then silence.'

While the rest of the patrol dealt with the occupants of the third pillbox, Stephenson attended to Lassen. He had been shot in the lower chest and he knew he was dying. 'It's been a poor show,' he told Stephenson. 'Don't go any further with it. Get the others out.' Lassen died a few minutes later.[26]

Of Lassen's 17-strong patrol, four were killed attacking the spit and another four suffered serious wounds. But the commandos had established their bridgehead. Ken Smith's patrol had not even got ashore before they were spotted and fired upon. 'I turned turtle and all we could do was swim back to our mud flat,' he recalled. 'Then they [Lassen's patrol] came in in ones and twos, and someone said, "Lassen's had it."'[27]

Colonel David Sutherland, the SBS commander, was thunderstruck by Lassen's death but when he heard the exact details he had no doubt the Dane deserved a Victoria Cross. The medal was presented by King George VI to

Lassen's parents at Buckingham Palace in December 1945, and the citation ended by stating:

> By his magnificent leadership and complete disregard for his personal safety, Major Lassen had, in the face of overwhelming superiority, achieved his objectives. Three positions were wiped out, accounting for six machine guns, killing eight and wounding others of the enemy and two prisoners were taken. The high sense of devotion to duty and the esteem in which he was held by the men he led, added to his own magnificent courage, enabled Major Lassen to carry out all the tasks he had been given with complete success.

✦ ✦ ✦ ✦

Unlike the other men featured in this book, Lassen was neither a great strategist nor a great tactician. The war's 'bigger picture' didn't really concern him; he was more interested in the here and now. He was a man of action, as much a born fighter as Paddy Mayne. Lassen was also not a natural leader of men in the way that David Stirling, Friedrich August von der Heydte or Evans Carlson were. Yet few soldiers who fought in World War II were as respected and admired by their men as Anders Lassen. He was an officer who led by example, whose courage and boldness inspired his men and struck fear into the enemy. Small wonder that the Germans were purported to have put a price on the head of 'that damned Dane'.

Perhaps the most telling assessment of Lassen's contribution to Britain's Special Forces was that of David Sutherland, his former commander. At a ceremony in Copenhagen in 1987 to celebrate the unveiling of a new bust to Lassen, Sutherland gave this address to the assembled crowd:

> Anders caused more damage and discomfort to the enemy over five years of war than any other man of his rank and age ... we know now that the sustained SBS attacks in the Aegean early in 1944, before D-Day, gave the impression that a second front would be opened in the Balkans. In April, Anders' patrol eliminated the entire army garrison on

Santorini. The German High Command reacted by reinforcing their Aegean positions. These troops stayed in place for the rest of the war when they could have been used elsewhere. Anders saved Salonika from demolition by the retreating Germans through the timely arrival of his squadron. In response to his ferocious attack at Comacchio on this day 42 years ago ... the Germans moved troops towards the Adriatic coast allowing the British Eighth Army to break out through the Argenta Gap shortly afterwards.[28]

DAVID STIRLING

SPECIAL AIR SERVICE

In the summer of 1939 a tall, slim young Scot was pursuing his dream of becoming the first man to climb Mount Everest. He had chosen as his training ground the Rocky Mountains of America. Moving south on horseback through Colorado, tackling the ranges in Park, Gore and Sawatch, 23-year-old David Stirling interrupted his ride south to pay a visit to Las Vegas to win some money on the gaming tables. That done, he continued on towards the Rio Grande, arriving in early September, where he heard the news that Britain and Germany were once again at war.

Stirling, a member of the Scots Guards Supplementary Reserve, was soon heading back to Britain, returning first-class by air and presenting himself at the regimental depot in Pirbright, Surrey. It was a flight that would lead to the formation of one of the world's most famous Special Forces units.

✦ ✦ ✦ ✦

The 6ft 6in Stirling was not one of life's natural Guards officers. Born into an aristocratic family in November 1915, there was a slight Bohemian side to his character (he had studied art in Paris in the 1930s) that didn't sit well with the drill sergeants. On one occasion Stirling was reprimanded for the state of his rifle. 'Stirling, it's bloody filthy. There must be a bloody clown on the end of this rifle,' exclaimed the sergeant. 'Yes, sergeant,' agreed Stirling, 'but not at my end.'[1]

Neither did Stirling endear himself to those senior officers whose job it was to lecture their young protégées on the art of war. In Stirling's view, most of them held opinions that had changed little since World War I and were 'quite irrelevant to tackling the Hun', and none of them were interested in dialogue or the exchange of views. It was a pupil/master relationship that Stirling deplored and his response was to spend an increasingly large amount of his time drinking and gambling in London's clubs.

When Stirling eventually left Pirbright he was described by his instructors as an 'irresponsible and unremarkable soldier', a description with which he would not have demurred. 'I think I just wanted to be off to join the war,' Stirling told his biographer, Alan Hoe, in the late 1980s. 'I didn't mind where.'[2]

In January 1940 it appeared that Stirling was going to get his wish, for the British government had decided to come to the aid of Finland in their 'Winter War' against the invading Russians. The 5th Battalion Scots Guards were sent on a mountain warfare course in the French Alps and Stirling, already a skilled skier, was promoted to instructor. The battalion returned to Britain dubbed the 'Snowballers', but the mission to Finland never materialized because of objections raised by Sweden and Norway.

Back in his favourite London club, White's, in the early summer of 1940, Stirling learned that volunteers were wanted for a special service force. Unsure of the exact nature of the force, Stirling nonetheless applied in the hope it might break the monotony of his own 'phoney war'. In fact what Stirling had joined was the nascent Commandos, raised on the orders of Prime Minister Winston Churchill himself.

Stirling took an instant shine to his new unit. The commanding officer of 8 Commando (there were five commando units in total) was Robert Laycock and the instructors were men whose ideas on how modern warfare should be conducted were similar to Stirling's.

Laycock's 8 Commando was sent to the Isle of Arran off the west coast of Scotland to undergo training and Stirling, now a lieutenant, found himself a section commander in 3 Troop under the command of Major Dermot Daley. The youngest man in the section was Guardsman Johnny Cooper, who had just turned 18. 'Because of his height and his quiet self-confidence he could appear quite intimidating but he wasn't a bawling leader,' recalled Cooper. 'This quietly spoken young lieutenant commanded far more respect and confidence with his ability to put soldiers at their ease and his willingness to help.'[3]

The training on Arran challenged the commandos physically and mentally. As well as the emphasis on physical fitness, they were schooled in explosives, unarmed combat, navigation and weapons. The instructors wanted the men to become self-sufficient and initiative was encouraged; it was the opposite of everything that had been drilled into Stirling at Pirbright.

For a man who had grown up on the family estate of Keir in the wilds of central Scotland, Stirling thrived on Arran and demonstrated an uncanny ability for such a gangly man to move noiselessly across the countryside.

'There was a tremendous air of expectancy,' Stirling said later. 'We didn't know where we were to be deployed or when, but we knew damned well that we were going to be good … the constant exercises, broken by short periods of equally hard play, kept one pretty well occupied.'[4]

In January 1941 it was decided to send three of the five commando units to the Middle East. The reason behind the decision was simple: the Special Forces had been raised to operate in conjunction with a large-scale offensive but in 1941 the British Army was not in a position to launch such a strike in Europe. But in the Middle East it could, particularly against Italy's lines of communications along the North Africa coast and against their lightly defended islands in the Mediterranean.

In February 1941, 7, 8 and 11 Commandos sailed from Scotland for the Middle East. On board one of the troop ships were Stirling and two other notable officers of 8 Commando, the novelist and satirist Evelyn Waugh and Randolph Churchill, son of the Prime Minister. The trio whiled away the voyage playing cards, drinking pink gins, and doing their utmost to escape the signalling courses and physical training organized by their commanding officer.

The Commandos arrived in Egypt on 11 March and were soon in camp in Geneifa near the Great Bitter Lakes, under inspection from General Archibald Wavell, Commander-in-Chief Middle East Forces. He told them that they were now to be known as 'Layforce' under the command of Lieutenant-Colonel Laycock.

The commando units separated, and while 7 Commando took part in a botched raid on the Libyan port of Bardia and 11 Commando were posted to Cyprus (and then attacked Vichy French forces in Syria), 8 Commando spent their time in more mundane pastimes. There were daily route marches into the hills, lessons in map reading and fatigue duties such as mending fences blown down by the frequent sand storms. In what free time they had the men went swimming in the Suez Canal.

On 9 April, 8 Commando boarded a troop ship and sailed for Port Said from where they entrained to Alexandria, Egypt's second-largest city. They were not there long before being ordered to move once more, to Cairo, where they were allowed to spend a day at the race track. Stirling lost a lot of money on the horses but some of his men had better luck and later blew their winnings in the city's many bars.

By early May Stirling and his men had still seen no action. They idled away their time on the banks of the Suez Canal and on 3 May Evelyn Waugh, Layforce's Intelligence Officer, wrote in the brigade war diary: 'Repeated cancellations and postponements of LAYFORCE is engendering an attitude of cynicism in all ranks.' As to prove his point, Waugh noted some graffiti found scrawled on the *Glengyle*, one of their troop ships: 'Never in the whole history of human endeavour have so few been buggered about by so many.'

Not long afterwards 8 Commando sailed to Mersa Matruh, an Egyptian port approximately 150 miles from the border with Libya. They began practising for a raid on a German airfield 30 miles from Tobruk but the mission was then scrubbed because of bad weather. The sense of frustration was palpable and it was almost too much to bear for David Stirling, but at least he had a haven to which he could escape when the opportunity presented itself – his brother's flat in Cairo.

Peter Stirling was a secretary at the British Embassy in the city who was in the habit of throwing wild and raucous parties for the expatriate community. David was present whenever possible and after one particular shindig discovered the elixir of life. 'I chanced, after a somewhat vigorous party, to be in the company of a charming young nurse from the Scottish Hospital,' recounted Stirling in his biography. 'And I must have bemoaned the fact that the next day was going to be quite intolerable because of the inevitable hangover. She told me to pop around to the hospital the next morning and ask for her. This I did and was introduced to the magical effects of taking a couple of deep snifters from the pure oxygen bottle. Wonderful. The hangover vanished in seconds.'[5]

In June 1941 Middle East HQ (MEHQ) informed Laycock that his force of commandos was being disbanded and its men either returned to their original unit or used as replacements for undermanned regiments in North Africa. The decision by MEHQ had been prompted by two factors: first, Layforce had taken heavy casualties during operations in Syria, Crete and Bardia. There just weren't enough men to replenish their diminished ranks, particularly as the British were launching a large offensive against Rommel's

Afrika Korps called Operation *Battleaxe*. Secondly, British intelligence reported that since Layforce had begun raiding targets along the Mediterranean coasts, Axis forces had strengthened their defences and they were now largely immune to the type of raids envisioned by the British commandos.

While Laycock wrote to Major-General Arthur Smith, Chief of the General Staff, Middle East Forces, expressing his 'bitter disappointment at witnessing the disbandment of a force on which they had set their hearts', Stirling wrote to his family in Scotland to tell them: 'The Commandos are no more. I am not sure what I shall do now but I am attempting and may succeed in establishing a permanent parachute unit. It would be on a small scale but would be more amusing than any other form of soldiering.'[6]

Dismayed as he was by the breakup of Layforce, Stirling was far from despondent. He had seen in 8 Commando the potential capability of small bands of highly-trained soldiers, but he had also glimpsed their weaknesses. So had Jock Lewes, a puritanical officer in the Welsh Guards, whose inspiration for a force of paratroopers came from the recent history of Crete and what the German Fallschirmjäger had achieved in capturing the island from the Allies in May 1941.

Lewes and Stirling were granted permission to intercept a consignment of parachutes destined for India and experiment with their idea of forming an airborne unit. Mick D'Arcy of the Irish Guards accompanied Lewes and Stirling as they collected the parachutes from an RAF officer at a base near Fuka. 'He showed us the parachutes we were to use,' recalled D'Arcy, who wrote a report on the first parachute exercise by British troops in North Africa:

From the log books we saw that the last periodical examination had been omitted but Lt Lewes decided that they were OK. Next along with Lt Stirling and Sgt Stone who were hoping to do a job in Syria, we made a trial flight. The plane used was a Vickers 'Valencia'. We threw out a dummy made from sandbags and tent poles. The parachute opened OK but the tent poles were smashed on landing. Afterwards we tried a 10ft jump from the top of the plane and then a little parachute control.

The following afternoon we flew inland in the Valencia which was used to deliver mail. We reached the landing field towards dusk, landed, fitted on our parachutes, and decided to jump in the failing light. We were to jump in pairs, Lt Lewes and his servant Gdsn Davies* first, the RAF officer was to despatch. The instructions were to dive out as though going into water. We hooked ourselves up, circled the aerodrome, and on a signal from the RAF officer, Lt Lewes and Davies dived out. Next time round I dived out, and was surprised to see Lt Stirling pass me in the air. Lt Lewes made a perfect landing, next came Davies a little shaken. Lt Stirling injured his spine and also lost his sight for about an hour; next myself, a little shaken and a few scratches, and lastly Sgt Stone who seemed OK.[7]

Stirling's parachute had caught on the aircraft's tail section as he jumped into the slipstream, an error that proved common among inexperienced army paratroopers. With a section of his canopy torn, Stirling descended at high velocity and hit the ground with a sickening thud. Temporarily blinded and paralysed (the injuries to his spine would plague Stirling in later years), Stirling was rushed to Cairo's Scottish General Hospital while a telegram was despatched to his parents in Scotland informing them that their son had been admitted to hospital on 15 June 'suffering from contusion of the back as a result of enemy action'.

As he lay in bed, slowly recovering the feeling in his legs, Stirling put his enforced rest to good use. The 'job in Syria' that D'Arcy tantalizingly referred to has been lost to posterity, but whatever Stirling and Sergeant Stone (a 31-year-old Londoner in the Scots Guards who was killed on the first SAS operation in November 1941) were planning it was now shelved.

But Stirling's enthusiasm for a parachute unit remained as strong as ever despite his accident. Propping himself up in bed, Stirling drafted a memo: *Case for the retention of a limited number of special service troops, for employment as parachutists.* In a subsequent summarization of the memo Stirling wrote:

---

* Davies was one of the original members of the SAS and was killed in Germany in April 1945

I argued the advantages of establishing a unit based on the principle of the fullest exploitation of surprise and of making the minimum demands on manpower and equipment. I argued that the application of this principle would mean in effect the employment of a sub-unit of five men to cover a target previously requiring four troops of a Commando, i.e. about 200 men. I sought to prove that, if an aerodrome or transport park was the objective of an operation, then the destruction of 50 aircraft or units of transport was more easily accomplished by a sub-unit of five men than by a force of 200 men. I further concluded that 200 properly selected, trained and equipped men, organized into sub-units of five, should be able to attack at least thirty different objectives at the same time on the same night as compared to only one objective using the current Commando technique. So, only 25% success in the former is equivalent to many times the maximum result in the latter.[8]

Stirling spent several weeks in hospital and upon his release resolved to put his memo into the hands of a senior officer at MEHQ. How Stirling actually achieved this has been shrouded in myth and hearsay ever since the publication of Virginia Cowles' *The Phantom Major* in 1958. Cowles interviewed Stirling and several other SAS veterans in the course of her research and produced a colourful description of Stirling, complete with crutches, sneaking into MEHQ in Cairo through a gap in the fence, having been denied entry because he lacked an official pass. This seems far-fetched in the extreme.

MEHQ was tightly guarded (the British were paranoid about spies in Cairo) and it is inconceivable that a 6ft 6in officer on crutches could have slipped through a gap in the wire and disappeared inside headquarters without being apprehended. Furthermore, according to Cowles, Stirling evaded an armed guard on his tail by slipping through the first door he encountered inside MEHQ. By an amazing coincidence it was the office of one of Stirling's lecturers from the Guards Depot at Pirbright, who recognized his former pupil at once and harangued him for his impertinence. Fleeing his abuser, Stirling tried the next office and found himself face to face with Major-General Neil Ritchie, Deputy Chief of General Staff (DCGS), Middle East Forces, who liked what the young lieutenant had to say about the potential of a parachute unit.

In the detailed six-page account of the formation of L Detachment, written not long after the war, Stirling recorded the far more prosaic reality of how he proposed his idea: 'Having submitted these proposals to the C-in-C [General Claude Auchinleck] I was three days later summoned to the DCGS, Major General Neil Ritchie. He took me along to the C-in-C and CGS [Chief of General Staff Arthur Smith] and after some discussion they agreed that the unit should be formed forthwith.'[9]

What had impressed Auchinleck above all was Stirling's comprehensive plan for a raid to coincide with the forthcoming large-scale offensive that was common knowledge among British forces in Egypt. Stirling outlined how his force would parachute into Libya in five raiding units two nights before the main attack was launched. 'The DZs [drop zones] of these sub-units were to be 12 miles south into the desert from their objectives and they were to be dropped at night without moon, thus preserving surprise to the utmost,' wrote Stirling. The men would lie up for 24 hours and then launch five simultaneous attacks against Axis forward fighter and bomber bases between Timini and Gazala. Once the raids had been effected the raiders would rendezvous at a pre-arranged spot in the desert where a patrol of the Long Range Desert Group (LRDG) would be waiting.

Auchinleck was sold on the plan. He promoted Stirling to captain and authorized him to recruit six officers and 60 other ranks to a unit called L Detachment, Special Air Service Brigade; the reasoning being that if – or more likely when – German intelligence got wind of the incipient force, they would be dismayed to discover that a British airborne brigade was in Egypt.

Thrilled that his idea had won official approval, Stirling nonetheless had one demand to make of Auchinleck. Stirling had a visceral dislike of staff officers, a species he termed 'fossilized shits' on account of their outdated ideas as to how a war should be run. Stirling 'insisted with the C-in-C that the unit must be responsible for its own training and operational planning and that, therefore, the commander of the unit must come directly under the C-in-C. I emphasized how fatal it would be for the proposed unit to be put under any existing Branch or formation for administration.'[10]

Auchinleck had no objections and a delighted Stirling departed MEHQ to begin the task of breathing life into his brainchild.

Stirling first appropriated the six officers, of whom Jock Lewes was a priority. It took Stirling a while to convince the sombre Lewes that the unit wasn't a 'short-term flight of fancy' and that he himself wasn't a 'good-time Charlie'. Eventually Lewes agreed, and soon he was joined by five more lieutenants: Englishmen Peter Thomas and Charles Bonington (the latter the father of the renowned mountaineer, Chris Bonington); and three ex-Layforce officers in Irishmen Eoin McGonigal and Blair 'Paddy' Mayne, and the fresh-faced Scot Bill Fraser.

Mayne also needed some convincing, but said later that one of the Scot's strengths was his way of 'making you think you are a most important person. Stirling was a master of that art and it got him good results'.[11]

Guardsman Johnny Cooper agreed with Mayne's assessment. The teenager from 2nd Battalion Scots Guards stepped forward to volunteer for L Detachment when Stirling arrived at their desert camp, dubbed 'Bug Bug', looking for recruits. 'He talked to you, not at you, and he usually gave orders in a very polite fashion,' recalled Cooper. 'His charisma was overpowering and we followed him everywhere.'[12]

Most of Stirling's recruits, however, were the disillusioned men from Layforce, the highly trained former commandos stuck in the desert waiting to be posted somewhere. 'We were just hanging around in the desert getting fed up,' remembered Jeff Du Vivier, who had fought under Mayne with 11 Commando at the battle of Litani River. 'Then along came Stirling asking for volunteers. I was hooked on the idea from the beginning, it meant we were going to see some action.'

Stirling established L Detachment's camp at Kabrit, a windswept spot 90 miles east of Cairo on the edge of the Great Bitter Lake. The HQ was christened 'Stirling's Rest Camp', an ironic moniker given the remorseless nature of the training that the men endured.

'In our training programme the principle on which we worked was entirely different from that of the Commandos,' remembered Stirling. 'A Commando unit, having once selected from a batch of volunteers, were committed to those men and had to nurse them up to the required standard. L Detachment, on the other hand, had set a minimum standard to which all ranks had to attain and we had to be most firm in returning to their units those [who] were unable to reach that standard.'[13]

When Guardsman Mick D'Arcy wrote an account of L Detachment's formation in May 1943 he recalled: 'Numerous exercises carried out in training. Actual training hardest ever undertaken in Middle East. Long marches starting from 11 miles working up to 100 miles with full load ... average training 9–10 hours daily plus night schemes.'[14] For the men who had come through the Layforce training on Arran there was nothing out of the ordinary in the physical training (except the heat and the flies) and the weapons training was also similar. But none of them had been asked to jump out of an aircraft before.

On the first day's parachute training, 16 October, disaster struck when the 'chutes of Ken Warburton and Joe Duffy failed to open as they left the aircraft, 900ft above the ground. The pair fell to their deaths as their horrified comrades looked on. 'Stirling assembled us all in one of the marquees and assured us that modifications would be made immediately [a subsequent investigation revealed that the snap-links on the men's static line had buckled],' recalled Johnny Cooper. 'He also told us parachute training would recommence the following morning, and that he would be the first to jump. He was quite right to get us into the air again as quickly as possible after the fatalities as otherwise our confidence would have evaporated.'[15]

As Stirling had envisaged, Jock Lewes proved his immense value to the unit with his diligence, hard work and especially his inventiveness. It was he who designed what was to become L Detachment's most effective weapon in the Desert War – the Lewes bomb, a small but potent mix of plastic explosive, thermite and engine oil, fitted with a No. 27 detonator, an instantaneous fuse and a time pencil. A Lewes bomb could blow the wing off an enemy aircraft, but crucially it was also light enough to carry on long marches through the desert to the target.

Jimmy Storie, the last surviving member of the original L Detachment, recalled how Lewes complemented Stirling: 'David was a good soldier and he had the pull that Jock never had because he came from a well-known landowning family. He was born a gentleman and he was a great man ... [but] while Stirling was the backbone Lewes was the brains, he got the ideas such as the Lewes Bomb and without that we couldn't have done a lot. To us Lewes was the brain and David had the power to get things done; he

43

[Stirling] was there for a certain amount of training but he was looking further ahead. Jock liked things right, he was a perfectionist and he thought more about things in-depth.'[16]

On 15 November 1941 Stirling celebrated his 26th birthday. The next day he and 54 men left Kabrit for the RAF base at Bagoush, approximately 300 miles west. It was the eve of L Detachment's first raid, the one Stirling had sold to General Auchinleck in the summer, and there was an air of cool excitement among the men as they were looked after like royalty by the RAF personnel at Bagoush.

Stirling, meanwhile, spent 16 November anxiously monitoring the latest weather reports handed to him by the RAF. A fierce storm was forecast for the target area with winds expected to reach speeds of 30 knots. The Brigadier General Staff Coordinator, Sandy Galloway, advised Stirling that the mission should be aborted. Dropping by parachute in those wind speeds, and on a moonless night, would be hazardous in the extreme. Stirling absorbed the reports and the advice of Galloway and chose to let his men decide: did they wish to cancel the mission, or press on and to hell with the storm? The answer was an emphatic wish to continue.

Stirling had divided L Detachment into four sections under his overall command. Jock Lewes was to lead numbers one and two sections and Blair Mayne would be in charge of sections three and four. At 1830hrs on 16 November a fleet of trucks arrived at the officers' mess to transport the men to the five Bristol Bombay aircraft that would fly them to the target area. Stirling was in the lead aircraft, along with nine other ranks including Sergeant Bob Tait, who wrote a report of the raid upon his return a while later:

We were scheduled to arrive over the dropping area about 2230 hours but owing to the weather which I think was of gale force, and the heavy A.A [anti-aircraft] barrage we were much later. The pilot had to make several circles over the area, gliding in from the sea, coming down through the clouds right over Gazala, which was well lit up by flares dropped by the bombing force, covering our arrival. During this glide, we came in for an uncomfortable amount of A.A. We finally were dropped about 2330 hours, and owing to the high wind (I estimated this about 30 miles per hour) we all made very bad landings. I myself being the only one uninjured. Captain Stirling himself sustained injuries about the arms and legs, Sergeant Cheyne, we never saw again. We had considerable difficulty in assembling, the wind having scattered us over a wide area but finally set off at about 0100 hours [on November 17].[17]

Stirling and his men laid up at dawn, and it soon became clear to him that the extent of the injuries suffered on landing made the original plan unfeasible. He instructed Sergeant-Major George Yates to lead the men to the rendezvous with the LRDG (70 miles to the south-west) while he and Tait continued on to the target.

At nightfall Stirling and Tait broke cover and began marching towards their target, but at 2000hrs they were engulfed by an electrical storm, one of the worst to hit that part of Libya in living memory. 'We were unable to see more than a few yards in front,' wrote Tait, 'and within fifteen minutes the whole area was under water. Eventually reaching the fork wadi we endeavoured to make our way down on to the flat coastal strip, but found this impossible owing to the water which rushed down with great force. From then until long after midnight we moved along the escarpment, attempting to go down the various wadis but with no success, so accordingly about 0100 hours [18 November] Captain Stirling abandoned the attempt and we turned away and marched south.'[18]

When Stirling and Tait finally reached the rendezvous they were met with the disastrous news that only Mayne and Lewes had brought their men in safely. The rest of the raiding force, 34 men in total, were presumed either dead or captured (six of the soldiers were killed).

Dismayed as Stirling must have been, he refused to countenance that this was the end for L Detachment. According to Captain David Lloyd-Owen, who was in command of the LRDG rendezvous party, Stirling was thinking of the future even as he gratefully accepted a mug of tea. 'He was so certain he could succeed and nothing was going to stop him,' wrote Lloyd-Owen in his memoirs, *Providence Their Guide*. 'He was convinced that he had been only thwarted by bad luck and certainly not by any lack of preparation or training.'

But it was Lloyd-Owen who came up with the solution to Stirling's quandary: if parachuting was too hazardous a form of transport in the desert, why not let the LRDG drive Stirling and his men to the target area? Having operated in the region for nearly 18 months he knew the desert intimately and could not only drop the raiders within marching distance of the target, but pick them up after and avoid detection on the long journey back to base.

Stirling put the idea to Lloyd-Owen's commanding officer, Colonel Guy Prendergast, once they were back at Siwa Oasis on 25 November, and the approval was given. Stirling also benefited from the fact that the main British offensive, Operation *Crusader*, which L Detachment's raid had been timed to coincide with, had not gone well. General Rommel's Afrika Korps had counter-attacked and pushed the British back into Egypt. The fate of 34 British paratroopers, therefore, was not an overriding concern for MEHQ. In fact Auchinleck, who shared Stirling's eye for an opportunity, saw that Rommel's supply lines along the Libyan coast were over-extended and ordered two flying columns under the command of brigadiers Denys Reid and John Marriott to attack the Axis forces hundreds of miles behind the frontline. In the meantime, Eighth Army would launch a secondary offensive against the Afrika Korps.

The LRDG had been allocated the task of attacking Axis aerodromes at Sirte, Agheila and Agedabia, timed to coincide with the attacks of the two flying columns, but Prendergast thought this was a mission best suited to Stirling's L Detachment. His suggestion, cabled to MEHQ on 28 November, was accepted and Stirling received the go-ahead to attack the aerodromes in the second week of December.

In the event, a party of seven men led by Mayne achieved complete success, destroying 24 aircraft and a barracks full of Axis pilots at Tamet aerodrome. Thirty miles to the east, at Sirte landing strip, Stirling could only watch in bitter frustration as the 30 aircraft he was intending to attack took off a few hours before the raid. A party of five men under Bill Fraser accounted for 37 aircraft at Agedabia.

At the end of December 1941 Mayne returned to Tamet and blew up 27 aircraft that had only recently arrived to replace the ones destroyed in his previous visit to the airfield. Stirling tried for a second time to inflict damage on Sirte but again was foiled, this time by a newly installed perimeter fence and an increased guard detail.

Upon his return to base Stirling learned that Jock Lewes had been killed, shot by a marauding German fighter plane as his party of men returned from a raid on Nofilia aerodrome. 'Stirling was rocked by Lewes' death,' recalled Jimmy Storie, who was with Lewes when the Messerschmitt attacked their patrol.

The death of Lewes robbed Stirling of his natural successor. Paddy Mayne was the unit's most successful operator, but he was first and foremost a man of action who led from the front. Lewes was not only a brave, tough and resourceful Special Forces soldier, but also an intelligent and innovative thinker, and someone whom Stirling had hoped would help him develop L Detachment in the coming months and years.

But Lewes was dead and Stirling didn't have the time to mourn him. Instead he was eager to capitalize on the unit's success since forming their partnership with the LRDG. Auchinleck agreed to Stirling's request to recruit six new officers and up to 40 men. He was also promoted to major and given permission to approach a group of 50 French paratroopers, led by Captain Georges Berge, who had recently arrived in the Middle East from Britain. Stirling went to see General Georges Catroux, Commander-in-Chief of the Free French Forces, to ask if the paratroopers could be seconded to L Detachment. Stirling later recalled:

As soon as introduced he demanded 'explain why you are here?' I tried in my appalling French to state the purpose of my visit but the general replied 'No, absolutely out of the question'. He was still standing in his formidable straight up posture and although a little taller than him I felt in that instant minuscule... I persisted in arguing further the purpose of my mission. He stared at me with cold eyes and answered flatly 'no, positively not, goodbye sir'. 'Hell,' I said under my breath, but so that he could just hear me. 'He is as pigheaded as those bloody English at MEHQ', and still listening he overheard my observation. Suddenly a tiny grin transformed his expression and he commented, 'well, it appears as though you are not English'. 'Wholly not, mon general, I am Scottish and was brought up in the tradition of the Auld Alliance between the French and the Scots against the English'. After this incident he invited me to sit down and began what turned out to be a series of very exacting and precise questions. It took only half an hour for my proposal to be agreed.[19]

One of the men recruited was Reg Redington, a pre-war regular soldier who had won the Distinguished Conduct Medal (DCM) a couple of months earlier for his conduct during the battle for Sidi Omar the previous October. Redington saw an appeal for volunteers pinned to his barracks' noticeboard, and was soon standing before Stirling. 'He asked me how I won the DCM and I told him, and he congratulated me. "But what makes you want to join our lot?" he said. I told him I was a regular soldier and I wanted to see more of life and a bit more action, and I thought it would be a change.'[20] For a fortnight Redington heard nothing, then he was called to see his commanding officer and informed that he had been selected for L Detachment.

Another arrival was Captain Malcolm Pleydell, a London doctor before the war and then an officer in the Royal Army Medical Corps, who was recruited as L Detachment's medical officer. 'Stirling was terribly informal when I arrived at Kabrit. It was clear he wasn't much interested in paperwork and the way he talked about operations one would have thought he was talking about something quite harmless,' reflected Pleydell. 'He inspired in a quiet way, he was so charming you would do anything for him.'[21]

On 21 January the ebb and flow of the Desert War continued when Rommel launched a counter-attack to regain territory ceded to the British the previous month. The Libyan port of Benghazi fell into German hands, along with most of Cyrenaica. On the plus side, the losses at least allowed Stirling to launch a fresh round of raids against Axis airfields in March, involving some of the men recruited at the start of the year. Stirling led a daring raid against Benghazi with the intention of blowing up enemy shipping in the harbour, but the collapsible canoe carried by the seven-strong party was defective and the mission ended in another failure for Stirling.

By now the strain of operations was beginning to tell on Stirling. With no Jock Lewes to lean on, Stirling was burdened with operational and administrative tasks. He spent an increasing amount of his time at his brother's Cairo flat, planning raids and chasing up stores and supplies. More often than not Johnny

Cooper and Reg Seekings (arguably the most skilled operator in the detachment after Mayne) were present at the flat and despite the difference in age, class and rank there was no insistence on formality. 'With Paddy we addressed him as Blair and Stirling as David when there was no one about or when we were on patrol,' remembered Seekings. 'There was no rank, they called us Reggie and Johnny. But we never took advantage when other people were around, then it was always sir. Stirling was always very open to suggestions and if John and I made a suggestion we would never get an off-hand answer from him.'[22]

Cooper recalled that it was around this time that Stirling 'suffered from migraine which meant wearing dark glasses and [he] was often sick with desert sores which refused to heal'. Nevertheless, Stirling maintained his relentless pace, fearful that those staff officers at MEHQ who had been opposed to L Detachment from the outset would jump at the chance to disband the unit if they thought the commanding officer was not up to the job.

Throughout the spring of 1942 the pressure was mounting on General Auchinleck to break the stalemate in the Western Desert. It was Churchill's view that the commander-in-chief was not being proactive enough in confronting Rommel and he feared that Malta, the invaluable island in the Mediterranean, could fall into the enemy's hands while Auchinleck dithered.

Auchinleck's defence was that he needed time to build up his reserves after the winter offensives, but when Churchill was told a large convoy would sail for Malta during a moonless period in June he issued Auchinleck with an ultimatum: either launch an offensive against the Axis forces before the middle of June or be relieved of your command. 'There is no need for me to stress the vital importance of the safe arrival of our convoys ... and I am sure you will both take all steps to enable the air escorts, and particularly the Beaufighters, to be operated from landing-grounds as far west as possible.'[23]

Stirling was issued with instructions to come up with a plan to help the two-pronged convoy (from Gibraltar and Alexandria) reach Malta. What he produced was L Detachment's most ambitious operation to date. On the night of 13 June they would launch simultaneous attacks against a string of enemy aerodromes in the Benghazi sector while a party of men under the command of Georges Berge and Captain George Jellicoe (the son of the famous World War I admiral) would attack Heraklion airfield on Crete, having been transported to the island by submarine.

The raids met with mixed success. A group of French soldiers who raided Berka Main airfield destroyed six aircraft but their timing was slightly awry, so as Paddy Mayne closed in on Berka Satellite the sight of their explosions lighting up the night sky prompted him to abort his attack. In Heraklion, more than 20 German aircraft were blown up but Berge was captured. The most productive sabotage that night was accomplished by Stirling who, along with Johnny Cooper and Reg Seekings, had wreaked havoc on Benina aerodrome, which was used by the Germans as a repair base. Cooper recalled that as he, Seekings and Stirling lay concealed in the dark, waiting for the RAF to begin a diversionary raid on nearby Benghazi, 'David gave us a long lecture on deer stalking, including methods of getting into position to stalk, the problems of wind and the necessity for camouflage and stealthy movement. Absorbed in his Highland exploits we could forget the job in hand and the time passed very quickly.'[24]

When they did move, the trio did so with noiseless precision, creeping from hangar to hangar and placing bombs on aircraft and engines. As they withdrew from the target area they passed a guardhouse and Stirling, perhaps with Mayne's destruction of the pilots' mess at Tamet still on his mind, kicked open the door and tossed in a grenade. Stirling subsequently regretted the act, saying: 'It was a silly show of bravado, I suppose. In a fight I would shoot to kill with the same enthusiasm as the next man but I was not at ease with that action. It seemed close to murder.'[25] Such thoughts never troubled Paddy Mayne, who talked of going on raids in the hope of some 'good killing', and whose ruthlessness at times unnerved Stirling.

The immediate consequence of the grenade attack was the onset of a violent migraine and as the three raiders made good their escape from Benina, Cooper and Seekings grabbed their commander and 'led him staggering and half-blind to the top of the ridge'. By the time Stirling encountered Mayne at the LRDG rendezvous he had recovered his old self and on learning of the Irishman's misfortune at Berka he couldn't help but gloat – for the first time the great Paddy Mayne had failed to destroy any German aircraft. Mayne jokingly doubted the veracity of Stirling's account of what had happened at Benina, so the pair decided to borrow an LRDG truck and see for themselves.

They took with them Seekings, Cooper, Jimmy Storie, Bob Lilley and Karl Kahane, an Austrian Jew attached to L Detachment. 'It was a bloody silly thing to do, but funny at the time!' remembered Cooper. 'David, in his usual self-confident way, reassured us that there wouldn't be any roadblocks along the way. We didn't waste time taking back routes, just went straight along the main road towards Benina all unconcerned at the potential danger we were driving into.'[26]

Six miles down the road they ran into a well-manned enemy checkpoint. As Storie recalled:

A German sergeant major came up to the truck and took a good look at it and at us. Kahane spoke German and said we were on a special mission, but he could see we were British. But at the same time the German could hear the sound of weapons being cocked, and he was obviously a wise man. He knew that if he made a false move he would be the first to go. So he turned to the men on the roadblock and told them to open the gates.[27]

The truck raced on down the road, crashing through a smaller checkpoint with Seekings scattering the Italian soldiers with a burst of machine-gun fire. At the village of Lete, approximately five miles east of Benghazi, they attacked a roadside café and killed a number of German and Italian soldiers enjoying a late-night drink on the terrace. Then Stirling told Mayne (who was driving) to head for home across the desert. Chased by the Germans for much of the way, only the brilliance of Mayne's driving allowed the men to evade their pursuers, and Stirling later admitted that had been 'a little pomposo' in trying to return to the scene of his crime.

When Stirling led his men back to their base at Siwa Oasis on 21 June it was to learn the alarming news that the Germans were once more on the attack, advancing at breakneck pace across the desert with the British retreating rapidly. They had already ceded 150 miles to the Germans and Tobruk was in Rommel's hands. The Royal Navy was pulling out of Alexandria and in Cairo there was a genuine fear that the city would soon fall. The Eighth Army did eventually manage to hold the German advance at El Alamein, by which time L Detachment had returned to Kabrit to see how they could be of use at this dire juncture of the Desert War.

Stirling visited MEHQ in Cairo and informed them that his unit had destroyed 143 enemy aircraft in the last six months, although this was on the conservative side. In truth it was probably more, but as Reg Seekings later recalled: 'Stirling reduced all tallies by ten percent, he wouldn't let anyone claim higher. At first they [MEHQ] couldn't believe we were destroying so many. Impossible. We were destroying more than the best fighter squadrons.'

In addition L Detachment had destroyed myriad petrol bowsers, repair bases and bomb dumps. It was said that the Germans now called Stirling 'The Phantom Major', such was his ability to ghost onto airfields, wreak havoc and then melt into the night. There was a downside to all the success, however, as Stirling himself noted: 'By the end of June L Detachment had raided all the more important German and Italian aerodromes within 300 miles of the forward area at least once or twice,' he wrote later. 'Methods of defence were beginning to improve and although the advantage still lay with L Detachment, the time had come to alter our own methods.'[28]

The opportunity to alter their methods of attack presented itself on the night of 7/8 July when L Detachment carried out a sequence of raids to coincide with the Eighth Army's offensive to regain control of the coastal region of Mersa Matruh. Stirling and Mayne headed to Bagoush (the airfield from which L Detachment had departed on their first fateful raid in November 1941, now in Axis hands) with the intention of going in on foot. Mayne penetrated the airfield without problem, but on setting the explosive charges he discovered that the primers were damp. Returning to the rendezvous, Mayne discussed with Stirling what they should do and they agreed to 'drive on to the field and shoot the beggars up'.

With Stirling driving the 'Blitz Buggy', a stripped-down Ford V8 staff car, and Mayne at the wheel of the jeep, the raiders set off. Both vehicles had been fitted with single and twin Vickers K machine guns from obsolete Gloster Gladiator biplanes, which could fire 1,200 rounds per minute. Johnny Cooper was alongside Cooper in the buggy: 'I was on the single Vickers and you really couldn't miss,' he reflected. 'The rear gunner was on the twin Vickers in the back and David was driving, shouting words of encouragement as we cruised up the airfield. We were doing about 20mph and yet I can't remember any fire coming our way.'[29]

Having destroyed 37 aircraft, the raiders departed and headed south towards their base some 70 miles distant. 'Paddy joined us in the buggy and he stretched out in the back and went to sleep while I drove,' recalled Cooper, whom Stirling had allowed to take the wheel of his prized buggy for the first time. 'It was just before dawn when I heard aircraft approaching. David jumped into the driving seat and made for a wadi just as a couple of Italian CR42s [fighters] appeared. David did his best to lose them but there was no cover. We jumped out of the Blitz Buggy as they came in low and got clear just before it exploded.'[30]

Despite the loss of the buggy, Stirling was delighted with the results of the motorized foray onto Bagoush airfield. On 13 July he returned to Cairo to acquire a fleet of jeeps as well as rations, equipment and Mike Sadler – a respected navigator for the LRDG who had been persuaded to join L Detachment. 'Stirling had a very good social manner and also had a compelling personality,' recalled Sadler. 'He was a terribly quiet chap and didn't raise his voice but he would come to one and say "I want you to take a party on this raid" and you would never think of saying no as he was so persuasive, but in a very charming way.'[31]

The operational strength of L Detachment was up to 100 men, and Stirling appointed as his second-in-command George Jellicoe. In November 1942 Jellicoe wrote a report on this period of operations that gave an interesting insight into how Stirling, quiet and charming though he might have been, set standards of utmost rigour:

I should like to lay emphasis on the great strain imposed on personnel of SAS regiment and the LRDG patrols before the actual operations began.

1SAS* regiment had never before been motorized. Four days only were available for preparations. 15 jeeps had to be prepared with special equipment and guns and twenty 3-ton lorries loaded. This meant that the drivers and maintenance crews had to work, for some times, as long as 72 hours almost without a break.[32]

Their industry, however, was not in vain and when L Detachment launched its first large-scale jeep attack it was a stunning triumph. On the night of 26/27 July Stirling arrived at Sidi Haneish, an airfield approximately 30 miles east-south-east of Mersa Matruh, at the head of two columns of heavily armed jeeps, with tracer, armour-piercing and incendiary bullets loaded into the drums of their Vickers guns. As the raiders drove slowly down the landing strip they could hardly miss the stationary aircraft either side of them: 'The whole place just erupted in this deafening roar,' recalled Cooper, who was in Stirling's vehicle. 'It was like a duck shoot, pouring Vickers fire into the planes and seeing them explode. But in fact there was return fire, although not that accurate – partly because the planes and the smoke obscured us from the Italian defences as we drove back down the runway. We got a shell through the cylinder head and had to abandon our jeep. Sandy Scratchley's pulled up alongside and we hopped on board.'[33]

The raid was the perfect climax to end a month in which, operating self-sufficiently from their remote desert base, L Detachment had destroyed a minimum of 86 enemy aircraft and between 36 and 45 motorized vehicles. Nonetheless when the raiders reassembled at their desert hideout after the Sidi Haneish raid, they were given a dressing-down by Stirling for their profligate shooting. Though approximately 40 aircraft had been damaged or destroyed, it could have been more if the gunners' accuracy had been better. 'Privately I was very pleased,' Stirling reflected in his biography, 'but I didn't want the men to become too blasé about the business. What we had proved to my satisfaction, and it was something I could use to positive effect at MEHQ, was that we could operate under a variety of tactics to the same end.'[34]

---

* Note that it was not until September 1942 that L Detachment was expanded into the 1st Special Air Service Regiment, abbreviated to 1SAS.

But despite this confirmation of L Detachment's versatility, the unit was recalled to Cairo in early August 1942. Stirling arrived in the Egyptian capital to discover that Churchill had sacked Claude Auchinleck and replaced him with General Harold Alexander. There was also a new commander of Eighth Army, General Bernard Montgomery, who was in the throes of planning a big offensive for the end of October to start from the Alamein front. Stirling was summoned to MEHQ and informed of what would be expected of L Detachment in the forthcoming attack. With the Afrika Korps receiving regular supplies through the ports of Tobruk and Benghazi, Montgomery instructed L Detachment, together with elements of Middle East Commando and the Special Boat Section (SBS) to raid Benghazi on the night of 13/14 September, while a combined force of commandos and infantry would launch a simultaneous seaborne strike against Tobruk.

Stirling was horrified at the plan, considering it anathema to L Detachment's *modus operandi*. They were suited to small-scale raids, lightning guerrilla warfare, yet the Benghazi raid – codenamed Operation *Bigamy* – was large and cumbersome, with 200 men and a pair of Honey tanks.

Stirling's fears proved well-founded. On the approach to Benghazi the force was ambushed and the survivors were forced to race across the open desert in the hour before dawn, before the inevitable enemy aircraft appeared. Not all of them reached the safety of the nearby mountains, 25 miles away, and 12 vehicles were destroyed. Casualties were mercifully light but Stirling still had to order Malcolm Pleydell, the unit's medical officer, to make a decision about which of the wounded could manage the long trip back to base and which would have to be left behind. Once the main party had moved off, Stirling remained in the mountains for several days with a small party of men and three jeeps in case any stragglers arrived. None did. When Stirling returned to Kufra Oasis, Pleydell expected him to be downcast but he gave no indication of being morose:

On the contrary his view was that, since the enemy had known of our raid, none of us could be blamed for what had taken place. 'The raid simply wasn't on!' But now, he continued, looking round at us eagerly, there was an easy target we ought to be getting busy on: the railway line from Tobruk to Alamein. That should make a lovely objective… In addition David had some fresh ideas concerning the future of the Special Air Service. He wanted it divided into two squadrons which, by relieving one another, could constantly maintain a force in the rear of the enemy.[35]

How the enemy came to learn of the attack on Benghazi remains unclear. After the war Mike Sadler blamed it on loose tongues in Cairo bars, and the sharp ears of German agents, though according to Brian Dillon, an intelligence officer in Cairo: 'The US had a military mission in Cairo and had access to British Operation Orders and they sent details of the Benghazi raid to Washington in low grade cipher and Germans intercepted it and broke it.'[36]

Perhaps as a form of compensation for the misuse of L Detachment, MEHQ promoted Stirling to lieutenant-colonel on 28 September 1942 and authorized the expansion of the unit to a full regiment comprising four squadrons: A, under the command of Major Paddy Mayne; B, under Stirling; C, a French squadron; and D, a Special Boat Section squadron under Jellicoe. Mayne took the experienced men into his squadron and, in October, disappeared into the desert to cut railway lines and attack vehicle convoys in an area between Tobruk and Matruh.

Stirling meanwhile oversaw a recruitment drive to bring the regiment up to its fighting strength of 29 officers and 572 other ranks. He was also, with his brother Bill, pressing for the formation of a second SAS regiment, permission for which was granted with surprising speed. Stirling had always viewed middle-ranking staff officers with distaste, because in his view they were jealous, spiteful, mediocre men who resented any young officer with ideas and initiative. The fact that L Detachment had been expanded into two regiments proved that even the 'fossilized shits' in MEHQ were powerless to prevent his rise. But all this frenetic activity did little for Stirling's health and when he led B Squadron into the desert at the end of November to link up with A Squadron he was again suffering from intermittent migraines, solar conjunctivitis and desert sores.

However Stirling didn't intend to deviate from his plan to lead B Squadron in a series of operations against the Axis forces – now in full retreat west following their defeat at the battle of El Alamein – in an area between Tripoli and Misurata. Operating in an area swarming with enemy soldiers, casualties for B Squadron were heavy during this period, but by the start of 1943 the indefatigable Stirling had envisaged the future for his regiment, as he outlined in his biography. 'With the end of the war in North Africa in sight … I had to be ready with a plan to move out of the desert and into other pastures,' he explained. 'To gain credence for the plan, which would first have to be presented to Montgomery, I must ensure that we had maximum impact in Africa before the end of the [desert] war. We had to be remembered.'[37]

Stirling thus arranged for Mayne to take A Squadron on a ski course at the British Army Mountain Warfare training centre in the Lebanon, in readiness for deployment to deal with the German threat in the Caucasus. He himself would head in the other direction, west into Tunisia, continuing to attack the retreating Germans while also reconnoitring to see if Rommel was preparing to dig in on the Mareth Line, a defensive wall from an earlier era of warfare. There was also the possibility of becoming the first unit from Eighth Army to link up with First Army.

On 21 January 1943 Stirling's patrol rendezvoused with Augustin Jordan and his 21 Frenchmen at Bir Soltane in central Tunisia. Word had just reached Stirling that Tripoli and Gafsa had fallen to the Allies and it was imperative that they attack the Axis lines of communication between Sfax and Gabes forthwith. Jordan left at 1600hrs on the 21st for the Gabes Gap, a geographical bottleneck between the Tunisian salt flats and the Mediterranean Sea. Stirling followed 12 hours later, his 14 men travelling in five jeeps.

They passed through the Gabes Gap at dusk on 23 January, and early the next day were on the road to Gafsa in bright early-morning sunshine. After a while they turned off the road and headed into the hills to lie up for the day. On finding a deep wadi, the patrol dismounted, camouflaged the jeeps and lay down to rest.

One of the men with Stirling was Reg Redington, the former artilleryman who had won the DCM in 1941. 'We could see the Germans from the wadi and some Arabs came up to us and they asked us if we could give them some tea,' he remembered. 'I'm sure it was the Arabs who gave us away. I put my Smith & Wesson by my side, and I'd had my boots on for weeks and weeks so I put them by the side and lay down. Next thing I know someone was kicking my feet shouting 'Raus, Raus'. I reached for my Smith & Wesson but it was gone.'[38]

Further up the wadi Mike Sadler and Johnny Cooper, along with a French soldier called Freddie Taxis, were also rudely awakened by the company of Luftwaffe troops – who had been on the hunt for Allied soldiers since encountering Jordan's patrol the previous day. Strangely, the Germans motioned for the trio to stay where they were and continued up the wadi looking for more men to capture. The moment they were out of sight, Cooper, Sadler and Taxis scrambled up the steep side of the wadi and escaped into some thick camel scrub.

Stirling and the other 11 men were herded into lorries and after a two-hour drive were forced from the vehicles at gunpoint. 'They took about four of us to a hut,' recalled Redington. 'Stirling wasn't with us because he was an officer. I thought we were going to [be] bumped off. The hut was just four walls, and it looked as though it had already been peppered with holes. In the hut they roughed us up a bit and I got it a bit worse than the others because I was a corporal. They knocked us around, hit us with rifle butts. I thought we were going to be shot.'[39]

Stirling was not beaten but was threatened with execution, although he believed his captors to be bluffing. Nevertheless, he decided to try to escape, and did so that night when he was escorted outside to answer the call of nature. Sprinting into the darkness, Stirling was soon out of sight of his pursuers, and he kept running until dawn. At daybreak he encountered a friendly Arab, who fed him and allowed him to rest in his barn. When it was dark Stirling moved off in the direction of Bir Soltane where he hoped to encounter Allied forces. He saw another local and asked for food and water. The man smiled and told Stirling to follow. He did, and was escorted to a waiting Italian patrol.

The capture of the 'Phantom Major' was a rare slice of good fortune for Field Marshal Rommel at a time of otherwise gloomy news for his forces in North Africa. In a little over a year, the Special Air Service had destroyed 327 Axis aircraft, innumerable motorized vehicles and petrol dumps, and seriously disrupted his lines of communication. Writing to his wife at the start of February, Rommel explained that with Stirling's capture, 'the British lost the very able and adaptable commander of the desert group which had caused us more damage than any other British unit of equal size'.[40]

Some of Stirling's comrades were also writing letters, although of course their emotions were anything but triumphant. Colonel Robert Laycock, who had commanded Stirling in 8 Commando, wrote to Stirling's mother to tell her that her son 'has done more for his country than any single individual of his rank in the army'. Mrs Stirling also received a letter from George Jellicoe in which he said: 'I don't think it is necessary for me to tell you what even a temporary loss of David's company – and his genius for command – means to me ... I am quite unashamed in avowing my devotion to him.'[41]

When Malcolm Pleydell heard the news of Stirling's capture, he wrote to his fiancée in England: 'There is no one with his flair and gift for projecting schemes. He ran the unit ... so now the ship is without a rudder.'

Though the immediate future of the SAS appeared in doubt following Stirling's capture, it survived the grievous loss of its leader. Stirling was flown to Europe and in 1944 was transferred to the notorious prisoner-of-war camp at Colditz. With the Allies winning the war against Germany, Stirling spent much of his time in Colditz thinking how best the SAS could be deployed in the Far East. Within days of his release from captivity in April 1945, Stirling was discussing with Brigadier Mike Calvert, commander of the SAS Brigade, the feasibility of sending the SAS into China to sever the Japanese supply line to Malaya. In the end they were overtaken by events in the Far East and the decision of the Americans (a decision with which Stirling disagreed) to drop atomic bombs on the cities of Hiroshima and Nagasaki.

✦ ✦ ✦ ✦

Like so many young men who make their mark in war, the years that followed proved anti-climactic for David Stirling. At the start of 1946, just a few months after the SAS had been disbanded, Stirling emigrated to Rhodesia. He went to seek his fortune in business but in 1948 formed the Capricorn Society, the aim of which was to establish a 'modus Vivendi by which all races, colours and creeds in Africa can live in harmony'. A little over ten years later, with the Society making little headway in an Africa in the throes of decolonization, Stirling resigned as president. By the early 1960s Stirling's health was deteriorating and he was in debt because of the money he had poured into the Capricorn Society. He went back into business, founding Television International Enterprises, and in 1967 formed Watchguard International Ltd, a company whose services were aimed at 'preventing the violent overthrow of a government' – in other words offering mercenaries to beleaguered governments in Africa and the Middle East.

Stirling continued to suffer from a bad back as a result of his parachute accident in the summer of 1941, and in 1970 he was involved in a serious car crash that exacerbated his health problems. In 1972 he ceased all involvement with Watchguard International Ltd.

In 1990 Stirling received a knighthood to go with the Distinguished Service Order (DSO) he had been awarded for his leadership of L Detachment in North Africa nearly 50 years earlier. But the accolade that pleased Stirling most was when he was the guest of honour at the unveiling of Stirling Lines, the refurbished SAS base in Hereford, in June 1984. In front of hundreds of past and present members of the regiment, Stirling gave an address which holds even more resonance now – nearly 30 years on – than it did at the time: 'The very survival of the regiment, in a society wary of elitism, depends on the calibre of each individual recruited,' said Stirling. 'This was, is and must remain the cornerstone … [but] the regiment must never regard itself as a corps d'elite, because down that road would lie the corruption of all our values. A substantial dash of humility along with an ever-active sense of humour must continue to save us from succumbing to this danger.'[42]

Stirling died on 4 November 1990, 11 days before his 75th birthday. In February the following year a memorial service was held in the Guards Chapel in London, on the same day that the Irish Republican Army – who had suffered two costly attacks by the SAS in the preceding three years – launched an audacious mortar attack on Downing Street. A coincidence? Who knows.

Stirling was without doubt one of the founding fathers of Special Forces warfare. Like many great men in their chosen field, Stirling glimpsed the future while the rest were stuck in the present, or in the case of the British

Army in 1940, the past. Stirling had grasped that the advances in weaponry and technology that had taken place since World War I could change the very nature of warfare. No longer would vast opposing armies confront each other on battlefields with the spoils going to the biggest, or the bravest, side. Now small units of highly trained soldiers with the right weapons could be just as destructive as an entire division.

Allied to this vision was Stirling's character, his determination, defiance, humour and his unshakeable belief in his conviction. As Sir Fitzroy Maclean – who served with the SAS in 1942 – said in Stirling's eulogy: 'There was about him, as about many great men, an element of mystery, an intangible quality, akin perhaps to what [T.E.] Lawrence called "the irrational tenth, like the kingfisher flashing across the pool".'[43]

EDSON RAFF

82ND AIRBORNE

To his men Edson Duncan Raff was known as 'Little Caesar' and to the rest of the US Army his men were known as 'Raff's Ruffians'. Both monikers were uttered with respect, and not a little affection, for in World War II Colonel Edson Raff proved himself an outstanding leader of men, and the soldiers who served under him fought with courage from North Africa to Normandy and on into Germany. As the commander of the 2nd Battalion, 503rd Parachute Infantry Regiment, Raff led the first American airborne operation of the war as part of Operation *Torch* in November 1942. Later he saw action in North-West Europe where he combined great personal courage with astute military thinking, and in the years after World War II Raff was at the forefront of the development of American Special Forces.

◆◆◆◆

Edson Raff was born in New York City in November 1907 to Edson and Abell Raff, one of four children. Little is known of his formative years, other than that he attended a small preparatory school in Winchester, Virginia, the Shenandoah Valley Academy, where he excelled at sport and was captain of the cadet force. The academy's superintendent was a reserve colonel. 'From that tough old guy I learned three things,' recalled Raff years later. 'One, I don't give a damn for any man who doesn't give a damn for me; two, be able to look any man in the eye and tell him to go to hell; three, Stonewall Jackson's battles in the Shenandoah Valley [during the American Civil War], which I remembered in Tunisia later on.'[1]

In 1928 Raff enrolled in the Military Academy at West Point and five years later he graduated, one of 347 graduates whose passing-out parade was attended by Douglas MacArthur, Chief of Staff of the US Army. For the next few years Raff's military career meandered slowly along, and when Germany invaded Poland in September 1939, the act that triggered the outbreak of World War II, he was a junior infantry officer and stationed at Schofield Barracks in Hawaii.

Raff subsequently claimed in his wartime memoirs, *We Jumped to Fight*, that in August the following year he noticed an article in the *New York Times* about the raising of a test platoon of American parachutists at Fort Benning,

Georgia. The one officer and 48 men had been assigned to the Infantry Board from the 29th Infantry Regiment following the War Department's decision the previous January to explore the possibility of American airborne troops.

'Not being sure if a first lieutenant of infantry having a C.A.A [Civil Aviation Authority] commercial pilot's license and a yen for adventure possessed the necessary qualifications I nevertheless decided then and there to be a parachutist,' wrote Raff in his memoirs.[2]

Raff fired off letters, the first to the Adjutant General in Washington requesting his 'six month extension in the Hawaiian Department be curtailed immediately', the second to the Chief of Infantry asking for permission to join any putative paratroop unit. The Adjutant General denied his request and the Chief of Infantry, Major General Stephen Odgen Fuqua, prevaricated and said he'd be in touch.

Six months later Raff did receive a new posting, but it was to the 23rd Infantry at Fort Sam Houston in Texas and not to the airborne unit he so craved. For two miserable months Raff undertook 'field manoeuvres in the Texas rattlesnake country' until one day an order arrived, stating simply: 'Detailed to report not later than June 1st [1941] to the 501st Parachute Battalion at Fort Benning, Georgia.'

Raff arrived in Georgia in a state of high excitement and was cordially welcomed by his commanding officers, Lieutenant Colonel William Miley, and Lieutenant Colonel William Lee, head of the Provisional Parachute Group, who had taught Raff tank tactics at the Infantry School in 1937.

On 4 June Raff began training to become a paratrooper. He and his fellow recruits began with physical training, such as long runs and calisthenics 'to harden the muscles' as well as learning the parachute roll on landing. 'Our class started like all the others before us, full of vim and raring to jump' wrote Raff in a letter to an aunt on 26 June 1941. 'It wasn't long before most of us realized the course was downright hard labor ... in the rest period we'd make a rush for the water spigot to drink until all the perspiration just lost could be replaced and the vicious circle would start once more – sweat and drink, sweat and drink.'[3]

From rolling around on mats, the aspirant paratroopers progressed to leaping off raised platforms, first 3ft and then 5ft in height. The next jumps were from a dummy fuselage, from where the troops learned not just how to land but also how to leap into space, individually and en masse. After the fuselage the instructors had the recruits use a 'Lulu', a contraption that Raff explained to his aunt: 'It's a trolley affair on an inclined rail down which rolls the would-be parachutist hanging in a suspension harness. At some uncertain moments during the downward roll the instructor gives a jerk on a control in his hand releasing the student. No one ever knows when he'll be released so all during the roll he has to be prepared to land feet apart, then make the somersault. Most of the time we were eating sawdust from the pit into which we drop.'

If there was sufficient wind at Fort Benning, the recruits would don parachutes and allow themselves to be dragged across the grass so they could learn how to arrest the chute in a heavy breeze. They were also given endless lessons in folding and packing the 'silk', with their instructors telling the volunteers that his parachute was as important to an airborne trooper as a rifle was to an infantryman.

Having learned how to leap from a 90ft tower, the day arrived when Raff and his fellow recruits were given the chance to make their first jump proper. Raff, who was known by his middle name of 'Duncan' to family members, described the experience to his aunt:

Our novice jump took place on a day which was clear and still. The engines of two C-39 transport planes warmed up as we lined up for inspection … when we passed over a certain spot on the ground, lieutenant Walters, the jumpmaster said, 'Number One, stand up!' The first man stood on his feet. Walters looked him over, then gave the command, 'Hook up!'

Number One snapped the static line attached to his parachute on the steel anchor cable running down the centre of the transport. Next came the command, 'stand in the door!' The student obeyed; for a few tense seconds he stood there ready for the leap into space. Then lieutenant Walters said 'Go!' Out went the tyro on his first trip to mother earth. The rest of us watched him gradually lose altitude and disappear far to the rear of the plane … then came number Seven. 'captain Raff, stand up!' yelled lieutenant Walters.

'Hook up!'

I hooked up.

'Stand in the door!'

There I stood, looking out at the earth moving slowly by 1,500 feet below. My hands lightly touched the metal fuselage, ready to make the push off. The propeller wash (we call it the 'prop blast') came through the door in intermittent gusts. Thus, on the threshold of a new world, I waited for the fatal 'go'.

I felt a tap on my right leg. Walters was saying 'Go! Go!' and out I went.

Deep down a submerged voice seemed to be counting 'one thousand, two thousand, thr-' but before I could finish 'three thousand' there was a jerking on my shoulders and I knew the chute had opened. It was a peculiar pain, strangely exhilarating. In spite of the frequent shoulder bruises from the opening jar the real joy of having that 'chute open knows no bounds. There was plenty of time to gaze around as a slight breeze drifted the chute and me to the south. After looking up at the canopy to see that it was completely open, I tried some turns and slips. Then I gazed around some more ... I noticed as I looked down that the earth seemed to be coming up toward me. The speed of its approach increased and, for the first time, I realized my drift was rearward. Working the risers (they run from the shoulders to the lines running down from the chute) I prepared to land. Both feet hit the ground at once, then a backward somersault, and the jump was over. The grassy field underfoot felt solid and good.[4]

Having qualified as a parachutist, Raff was appointed executive officer of the 504th Parachute Battalion on 6 December 1941. The following day the Japanese air force attacked Pearl Harbor on what President Franklin Roosevelt declared to be a 'day of infamy'. On 8 December the United States of America declared war on Japan and three days later a similar announcement was made concerning Germany.

The declarations of war affected Raff little in the short term. In March 1942 the 504th Parachute Battalion was renamed the 2nd Battalion of the

503rd Parachute Infantry* and Raff – now a major – was appointed its commanding officer. He trained his men at Fort Bragg, North Carolina, night and day, recalling in his memoirs that 'when I told them that we were going places some day, that our battalion would do any and all jobs, fighting either the Japs, the Germans or both, if I had to volunteer to do it, they cheered'. Behind his back, however, Raff had been christened 'Little Caesar' for the relentless way in which he drove his men. They respected their chief's toughness and his willingness to train alongside his men, but they disliked his autocratic style of leadership. Unlike the democratic Evans Carlson, who at the same time was whipping his 2nd Raider Battalion into shape in California, Raff believed unequivocally in the military chain of command and he did not tolerate indiscipline from the men in his battalion.

In May 1942 Raff received orders to ship out for England, and the new airborne battalion did so in the utmost secrecy. Before leaving Fort Bragg they removed all airborne insignia from their battledress and travelled to New York as an infantry battalion. On 6 June Raff and his men sailed from New York on board the erstwhile luxury liner, *Queen Mary*, and by the end of the month they were encamped on the sprawling Berkshire estate of Chilton Lodge, a 16th-century manor house that belonged to Mrs Jean Ward, the daughter of Whitelaw Reid, who was the US Ambassador to Britain from 1905 to 1912. Mrs Ward loaned the house's extensive grounds to the American military for the duration of the war and Raff's battalion was the first unit to take up occupancy in the Nissen huts erected on the estate.

Upon arrival in England, Raff (now a lieutenant colonel) came under the operational command of Major-General Frederick 'Boy' Browning of the British 1st Airborne Division. Raff welcomed the association and in the weeks that followed he learned much from his Allies. A two-week field exercise was conducted in Devon and the American paratroopers travelled to the British parachute training school in Ringway, Manchester, to practise low-level drops from 650ft.

Despite the rigorous training there was still no indication that the 2nd Battalion, 503rd Parachute Infantry would soon be in action, and by late July

---

* In December 1943 it was redesignated the 509th Parachute Infantry Battalion.

1942 the men were suffering from every soldier's worst enemy – boredom. Raff's men chafed at the inactivity, as Baron Frederich von der Heydte's had in the weeks before the invasion of Crete 15 months earlier, though at least the American airborne troops had a plentiful supply of local girls on hand to help while away the hours off-duty.

When Raff and his men were waiting impatiently to put their training to the test, events that were unfolding elsewhere would grant them their wish. On 13 August Lieutenant General Dwight Eisenhower, who had arrived in England two months earlier in command of American forces, was appointed to command Operation *Torch*, a mission designed seemingly to appease Stalin, who for several months had been pressing the Americans and the British to open a second front to ease the pressure on Soviet troops engaged in repulsing the German invaders on the Eastern Front.

The Americans believed the best course of action would be a landing in northern France in September 1942, codenamed Operation *Sledgehammer*, but the British convinced their Allies that they lacked the men and equipment to successfully establish a foothold in France. In addition the British were still fighting Axis forces in North Africa, and their priority was to win that campaign so that they could control the Mediterranean. Eventually the Americans agreed to Operation *Torch*, an invasion of French north-west Africa, understanding that with the whole of Africa in their possession they could use the continent as another base from which to attack Germany.

The great imponderable concerning Operation *Torch* was the French and how they would react. Though France was now governed by the collaborative Vichy government, many of its overseas territories were Vichy in name only, with French soldiers desperate to fight against the Germans.

The Allies drew up a plan for an invasion of French north-west Africa in November, in which three task forces would seize the main ports and air bases in Morocco and Algeria, enabling the invasion force to then strike east into Tunisia and attack the German forces – which by that time were in retreat from Egypt following the British Eighth Army offensive at El Alamein in late October. The ultimate aim of *Torch* was to crush the Axis forces in a pincer with the British applying the force from the east and the Americans from the west.

Eisenhower tasked Major General Mark Clark of II Corps with planning the airborne phase of Operation *Torch*. Clark had seen the potential of paratroopers from the very first days of their existence in the States, and at his headquarters in Norfolk House in London he devised a mission for Raff's battalion.

What he produced was a daunting challenge for Raff. Flying 1,500 miles from England to Algeria, his men would seize the military airfields of La Sénia and Tafaraoui and thereby prevent French fighter planes from attacking the main invasion fleet as it came ashore. No large-scale airborne assault had ever flown such a distance to its target but despite that, and the fact his men had no combat experience, Raff had every confidence in his battalion, informing Clark in a note:

There is no doubt in my mind that we can accomplish the mission, provided: (1) we get a break by the Air Corps and (2) by the weather. And provided (3) I am permitted to command my paratroopers when we hit the ground.[5]

Granted permission to lead his men into battle – and ordered not to disclose to them their destination until instructed – Raff returned to his battalion's training camp and pushed the men even harder, telling them they would soon see action. They asked where, but Raff refused to reveal the target, leading his paratroopers to speculate on where they might be headed. Most guessed France, but there were one or two extravagant claims suggesting they were to drop into Berlin and kill Hitler himself. In his memoirs Raff described how 'all our battalion training and manoeuvres were directed towards the accomplishment of the mission ... [we] hiked across country the exact distance [we] actually would march to the objective, which, in the exercises was always an airfield with planes to be destroyed thereon. The remainder of the battalion moved the same distance it would have to move, then assumed firing positions which were similar to the ones to be taken on D-Day.'[6]

They practised jumping at night, as they would have to do in Algeria, and before long Raff's battalion could land in any given area and be assembled

70

within 20 minutes. 'Little Caesar', though he didn't let on, was delighted with the discipline and professionalism of his battalion.

Hours were spent studying models of their target (whose identity was still unknown to the men), with everyone from company commanders to buckshee privates instructed in their own individual task. 'It was also intended,' commented Raff, 'to divert personnel from rushing into the first fight they heard or saw, thereby forgetting their primary role.'

Shortly before the battalion flew to Ireland for a final dress rehearsal, a war correspondent from *Time* magazine visited Chilton Foliat to watch the battalion at work. The article appeared in the edition dated 12 October, and described Raff's men as 'swashbuckling Hell's Angels'. The article continued:

[They] make up the most justifiably pampered outfit in the A.E.F. [American Expeditionary Force]. U.S. paratroopers get top pay—$50 extra for men, $100 for officers. They were the first taken off the monotonous English ration and given American victuals, including Southern fried chicken; they have the most cats & dogs (which they carry around in musette bags and take up in their planes), the smartest outfits (sleek high boots for town wear) and the latest and best equipment (including the 4-lb., 30-calibre automatic carbine, light field pieces, mortars, grenades, knives, bayonets, Garands and antitank guns).

Their leader, Lieut. Colonel Edson Raff, 34, fatalistically explains the extra fire power: 'We want to keep from being eliminated any quicker than we have to.' Chafing to become advance agents of a second front, the troops keep on jumping, make exhaustive night marches over stone-wall-patched English fields, learn to use knives, to drive continental locomotives. When not included in the Dieppe raid the jumpers moped. One drank himself into the town jail.

Upon arrival in Britain the doughboy jumpers went to work at their 800-ft jumps (U.S. Army minimum). Tommy counterparts were making jumps from even lower altitudes. Sensitive Colonel Raff cabled for permission to lower the jumps and shortly made a new record for the lowest (secret) mass jump without casualties.

Although Colonel Raff is a physical culturist and does not smoke, drink or play cards, his men have more than usual liberty. They gamble extra pay as they must soon gamble their lives. The galloping dominoes were so profitable for one Alabaman that he sent $4,000 home to the folks. After a round of poker, blackjack and craps the cash-lousy chutists took over an entire hotel for a clambake. Camaraderie between officers and men is encouraged by Colonel Raff, whom they call 'Little Caesar.' He is tough enough himself not to lose authority by personal contact. Says Raff: 'In a plane, I'm just another guy named Joe.'[7]

After the satisfactory rehearsal in Ireland, Raff's battalion broke camp on 3 November and travelled south by train to St Eval and Predannack, two Royal Air Force bases in Cornwall. By now the main invasion fleet was already sailing south for North Africa and finally, on 5 November, Raff revealed to his men their target and the drop date – 0130hrs on 8 November. He also added that as of that moment it was still not clear whether the French would welcome them or fight them. The day before the battalion embarked for North Africa word reached Raff that the French would be hospitable towards the Americans and they would be able to land unopposed at La Sénia airfield, resulting in the drop hour being rescheduled to mid-morning.

The 556 paratroopers of the Airborne Task Force left England at 2130hrs on 7 November, beginning the 1,500-mile flight south in 39 C-47 aircraft. Twelve hours later the lead aircraft began making their final approach to La Sénia. Suddenly the French opened fire with anti-aircraft batteries and small-arms fire, forcing the C-47s to break off the approach and land some distance from the airfield on a dry salt lake known as the Sebkra. Alerted to the French resistance on the airfield, the remaining aircraft headed for the salt lake, but as Raff approached he saw three tanks heading towards the three planes already on the ground. Assuming them to be Vichy French tanks, Raff gave the order for his men to jump and attack the armoured vehicles from the rear. 'The air seemed filled with white silk,' recalled Raff, 'the paratroopers underneath twisting, turning and striving to make a safe landing. On the ground, others, already disengaged from their equipment, were springing at the containers and dragging out musette bags, extra ammunition and anti-tank guns.'[8]

Raff had a bad landing, hitting his chest against a jagged rock with such force that he broke two ribs, but he ignored the pain to assemble his men and prepare to attack the enemy armour. Then he heard one of his scouts yell 'Colonel, those tanks have big white stars on them – they're American tanks!' The tanks belonged to the American Combat Command Force that had come ashore earlier at the beaches west of Oran and were now making for their own objectives.

By now 30 of the 39 planes had landed. Four others had landed in other parts of North Africa and been taken prisoner, one had got lost and landed in Gibraltar, and the other four had ditched in Spanish Morocco and were interned for three months. After a quick examination by his medical officer, Raff ordered his men to follow him on foot to Tafaraoui airfield – 35 miles away. Ten miles into the trek, Raff received word over the radio that American tanks were already in possession of Tafaraoui, but were in need of troops to guard the large numbers of French prisoners. It was decided to send one company from the battalion ahead in three aircraft to fulfil this request while the rest continued on foot towards the airfield. Captain John Berry led the 80-strong unit but halfway to Tafaraoui they were attacked by two French fighters, and in the strafing seven paratroopers were killed and 20 wounded.

Berry and Raff were finally reunited at Tafaraoui on the afternoon of 9 November. Though they were pleased to hear that the invasion was making swift progress – with Algiers in Allied hands and Casablanca and Oran on the brink of following – there was also a feeling of despondency that the first airborne operation in American history had achieved next to nothing.

However, that was not the angle taken by the American press. On 12 November the *New York Times* ran an interview with Raff's mother, Abell, in which she declared herself 'very happy and I'm very proud of my son'. The *Times* told its readers that Edson Raff had led parachutists in the longest airborne invasion in history and was the 'latest army hero', as well as filling in some details about the 34-year-old officer. Not only was he a devoted son but he was married to Mrs Virginia Chaney and was also the proud father of two boys, Thomas, aged four, and one-year-old Chaney.

Even as Raff and his men secured Tafaraoui airfield, events elsewhere were developing rapidly. Having resisted the Allied invasion on the orders of the Vichy government, French forces in north-west Africa quickly began surrendering when they realized the size of the invasion force. As Axis forces were brought in to try to repel the landing force, the German High Command ordered the invasion of southern France (hitherto unoccupied by the Germans and under the jurisdiction of the Vichy government), a move that prompted Admiral François Darlan, commander of the Vichy French forces and in Algeria to visit his sick son, to declare his allegiance for the Allies and order his troops to lay down their arms.

There now began a race between the Allies and the Germans to occupy air bases and towns of strategic importance in north-west Africa. Raff became involved in the competition when, on 12 November, he was instructed to lead a mission to capture the French airfield at Tebessa in the east of Algeria, 15 miles from the border with Tunisia and within range of the German forces streaming west from Libya.

As Raff began to plan for the insertion onto the airfield at Tebessa on 15 November, he learned from a French civilian of a second, larger air base close to the Tunisian border at Youks les Bains. Raff contacted headquarters with the intelligence report and was ordered to seize the base at Youks les Bains with an airborne operation and then send one company overland to secure the airfield at Tebessa, about 10 miles distant.

Despite having had less than 48 hours to prepare the operation, at 0730hrs on 15 November Raff led his men on their mission as scheduled. Jumping from 22 aircraft at a height of only 350ft, the 350 men of Raff's battalion assembled on the drop zone in just 20 minutes without any incoming fire. 'The quick descent from 350 feet leaves little time for thoughts,' wrote Raff. 'I had only two. First, "There must be Frenchmen in those trenches. No shots are being fired." Then "How in the world did this carbine (which was in my hand) get tangled in the shroud lines?" when plunk – both feet hit the mud of the field and, like the others, I, in the prone position, was struggling to get out of the harness. This tense moment is always critical in a paratrooper's life and is really much shorter than one thinks.'[9]

As the French soldiers (belonging to the 3rd Zouaves) emerged from their trenches to greet the Americans, Raff ordered one company to dig in around Youks les Bains, and then he dispatched a second company to secure Tebessa, which was also accomplished without contact with the Germans.

For the rest of November Raff, whose forces at Youks les Bains were augmented by the arrival of an American tank destroyer company and some Royal Engineers, embarked on several reconnaissance patrols. Now operating under the sobriquet 'Raff Force', the Allies penetrated as far as Gafsa, a Tunisian town 80 miles south, only to learn that the Germans were approaching. Pulling back to Youks les Bains, Raff Force was soon bolstered by the arrival of a squadron of P-38 fighters and, on 22 November, Gafsa was cleared of Germans in a combined air and land operation. Further engagements occurred with the Germans at Ferriana, resulting in the destruction of 12 enemy tanks and the capture of 100 prisoners, and at Faid Pass to the east – a portal through the Dorsale mountains to the coastal plain, the control of which offered protection to the British First Army flank to the north.

The battle for the Pass raged for two days before finally, late in the afternoon of 4 December, the Germans began waving white flags from their positions behind the rocks. Casualties had been heavy, with 100 Allied dead or wounded and twice that number on the German side. 'From the battle that day there is one sound which sticks in my mind,' wrote Raff later. 'It is the rhythmic beat of a heavy German machine gun manned by a Nazi who played tunes by fanning the trigger. At first the monotoned songs were songs of positive confidence; later, when the artiste began to feel less sure of his position, the tunes changed to dejected small bursts and, as his ammunition ran out, they ceased altogether.'[10]

Raff remained in Tunisia throughout December and on New Year's Eve he and his men were stationed at Kasserine, close to the border with Algeria. Raff spent the evening at a lavish party where red wine flowed and there was an abundance of roast pig. Shortly before midnight, however, he slipped away from the party to spend it with his men outside. 'I felt that they, who had been with me through so much, should be greeted before the comparative strangers in the house,' reflected Raff, whose battalion was about to finish operations in north-west Africa.

Writing about the contribution of 'Raff Force' to the campaign in Tunisia, Dwight Eisenhower said after the war that 'under the command of a gallant

American, Colonel Edson D. Raff, the story of his operations in that region is a minor epic in itself. The deceptions he practised, the speed with which he struck, his boldness and his aggressiveness, kept the enemy confused during a period of weeks'.[11]

Withdrawn from the theatre of operations in early 1943, the 2nd Battalion of the 503rd Parachute Infantry established camp at Oujda in French Morocco and later returned to England where, in time, they began preparing for another invasion – that of Italy. However, the battalion would do so without Raff. Having assisted General Omar Bradley, commander of the US First Army, with the planning of airborne operations in the lead-up to the invasion of Normandy, Raff (now a colonel) was assigned the command of 'Task Force Raff'. This was a special strike force comprising 17 Sherman M4 tanks from the 746th Tank Battalion and 90 glidermen belonging to the 325th Glider Infantry. Its mission on 6 June 1944 was to land at Utah Beach and punch inland towards the village of Sainte-Mère-Église, six miles to the west (where Baron von der Heydte had one company of his 6th Parachute Regiment posted) and join forces with the 82nd Airborne Division.

Raff led his men ashore at 1300hrs on 6 June, several hours after the main landing on Utah, and raced inland towards Sainte-Mère-Église. As he neared a crossroads at Les Forges, two miles south of his rendezvous with the command post of the 82nd Airborne, Raff found a large number of American infantrymen pinned down by German artillery, which was coming from the high ground known as Hill 20 between the two villages.

Raff sent a scout car down the road towards Sainte-Mère-Église with a Sherman tank behind to offer covering fire. The two vehicles disappeared along the winding road, and then Raff heard a violent crash followed by another heavy noise. A couple of minutes later the lieutenant in the scout car ran back along the road, shaken but unhurt, to explain to Raff that a German shell had hit his vehicle head-on but failed to explode. Nonetheless, such had been the force of the impact that the scout car had smashed into the tank behind and rendered it immobile.

Undeterred, Raff advanced down the road twice more, but each time shells from the German 88mm guns forced his armour to withdraw. Raff began to fret; it was 2000hrs and a glider landing was scheduled at 2100hrs, bringing in reinforcements from the 82nd Airborne on a landing zone one mile south of Sainte-Mère-Église. Suddenly into view appeared the gliders and their tug ships, one hour ahead of schedule and right on top of the German artillery.

Incredibly most of the glidermen landed unharmed, though their presence wasn't sufficient to assist Raff in breaking past the German positions on Hill 20. That was achieved the next day when, with the help of the 4th Division, Raff reached General Matthew Ridgeway and his 82nd Airborne. A week later Ridgeway appointed Raff commander of the 507th Parachute Infantry Regiment, following the capture of its predecessor Colonel George Millett at Amfreville.

By March 1945, 507th Parachute Infantry Regiment were respectfully known among the American airborne troops as 'Raff's Ruffians'. So heavy had their casualties been in the Normandy landings that they were not deployed during the ill-fated Operation *Market Garden* in September 1944, the audacious but unsuccessful Allied attempt to seize a number of important bridges in Holland and expedite the advance into Germany. They did, however, take part in the Battle of the Bulge, helping drive back the German attack through the Ardennes in January 1945, and in March it fell to Raff's Ruffians to lead the drop into Germany.

Operation *Varsity* was an Anglo-American operation involving more than 21,000 paratroopers and glidermen, the biggest single airborne drop in warfare in one day. The object of *Varsity* was simple: for two airborne divisions to drop east of the Rhine, secure key bridges and roads, and hold them while the 21st Army crossed the river in amphibious landing craft. Opposing the Allies was the German Army Group H, consisting of approximately 85,000 troops, although their morale and fitness for combat varied. Nonetheless it was a daunting task for Raff and his ruffians as they boarded their aircraft in the early hours of 24 March, having digested a breakfast of steak and eggs.

The 507th's DZ was a clearing two miles north of the town of Wesel, just to the edge of the Diersfordter Forest. As ever, Raff insisted on being the first to jump. 'I was alone standing in the door of the plane looking down at the river passing beneath the plane, smoke partially obscured my view,' he later recalled. 'At that moment, I said a prayer to the infant Jesus, The Little Flower, "Little Flower, in this hour show Thy power." The prayer was given to me by my sister who was a nun. I said the prayer before every jump. A split second after I said the prayer, the green light came on, as I looked down, I saw several objects below me. The first thing that caught my attention was several German soldiers on the ground with rifles in their hands looking up. The second thing I noticed was a heavy equipment bundle that was swinging back and forth as it descended toward the ground. The bundle saved my life because the Germans thought it was a bomb and disappeared into the cellar of a nearby house. I landed in the chicken yard behind one of the homes.'[12]

Once down on the ground, Raff and his men rounded up the Germans and then took stock of their position. They had been dropped wide of the intended DZ and were two miles north-west of where they should have been. Raff led his 700 men through the woods and back to the DZ, engaging several German patrols as they went. By mid-afternoon the 507th, along with all other airborne units, reported that they had secured their objectives. Operation *Varsity* had been a stunning success, a brilliant demonstration of what airborne troops could achieve with thorough planning and swift execution. Of the American 17th Airborne Division, 359 men had been killed and 522 wounded, while the British 6th Airborne lost 347 men and suffered another 731 wounded.

On 26 March the Allied 21st Army Group under Field Marshal Bernard Montgomery began moving east into Germany and two days later they had penetrated 20 miles behind the Rhine across a front 30 miles wide. Though there would be much bloody and bitter fighting in the weeks ahead, the Allies were within sight of victory against Nazi Germany.

✦ ✦ ✦ ✦

Raff remained in the army after the war. Already something of a legend within the United States thanks to his wartime exploits and the publication in 1944 of his book *We Jumped to Fight*, Raff was a leading figure in the development of Special Forces in the post-war period. In 1952 he trained Turkish troops in commando tactics, and later he commanded the 77th Special Forces Group, Airborne, who specialized in guerrilla warfare. Raff is credited with introducing the 'green beret' as the headgear of the elite Special Forces unit.

His last appointment was as head of the Psychological Warfare Centre at Fort Bragg, North Carolina, from where a quarter of a century earlier he had prepared the 2nd Battalion, 503rd Parachute Infantry to become the first combat airborne troops of the American military. Though Raff died in 2003 aged 95, some of the philosophy that made him one of the greatest Special Forces soldiers in American history lives as 'Afterthoughts' in *We Jumped To Fight*. Among three of the most pertinent, nearly 70 years later, are the following:

Be simple in your every act, word and deed. Your men will like it and you'll get results, not excuses.

You will never win a war at the command post. It is just as safe and more inspiring for your men to see the commanding officer around whatever your rank may be.

Mere production will not win the war. It is the man with the gun, the man in the tank, the man at the stick of the plane who must do the actual fighting. You must have the best and sufficient quantities of it, to be sure, but you, individually, must be the best also.

EVANS CARLSON

MARINE RAIDERS

On 2 February 1943 Lieutenant Colonel Evans Carlson assembled his 2nd Raider Battalion of the United States Marine Corps at their camp on Espiritu Santo one of the islands of Vanuatu in the South Pacific Ocean, in order to celebrate their first anniversary. Just a year earlier Carlson had formed the battalion at the behest of President Franklin Roosevelt, 'the first organization in the history of the American armed forces to be organized and designed purely for raiding and guerrilla missions'.

Casualties had been high on the battalion's two major operations but the sacrifices had been worth it, explained Carlson, because they had 'proved to the world the value of democratic practices in connection with military operations'. Then the lean, wiry grey-haired Carlson, about to turn 47, told his men why the battalion had achieved such success. It was, he said with his customary zeal, because each of them possessed 'a deep spiritual conviction in the righteousness of the cause for which he fights and in the belief that victory will bring an improved social pattern wherein his loved ones and the loved ones of future generations will enjoy a greater measure of happiness and well being than was his lot. And so it has been an unfailing policy in this organisation to articulate for you and constantly remind you of the reasons why we endure and fight and sacrifice.'[1]

Yet despite the impassioned address of Evans Carlson the 2nd Raider Battalion never saw action again. The following month the Marines decided to incorporate the unit into the new 1st Marine Raider Regiment under the command of Lieutenant Colonel Alan Shapley, a far more conventional officer than Carlson, who was ordered back to the States to recover from the effects of disease and exhaustion. While Carlson was recuperating, Hollywood released *Gung Ho!*, a motion picture based on the exploits of the 2nd Raider Battalion. Randolph Scott portrayed Carlson, and while the film was a box-office hit it further alienated its real-life star from the Marine Corps, who bristled at the attention lavished on their maverick comrade. As a result Carlson never again commanded troops in battle, and when he retired from the Corps he did so a bitter and disillusioned man, yet one who was held in the highest regard by the men who served under him in the 2nd Raider Battalion.

✦ ✦ ✦ ✦

Evans Carlson was born in Sidney, New York, on 26 February 1896, the son of a New England minister. Like Orde Wingate, the founder of the Chindits, Carlson grew up in a household where the influence of religion was pervasive to the point of being restrictive to his development as a young man. And just as Robert Frederick of the 1st Special Service Force fled the nest as soon as possible to escape his overbearing mother, so Carlson sought a route away from the religious doctrine of his father – however he bore for the rest of his life a deep and abiding respect for the gospel.

Carlson went to work on a farm at the age of 14, and then had a spell as a railroad worker before, in 1912, he enlisted in the US Army, adding five years to his age to meet the minimum requirement of 21. After basic training Carlson was sent to the Philippines and for three years endured a series of exotic if ultimately unexciting postings. He showed aptitude, however, for the military life and by the time he was 19 he had risen in rank from private to sergeant major. In April 1917, when the United States declared war on Germany, Carlson was commissioned a second lieutenant and posted to the 13th Field Artillery Regiment.

Even at such a young age Carlson displayed an unorthodoxy in his views on leadership that was fostered as much by his independent spirit as by his avid reading of philosophical tracts by authors such as Ralph Waldo Emerson. In a letter to his father, Carlson explained that 'I love my men but I must keep them working. When the work is over, I must see that they have some recreation. I must always see that they have sufficient food and shelter wherever it is possible. I will lead a man, if he will be led. But I'll get him where he's got to go, even if I have to drive him. I never ask a man to do something I won't do myself.'[2]

Carlson's idiosyncratic leadership style drew comment from his fellow officers but did not prove a barrier to promotion; in 1918 – still only 22 – he was promoted to captain and assigned to the 334th Regiment. But before his unit reached France to participate on the Western Front, Germany sued for peace and the Great War ended.

Despondent at missing the chance to test himself in battle, Carlson resigned his commission in 1919 and tried to make a name for himself in business. But he missed the military life and in 1922 re-enlisted as a private in the Marine Corps. Within three weeks he was a corporal and in 1923

Carlson was once more an officer, a second lieutenant stationed on the west coast of the United States.

His first overseas posting was to China in 1927, a country for which Carlson developed a strong affinity that endured all his life, but it was in the Central American country of Nicaragua that Carlson first began to develop as an exponent of guerrilla warfare. He arrived in Nicaragua in May 1930 to command a local militia force called the Guardia Nacional in the face of terrorist attacks from the rebel army; when he left Carlson had won a Navy Cross for his courage in confronting the enemy, as well as gained five guiding principles that formed the cornerstones of the 2nd Raider Battalion.

Like David Stirling in North Africa, Carlson recognized that in inhospitable terrain – in his case the jungle of Nicaragua – small units of highly trained men were much more effective in confronting the enemy than an entire regiment. Secondly, superior firepower rapidly deployed would always demoralize the enemy. It was important, too, to have men under his command who were not afraid to seize the initiative and think for themselves, and this combined with his fourth tenet – to always keep moving – produced men who were swift in thought and action. Lastly, Carlson came back to the point he had explained to his father in the letter a decade earlier: to look after the wellbeing of the men under his command.

Upon his return from Nicaragua Carlson was posted to Warm Springs, Georgia, where he formed part of Franklin Roosevelt's protection guard. Despite the fact Carlson was only a junior officer he formed a friendship with the American president that was to endure for the rest of their lives. It was an imbalanced friendship; Carlson idolized Roosevelt and enjoyed the thrill of having the ear of one of the world's most powerful men. The bond between the two men was noted by other Marine officers and did little to endear Carlson to his peers. In 1937 Carlson was posted back to China as a military observer on the war between the Chinese and Japanese, a conflict that was in its seventh year. Roosevelt asked Carlson to write personally to keep him updated on developments.

Carlson learned much from the Chinese communists. Mao Tse-tung expounded his philosophy, and one of his generals, Chu Teh, taught Carlson much about his military beliefs and the best way to fight the Japanese, even inviting the American officer to accompany his men into the field. What struck Carlson most about his time with Mao's army was its democracy: officers shared the same hardships as their men and involved them in decision-making. Writing of his experience to Roosevelt, Carlson said: 'Before a battle the men are assembled and the military situation is explained to them so that they go into the battle with their eyes open. They are told the possibilities of victory, the consequences of defeat. The result is a strong bond of understanding between leaders and fighters.'[3]

While Carlson was in China he received a visit from the American author Agnes Smedley, who was in the country to learn more about communism. She was impressed by Carlson and described him as 'one of those dangerous men of lean and hungry look. He's a throwback from our own distant revolutionary past – a mixture of Tom Paine, John Brown – with a touch of Lincoln. But all of him is New England – craggy and grim in appearance, yet kindly and philosophical.'[4]

Not everyone was so enamoured of what Carlson was doing in China, and a candid report of his on Japanese ambitions in the Pacific resulted in rebukes from both Japan and the US Navy, which did not wish to upset Japan. Infuriated by the attitude of his superiors, Carlson resigned his commission in April 1939.

When America declared war on Japan on 8 December 1941, Carlson had been back in the Marines for eight months with the rank of major. He still had his vocal critics within the Corps but he still also retained the ear of President Roosevelt.

In the weeks immediately after the declaration of war, Roosevelt was desperate for a way in which to strike back at Japan and show the American people that they would take the fight to the enemy – as the Japanese had done in such devastating style at Pearl Harbor. When Roosevelt read a memo written by Colonel William Donovan, chief of the Office of the Coordinator of Information, in which he recommended establishing a commando-style unit similar to those formed by the British 18 months earlier, Roosevelt embraced the idea with alacrity.

With the Pacific Fleet in ruins and the factories not yet capable of producing the requisite machines and arms to launch a major attack against Japan, Roosevelt saw a small unit of Special Forces troops as the perfect way in which to take the offensive to the enemy. Simultaneously Carlson was trying to draw the military's attention to his own belief in the efficacy of guerrilla warfare against the Japanese, and eventually he did so through his connections to the Roosevelts. Not only was Carlson on friendly terms with the president but he also knew well his eldest son, James, who at 34 was still searching for a role in his life. James Roosevelt had worked for William Donovan in 1941 and it was James who helped promote Carlson's idea for a Special Forces unit in a paper entitled *Development within the Marine Corps of a Unit for Purposes similar to the British Commandos and the Chinese Guerrillas.*

Despite the resistance of several influential Marine Corps officers, who still viewed Carlson with distrust after his open support for the Chinese communists and his subsequent resignation, the idea won the wholehearted support of President Roosevelt. On 23 January Carlson received authorization to form a Special Forces unit capable of carrying out attacks against Japanese targets; a month later the unit was designated the '2nd Marine Raider Battalion'.*

British Prime Minister Winston Churchill was delighted when he heard the news in early 1942. By this stage of the war Britain's Special Forces – the Commandos, the Special Air Service and the Long Range Desert Group – had been successfully operating against Axis forces in North Africa and Western Europe and he wrote to Roosevelt to tell him: 'Once several good outfits are prepared, any one can attack a Japanese-held base or island and beat the life out of the garrison, all their islands will become hostages to fortune. Even this year, 1942, some severe examples might be made causing perturbation and drawing further upon Japanese resources to strengthen other points.'[5]

Carlson's first appointment was Captain James Roosevelt as Executive Officer of the Raider Battalion, even though the president's son was physically weak and suffered from flat feet that in normal circumstances would have precluded him from active service. Nonetheless Roosevelt wanted to serve, with the reluctant approval of his parents, and Carlson knew the benefit of having such a man in his outfit.**

---

* The 1st Battalion, under the command of Merritt Edson, was raised and trained on the east coast of America and later fought with distinction at Guadalcanal.
** A similar situation briefly arose in the SAS in 1942 when David Stirling accepted Winston Churchill's son, Randolph, into the unit even though he was overweight, unfit and a heavy drinker. Fortunately for the SAS Churchill soon acknowledged that he was out of his depth.

With Roosevelt on board, Carlson embarked on a recruitment programme for his nascent unit that he envisaged would be 'flexible, mobile, possess the maximum fire power commensurate with great mobility and be composed of men physically capable and mentally conditioned to endure the hardships and overcome the obstacles necessary to accomplish the mission. It follows, therefore, that the personnel must be volunteers for this type of work and that they must be trained, conditioned and indoctrinated for this particular type of work.'

Carlson got his 500 volunteers from the Marine bases near San Diego; they represented a broad cross-section of American society, from city boys to farm hands, from high school dropouts to Grade A students. Their overriding motivation was similar to that of the early volunteers for David Stirling's SAS – boredom and a thirst for adventure.

The recruits were split into four companies and sent to the unit's training camp at Jacques Farm in California, but before they began their training the men were addressed by Carlson. He explained that 'the Jap is a wily and rugged enemy, experienced in hardships. And so I can promise you nothing but the toughest life while we're in the States and the toughest battles when we're overseas.' For men who already considered themselves part of the military elite it was a stirring introduction to their new unit, as was the disclosure of their battle cry – Gung Ho!*

The training that followed was intense. Each day the men rose at 0430hrs and endured several hours of exhausting exercise, including route marches through the countryside, strengthening exercises such as giving a buddy a fireman's lift over 50 yards, and thousands of press-ups and sit-ups. Soon the men could cover seven miles in one hour carrying a full pack.

In addition the men were schooled in navigation, demolitions and sharpshooting, and there were lectures and practical demonstrations in all aspects of jungle warfare, including water discipline and tropical diseases. 'As training proceeded self-confidence grew,' wrote Carlson. 'There was little cockiness. These men were bent on whipping an enemy who sought to destroy the democratic way of life they hold dear.'[6]

---

* 'Gung' in Chinese meant 'work' and 'Ho' was 'harmony', so the 2nd Raider Battalion would 'work in harmony'.

Democracy was a prominent theme in the Raiders' training. Carlson implemented a similar philosophy to that which he had witnessed in China during his stay with the communists. The men and the officers bedded down together, queued for food together at mealtimes and cleaned their equipment together. There were no special privileges. 'My first step was to abolish all social distinctions between officers and men,' explained Carlson to the *Reader's Digest* in 1943. 'There must be obedience, of course. That was the cornerstone of everything. But I told my officers they must command by virtue of ability. Their rank meant nothing until they had proved their right to it.'[7]

Each week Carlson held 'Gung Ho!' meetings in which officers and men could speak their mind. The meetings began with the commanding officer greeting his men with a cry of 'Ahoy, Raiders!', to which came the response 'Gung Ho!' Once points had been raised or grievances aired, the meeting ended with everyone singing the National Anthem.

Carlson also encouraged his men to examine the causes of the war and learn why Japan had attacked Pearl Harbor and why America was determined to prevail in the Pacific. Though he never expressed a political point of view, despite his close relationship with the Democrat Franklin Roosevelt, Carlson was less reticent when it came to religion. Men who served in the 2nd Raider Battalion recalled their commanding officer speaking to them often about religion, a theme that was addressed by a war correspondent. 'I'm an out-and-out pacifist,' replied Carlson when asked how a man who professed to be religious could lead a Special Forces unit. 'But when an aggressor strikes I do not believe in calmly permitting his steam roller to run over me. It is necessary to resist, to whip the aggressor with one hand, while with the other we work even harder to build a social order in which war will not be necessary as an instrument for adjusting human differences.'[8]

Once the raiders were physically fit and technically proficient, they were schooled in Carlson's guerrilla warfare. Applying to his battalion what he learned from his time in Nicaragua and China, Carlson sub-divided each of the four companies into ten-man squads; the squads in turn were divided into three three-man fire-teams, each led by a non-commissioned officer. In doing this Carlson believed the squad leaders would be able to concentrate more on winning the contact with the enemy rather than worrying about all the men under his command; instead he gave orders to his three fire-team leaders who in turn passed the orders on to the men in their teams.

The fire-teams were also equipped with a devastating array of weaponry, comprising one M1 rifle, a Browning Automatic Rifle (BAR) and a Thompson sub-machine gun. Carlson was determined that in any fight with the Japanese, his men would have the superior firepower. To obtain the weapons, Carlson asked James Roosevelt to use his connections, much to the chagrin of fellow Marine officers who were increasingly hostile to the 2nd Raider Battalion. Brigadier General Alexander Vandegrift, commander of the First Marine Division, admitted that the 2nd Raider Battalion 'annoyed the hell out of me but there wasn't one earthly thing I could do about it'.

In March 1942 the Raiders spent three weeks practising beach assaults off the California coast, and the following month the battalion was strengthened by the arrival of 250 new recruits, expanding the number of companies to six. In May the battalion – with Carlson promoted to lieutenant colonel and Roosevelt to major – sailed to Hawaii, from where two companies were dispatched to help reinforce Midway Island in the North Pacific Ocean, a 2.4-square-mile atoll 3,200 miles west of San Francisco and 2,500 miles east of Tokyo that the Americans feared Japan wanted to seize as an air base.

Carlson sent C and D companies to the island with orders to 'sell out dearly' when the Japanese invaded. The aerial bombardment began on 4 June when 108 aircraft took off from four Japanese carriers and attacked; although they all but annihilated the inferior American fighter planes, they caused little damage to the defenders on Midway. In contrast when the US Navy engaged the Japanese aircraft carriers they sank all four, causing irreparable damage to Japan's fighting capabilities in the Pacific.

Carlson had only agreed reluctantly to send two companies to Midway; it was not the sort of guerrilla action for which his battalion had been formed. In July 1942, however, at the behest of Franklin Roosevelt, the Raiders were given the opportunity to prove their mettle. The president wanted the military to launch an audacious raid on a Japanese target, a feat that would boost the morale of the public to follow the Doolittle Raid on Honshu by the US Army Air Force in April.

The target chosen was Makin Island (present day Butaritari) and the unit given the honour of making the first land assault against Japanese forces was Carlson's 2nd Raider Battalion. Makin was a small island measuring eight miles in length and one and a half miles at its widest point, situated approximately 1,100 miles east of Papua New Guinea. It conformed to the stereotype of the tropical island with its lagoon, coconut trees and plentiful mangroves, along with two villages at opposite ends of the island and a number of government buildings.

The Japanese had landed on Makin on 10 December 1941, installing a garrison under the command of Sergeant Major Kanemitsu with a seaplane base, two radio stations and a weather station.

The aim of the raid, apart from a propaganda coup for America, was to obtain intelligence on the Japanese forces in the area (Makin was reported to be the base for all Japanese activity in the Gilbert Islands) and distract the enemy's attention from the impending invasion of the much more important island of Guadalcanal, 1,000 miles to the south-west. Carlson was informed by his superiors that intelligence on the strength of the garrison was vague, but it was believed to be anywhere between 100- and 200-strong. In fact Kanemitsu had no more than 100 men under his command.

Carlson selected his two most experienced companies for the mission, A and B, and several rehearsals were conducted using the limited information available of the disposition of the Japanese forces and the topography of the island. Included in the practice runs was James Roosevelt, even though Carlson was reluctant to include the president's son in the raid. Roosevelt had lived up to the standards of a Marine officer but Carlson was concerned for his welfare during the raid; if he fell into enemy hands the propaganda consequences would be unimaginable. Ultimately it was James Roosevelt himself who decided the issue, insisting to both his father and Carlson that he fulfil his role as executive officer of the Raider Battalion.

The 134 raiders left Hawaii at 0900hrs on 8 August 1942 for the 2,030-mile journey to Makin on board the submarines *Nautilus* and *Argonaut*. Inside the vessels Carlson briefed his men once more on the plan: they would assault the ocean side of the island, not the more heavily defended lagoon side, with A Company under First Lieutenant Merwyn Plumley hitting Beach Y and Captain Ralph Coyte landing on Beach Z. Once ashore the raiders would advance rapidly across the island and attack the Japanese from the rear, eventually the two companies closing to rendezvous at Makin's church.

On board the *Nautilus* the task force commander, Commodore John Haines, would expect the raiders to return in their rubber dinghies no later than 2100hrs on D-Day, which would be 18 August. Providing everything went according to plan the Marines would then attack Little Makin, one and a half miles to the north-east, the following morning.

A little after 0300hrs on 16 August, the *Nautilus* was by Little Makin, and at first light the submarine submerged and moved closer to Makin to take a series of periscope photographs. That evening the two submarines rendezvoused and the men began to prepare for battle, relieved at the imminent escape from the claustrophobia of the submarine. At 0330hrs on 17 August the submarines surfaced and the raiders emerged to driving rain and a strong wind. Seeing the weather, Carlson scrapped the original plan of landing on two beaches and ordered his men to head for Beach Z.

Cautiously the Marines jumped into their 20 dinghies and proceeded towards the shore half a mile away, with 19 of the inflatables landing on a 200-yard stretch of beach. The dinghy containing Lieutenant Oscar Peatross and 11 men beached a mile to the south-west; showing the sort of initiative with which the Raiders had been instilled, Peatross sent two men off on separate trails to search for the main party and positioned the others in what, unbeknown to the officer at the time, was the Japanese rear.

Minutes after landing the Raiders' hope of a surprise attack was dashed when one of their number accidentally discharged his weapon. The incident confused Carlson, already unsettled by the weather and the disappearance of Peatross, and he ordered A Company to launch an immediate attack on the Japanese garrison on the other side of the island – a role for which B Company had trained.

By 0630hrs Carlson's force was 'heavily engaged' and already nine Raiders were dead. Throughout the morning machine-gun nests were painstakingly dealt with by the Americans but the well-concealed snipers hiding in coconut trees were harder to silence. Carlson ordered his men to bring their superior firepower to bear, which accounted for many but not all of the Japanese marksmen. 'Snipers were cleverly camouflaged and their fire was extremely effective,' wrote Carlson in his report on the raid.

The raid on Makin had turned into a battle, a combat situation for which Carlson was unprepared. Thrown by the ferocity of the Japanese resistance, even though he had learned of their aggression during his time in China, Carlson's boldness dissipated and he ceded the initiative to the enemy, who grew in confidence in the face of American passivity. Instead of launching a flanking attack on the main Japanese force, Carlson positioned his men in a skirmish line so the fight, in the words of one Raider, resembled 'a shootout at the OK Corral'.

Nonetheless there were acts of great individual courage from the Raiders, such as the lone charge by Corporal Daniel Gaston, in which he destroyed a machine-gun nest and killed five of the enemy before dying himself. Some of the Raiders' finest non-commissioned officers were downed as they tried to wrest the initiative back from the Japanese. Sergeant Clyde Thomason fell to a sniper (he was subsequently awarded a Medal of Honor for his gallantry, the first such award in the war for a Marine serving in the Pacific) and Sergeant Norman Lenz was shot in the head and paralyzed by a sharpshooter's bullet.

Twice the Japanese launched counter-attacks but both times they were repelled by the Raiders. Then at 1320hrs the Japanese air force arrived, the Makin wireless station having radioed for assistance. Twelve aircraft spent more than an hour strafing the island, causing few casualties but pinning down the Marines and giving much-needed succour to the Japanese. Two flying boats attempted to land in the lagoon and disgorge reinforcements but both were destroyed by the Raiders' anti-tank weapons.

By now it was clear to some of the Raiders that the Japanese resistance was weakening. Dead littered the island and only sporadic sniper fire disturbed the afternoon tranquillity of the island. When Carlson questioned some of the locals on the strength of the Japanese garrison, estimates varied from 100 to 180. Carlson erred on the side of caution and believed the figure to be at the top end of the scale.

Carlson also inexplicably neglected to act when one of the two men sent by Lieutenant Peatross reached his command post at 1400hrs. Informed by the soldier that Peatross's section was in the unoccupied south-west of the island, Carlson failed to order his officer to attack the Japanese rear. It was a decision that later baffled Peatross, who wrote in his post-war memoirs: 'As he walked along the battle line and talked with the Raiders, saw with his own eyes the enemy dead strewn about the battlefield and heard with his own ears the marked diminution in the volume and variety of enemy fire until all that remained was intermittent sniper fire, Carlson should have realized long since that the prize was his for the taking. But he didn't.'

As dusk approached, Carlson decided to withdraw from the island rather than complete the mission by destroying the radio stations and wiping out all Japanese personnel. Instead, at 1930hrs the men climbed into their dinghies and began paddling for the submarine lying offshore. Exiting the reef proved a challenge, as time and again heavy breakers capsized the already exhausted men. At least one man appeared to be taken by a shark. At nightfall only 80 of the 200 men had succeeded in reaching the submarines. The other 120, including Carlson and Roosevelt, were stranded on the beach, many without their weapons.

During the night Carlson and Roosevelt discussed many options, among them surrender, but at dawn on 18 August some of the Raiders tried again to leave the beach, and two dinghies made it to the submarines. On hearing that surrender was being discussed, Commodore Haines sent a rescue party to the beach composed of five volunteers, all of whom were strong swimmers.

Before they arrived, however, Carlson had recovered his poise and his fighting spirit and resolved to fulfil his mission. Sending out patrols to probe the enemy's strength, he learned that the few Japanese who remained were dispersed over a wide area; emboldened by the intelligence, Carlson advanced across the island and destroyed what he could.

Carlson and his men finally made it off the island at 2300hrs on 18 August, and 53 minutes later the *Nautilus* and *Argonaut* set sail for Hawaii. Nineteen Raiders had been killed and several wounded during the raid, though it wasn't until later that it was discovered nine men had been left behind – five of whom were the rescue party sent by Haines. Although the oversight was blamed in part on the fog of war, Carlson's mistake further fuelled resentment among his detractors within the Marine Corps who in private considered it an act of gross negligence. The nine Marines were subsequently captured by the Japanese and after a few weeks in captivity were beheaded on 16 October, a Japanese holiday to honour departed heroes.

The fate of the missing nine men, however, was of little importance to the American press when the Raiders returned to Hawaii on 25 August. Despite the questionable success of the raid, Carlson and his men were acclaimed as heroes and afforded a military guard of honour at Pearl Harbor with Admiral Chester Nimitz, Commander in Chief, US Pacific Fleet, greeting Carlson as he stepped on shore. A Marine press release was hastily sent to media organizations in which it was said the Raiders had 'fought gangster fashion for 40 hours' with the soldiers showing 'they can give plenty of hot lead and cold steel to the Japs'.

Along with Sergeant Thomason's posthumous Medal of Honor, the Navy awarded 23 Navy Crosses (second only to the Medal of Honor) to members of the raid including Carlson and James Roosevelt, to help convey the impression that the raid on Makin had been an unparalleled triumph and a severe setback to Japanese prestige. But in truth the raid achieved little, other than to battle-harden the men who took part. An insignificant number of Japanese soldiers had been killed and a few buildings destroyed, at a cost of 28 dead or missing Marines. It also deepened the dislike among a cadre of Marine officers for Carlson, as they watched in distaste as he revelled in the limelight upon his return from Makin.

Carlson, however, was brutally honest in his assessment of the raid, even admitting in his operational report that he had considered surrender. Nimitz was astounded, and furious, when he read the report and demanded the passage concerning surrender be removed. When he himself analyzed the Makin Island operation, Nimitz criticized Carlson for failing to take the initiative in the early stages of the raid and he concluded that 'the old story in war of the importance of the offensive was again demonstrated'.

What was never brought into the open in the analysis of the Makin raid was the extent to which the presence of James Roosevelt had inhibited Carlson's decision-making. Though Roosevelt performed his duties admirably in difficult circumstances, some believed his presence on the island caused Carlson to act with unusual docility. The thought of the president's son being shot by an enemy sniper must have weighed on Carlson's mind at some level or other, and instead of showing characteristic Gung Ho! aggressiveness, the Raiders were hesitant and diffident in the face of a small, if determined, enemy.

Fortunately for Carlson, two months after the Makin raid Roosevelt was transferred to San Diego with instructions to raise what would be known as the 4th Raider Battalion (a 3rd Battalion was raised at the same time). By now, October 1942, the 2nd Raider Battalion was based on Espiritu Santo in the New Hebrides, 550 miles south-east of Guadalcanal, one of the southern Solomon Islands in the south-west Pacific.

Guadalcanal was an island at the centre of a bitter struggle between Japan and the United States. Situated 1,400 miles east of Australia, the island – 92 miles long and 33 miles wide – was in the hands of the Japanese, and a major threat to the supply lines between the USA and Australia. If America wanted to win the war in the Pacific they would need to oust the enemy from Guadalcanal and seize the airstrip for themselves.

In August 1942 the Americans landed on Guadalcanal and in the face of fierce Japanese resistance established a small foothold in the north, centred around an airfield under construction called 'Henderson Field'. But Japanese forces were in the dense jungle all around the Field and on top of the 1,515ft mountain overlooking the American positions, on which was located their artillery piece dubbed 'Pistol Pete' by the Americans.

Bitter as the fighting was on Guadalcanal, it offered Carlson and his men the perfect opportunity to re-establish their reputation after the confusion of the Makin raid. There they had been forced to fight like infantrymen, but in the jungles of Guadalcanal they could revert to being what they had trained to be: guerrilla fighters. On 22 October Carlson presented a plan to his superiors: landing on the unoccupied south side of the island, his Raiders would advance through the jungle and over the mountain and attack the Japanese from the rear. The idea was considered but rejected, and instead

Carlson was ordered to land two companies at Aola Bay, 40 miles east of Henderson Field, and provide a defensive ring to allow another airfield to be constructed so that aircraft could land safely.

On 4 November, C and E companies landed at Aola Bay and almost immediately found their mission altered; instead of acting as defensive troops they were to carry out a reconnaissance patrol to gauge the strength of the Japanese between the bay and Henderson Field, and eliminate any of the estimated 1,500 Japanese still at large following an earlier offensive by the Marines and Army.

Carlson was delighted at the change of plan. Now at last he could put into practice all the guerrilla skills he had acquired since arriving in Nicaragua 12 years earlier. On 6 November Carlson led his patrol into the jungle. As well as the 266 men of C and E companies, he was accompanied by 150 native scouts, the latter finding the going easier in the dense jungle – in which they covered only five miles on the first day.

Over the next few days the Raiders struggled to acclimatize to the enervating heat, a terrain that was a daunting mix of volcanic hills, jungles, rivers and open fields of kunai grass interspersed with ramshackle villages and the prevalence of venomous reptiles and aggressive insects. Though there were wasps on Guadalcanal that were 3in long, it was the millions of mosquitoes that made life miserable for the Raiders, for with the mosquitoes came malaria – the most common affliction to strike down men on the island, after dysentery and ringworm.

The first major contact with the Japanese occurred on the morning of 11 November when they intercepted 700 enemy troops evading a large-scale American offensive to the north-west of the Raiders' position. Throughout the day the Raiders fought a series of bloody engagements around Asamana, with Captain Richard Washburn's E Company fighting off a far superior force and in the process killing 120 of the enemy. C Company, on the other hand, was in disarray by mid-afternoon and it required Carlson to leave his command post and take charge of the company. Having assessed the situation at first-hand, Carlson called in an air strike and, in the aftermath, the Japanese withdrew to the south, leaving behind 160 dead in total. Raider losses were ten dead and 13 killed. As a consequence of C Company's performance, Carlson relieved its commanding officer – Captain Harold Throneson – of his duties.

The day after the battle at Asamana, the Raiders found one of their number staked out on the ground with his testicles cut off and stuffed in his mouth and dozens of other mutilations to his lifeless corpse. An enraged Carlson, adopting the Biblical exhortation of 'an eye for an eye', ordered the immediate execution of two Japanese prisoners and gave instructions that no mercy was to be offered to the enemy for the rest of the campaign.

On 12 November the Raiders began pressing west, following the trail of the Japanese survivors of Asamana who were trying to link up with the main army beyond Henderson Field. On 13 November Carlson and his men fought the Japanese in a series of short, sharp engagements that ended each time with the Americans drawing the enemy into the sights of their artillery. Satisfied that the Japanese had been cleared from the area around Asamana, Carlson established a new command post in the village and began probing further west and south.

At last Carlson was in his element, the leader of a band of guerrilla fighters operating in the perfect terrain for the warfare for which they had trained. In addition his fire-teams were proving their effectiveness in the almost daily contacts with the Japanese, overwhelming the enemy with their devastating concentrated firepower. Despite being twice as old as his Marines, the 46-year-old Carlson possessed limitless supplies of stamina that astounded his men, and he often insisted on walking with the lead scout in order to better assess the situation. 'Colonel Carlson was a fearless, inspirational leader,' recalled Captain Richard Washburn. 'He seemed to have a sixth sense as to where the enemy was located and what he was going to do.'[9]

Occasionally the Raiders would encounter a solitary Japanese sniper, more often than not concealed in the vast roots of a banyan tree, but the real enemy on Guadalcanal was the environment itself. It was the rainy season and the men were constantly wet as they moved through the steamy jungle; clothes rotted, boots disintegrated and skin chafed until it was red-raw. Nearly all the men suffered from one disease or another with dysentery causing the most misery: some soldiers were so badly afflicted they cut a opening in the seat of their trousers so they could evacuate their bowels on the move.

At night they slept where they pitched camp, a poncho over their emaciated bodies, and a string attached to the foot of their nearest buddy so they could alert one another to any approaching Japanese soldier. Day after day they ate the same rations – rice and bacon, heated in their helmet – with a little chocolate to follow. Often it was impossible to build fires so the men ate it cold.

On 24 November, 18 days after embarking on the patrol, the 2nd Raider Battalion had achieved what they had set out to do. The 40-mile area south of Henderson Field had been cleared of the Japanese, relieving the pressure on the American foothold at Guadalcanal.

The next day, Carlson's force was reinforced by the arrival of A Company, fresh and eager for the fray, and aghast at the sight of their comrades as they emerged from the interior of the island.

In the last few days of November Carlson established a new HQ close in the shadow of Mount Austen, and sent out patrols to search for 'Pistol Pete', the Japanese artillery piece that had been bombarding Henderson Field, as well as the main enemy supply trail that led up the mountain and down the other side towards the airfield. On 30 November, in the Lunga Valley, a section of Raiders discovered and destroyed 'Pistol Pete', together with a 37mm anti-tank gun. On the same day another section of Raiders consisting of seven men under the command of Corporal John Yancey ambushed 100 weary Japanese soldiers who had stopped for some lunch; without sustaining casualties themselves, the American patrol killed 75 of the enemy in the half-hour contact.

On 2 December Captain Peatross, one of the Raiders who had emerged from the Makin Island raid with his reputation intact, located the Japanese supply trail that skirted Mount Austen and branched out north-west towards the Matanikau River. Armed with the news, Carlson decided that rather than returning to Henderson Field as ordered, he would demand one final task from his men: to clear the summit of Mount Austen of Japanese.

By now all six Raider companies were on Guadalcanal. Carlson assembled them and explained that they had one final mission that would involve A, B and F companies, the three sections that had been on the island for the shortest amount of time. Having outlined the task, Carlson led his men in a rendition of 'Onward Christian Soldiers', and then he led them up the mountain.

It took six hours to reach the summit of Mount Austen and as they neared the top the Raiders encountered the Japanese. A desperate two-hour firefight ensued, but Carlson, unlike at Makin Island, never lost the initiative and deployed his men in flank attacks that slowly wore down the Japanese resistance. At the end of the engagement the Raiders had killed 25 of the enemy, though they had lost Lieutenant Jack Miller, one of their most popular officers.

With Mount Austen cleared of Japanese troops, Carlson led his men down the northern face and on to Henderson Field. After a month-long patrol he had led his Raiders back to base after a 120-mile march through some of the toughest and most unforgiving terrain on earth. Of the original 266 men whom Carlson had taken into the jungle on 6 November, 209 Raiders had been killed, wounded or evacuated suffering from disease.* The 57 that had made it through to the bitter end, however, were shadows of the men that had marched into the interior of Guadalcanal a month earlier. Some had shed more than two stone in weight.

Carlson and his 2nd Raider Battalion left Guadalcanal on 15 December and celebrated Christmas Day at their old camp at Espiritu Santo. Two weeks later *Newsweek* ran an article trumpeting the achievements of the Raiders on Guadalcanal: 'Carlson's boys – officially known as a Marine Raider Battalion – were something new in America warfare. They were America's first trained guerrillas, whose boast was that they "know how to do anything" and who could prove it.'

And prove it they had, claimed *Newsweek,* just one of several publications to pick up on the exploits of the Raiders.

On 28 December, the same day that the *Newsweek* article appeared in America, General Hajime Sugiyama and Admiral Osami Nagano informed Emperor Hirohito that their position on Guadalcanal had become untenable and a withdrawal was recommended. On 31 December the Emperor accepted the recommendation and an evacuation plan was immediately formulated, to begin in January 1943. By 7 February the Japanese Navy had successfully evacuated more than 10,000 soldiers from Guadalcanal without alerting the

---

* In his report on the patrol, Carlson stated that his battalion had killed approximately 488 Japanese soldiers and suffered 16 dead and 18 wounded in returning harmony.

Americans to the operation. Nonetheless, on 9 February the Americans were able to declare that the island was free of Japanese.

A week before the declaration Carlson and his men had celebrated the first birthday of the 2nd Raider Battalion, and there had been much to celebrate. Carlson had been awarded his third Navy Cross for his conduct on Guadalcanal, while a host of other men had been decorated for their gallantry during the arduous patrol. The most cherished honour, however, was the unit citation for the Battalion, which stated:

> For a period of thirty days this battalion, moving through difficult terrain, pursued, harried and by repeated attacks, destroyed an enemy force of equal or greater size and drove the remnants from the area of operations. During this period, the battalion, as a whole or by detachments, attacked the enemy whenever and wherever he could be found in a series of carefully planned and well executed surprise attacks. In the latter phase of these operations, the battalion destroyed the remnants of enemy forces and bases on the Upper Lunga River and secured valuable information of the terrain and enemy line of operations.

But in March 1943 Carlson's 2nd Raider Battalion was incorporated into the new First Marine Raider Regiment under the command of Lieutenant Colonel Alan Shapley. Carlson was sent back to the States to recover from the effects of Guadalcanal, but in a letter to a friend the same month he disclosed that he knew what was really behind the move: 'I have been kicked upstairs to the No2 job in the regiment. It means that I lost my command.'

The cartel of senior officers in the Marine Corps who had distrusted and disliked Carlson since his days spent in the company of Chinese communists, an antipathy fostered by his cosy relationship with President Roosevelt and his popular image with the press, had exacted their revenge by stripping Carlson of the one job he loved above all others – leading the Raiders. One of the few senior Marine officers who didn't bear a grudge towards Carlson was Lieutenant Colonel Merrill Twining, Chief of Staff of the First Marine Division. In his memoirs he reflected: 'If this Byzantine manoeuvre was conducted to relieve Carlson of command, it gives a momentary glimpse of the dark side of the upper levels of the Marine Corps showing its inflexibility of thought and a compulsive suspicion of all things new and untried. Evans Carlson was worthy of more generous treatment than he received.'[10]

✦ ✦ ✦ ✦

Though Carlson's enemies ensured he never again commanded Marines in battle, he nonetheless saw further action in the Pacific, participating in the battle for Saipan in June 1944. Wounds sustained in the battle ended Carlson's active service career and he was invalided home to California, where a month later he received a visit from President Roosevelt and his wife. In December 1946 Carlson suffered a heart attack, and the following May he died, aged 51, in Portland, Oregon. The Marine Corps refused to pay the costs of transporting his coffin from Oregon to Arlington National Cemetery in Washington, DC – much to the fury of James Roosevelt, who covered the expense.

Yet despite the treatment of Carlson and the fact that the 2nd Raider Battalion was not deployed as a guerrilla force following their amalgamation into the 1st Marine Raider Regiment in March 1943, their legacy lived on in the Marine Corps. In his 1995 memoirs Oscar Peatross, the young lieutenant who had performed so creditably on Makin Island and rose to become a major general in the Marine Corps, wrote: 'In spite of the fact that practically all other units hated and were jealous of the raiders, all Marine infantry squads were organized on the … fire team concept by the middle of WWII, and, as you know, are still organized that way today.'[11]

ROBERT FREDERICK
1ST SPECIAL SERVICE FORCE

There was nothing exceptional in the early military career of Robert Frederick to suggest that he would become the leader of one of the United States' most renowned Special Forces units of World War II. A second lieutenant in the Coast Artillery throughout much of the 1930s, Frederick was on a staff officers' course when Germany invaded Poland. But within four years he was the commander of the 1st Special Service Force, a unit so feared by the Germans that Frederick and his men were nicknamed 'the Black Devils', a sobriquet in which they revelled. Intended as a US-Canadian special winter warfare unit, the 1st Special Service Force fought in the bitter Italian campaign of the winter 1943/44, and Frederick's 'devils' played a vital role in the landings at Anzio. An unassuming but fearless Special Forces brigadier who often commanded his troops from positions of exceptional danger, it was Frederick's fighting record that earned him his place in military history, with Winston Churchill calling him 'the greatest fighting general of all time'.

✦ ✦ ✦ ✦

The inventor Geoffrey Nathaniel Pyke was an opinionated, argumentative, dogmatic English eccentric who rarely washed or shaved. Having read law at Cambridge, the physically fragile Pyke found work as a war correspondent during World War I, later working as a financier and educator before turning his first-class mind to invention.

The Times of London would describe him in his obituary as 'one of the most original, if unrecognized figures of the present century' and certainly Pyke was one of the first men in the 1930s to realise the extent of the dangers posed by Nazi Germany. He was also able to grasp quicker than most what would happen to British cities if the German Luftwaffe launched the same intensity of bombing raids that they had on Spain during the Civil War. It was Pyke's suggestion (which was ignored) that the chalk deposits in Wiltshire and Devon should be hollowed out and used as shelters for Londoners.

Pyke was 45 when war broke out in 1939, a middle-aged man bitter and disappointed that none of his ideas had received the acclaim he believed they deserved. But still he persevered and in 1940 produced a paper in which he outlined how a force of highly trained soldiers could wage a guerrilla war behind German lines with the aid of his mechanical innovation.

The paper was timely, coming shortly after Winston Churchill had replaced Neville Chamberlain as Prime Minister and instructed the War Office to raise a commando force. Yet despite this the paper received a muted response from the military and Pyke was left once more to fume against those who failed to recognize his genius. Then, in October 1941, Lord Louis Mountbatten was appointed Chief of Combined Operations, and among his tasks was the initiation of British commando attacks against German targets in Europe.

Mountbatten learned of Pyke's memo from the previous year and invited him to his headquarters to hear more. Within minutes Mountbatten was convinced that Pyke was on to something; having first explained to Mountbatten that 70 per cent of Europe was covered in snow for five months of the year, Pyke unveiled the mechanical innovation that would enable the British to exploit the continent's weather to their advantage: a motorized snow plough capable of travelling across the icy terrain at great speeds. Pyke's plan was for a small force of highly trained soldiers to parachute into Norway, Denmark and the Alps, along with several of the snow ploughs, and then attack key German targets such as bridges, tunnels and hydroelectric plants that the British feared would be used in the production of atomic weapons. With the Germans possessing no comparable form of winter transport they would have to counter the saboteurs by drafting in large numbers of troops, thereby causing them maximum inconvenience.

Pyke was thrilled that his intellect had at last been recognized. Within a short space of time he had his own office at Combined Operations HQ and answered to the title 'Director of Programmes' as he began work on 'Project Plough'.

On 11 April 1942 Mountbatten briefed Churchill on Project Plough at a meeting in which President Franklin Roosevelt was represented by Harry Hopkins, his unofficial emissary in London, and General George Marshall the US Army Chief of Staff. It was agreed that with America's greater resources, both in manpower and manufacturing, Project Plough would be a US responsibility, although with input from the Norwegians and Canadians, as well as the technical advice of Geoffrey Pyke.

One of the Americans' first moves was to appoint an officer to recruit volunteers for the project. The man eventually chosen was Lieutenant Colonel Robert Frederick, a 35-year-old native of San Francisco with a doctor for a father and a domineering woman for a mother. Kept on a tight leash by his mother as a boy, Frederick rebelled against her authority aged only 13 by enlisting in the California National Guard. Three years later he was commissioned in the Cavalry Reserve as a second lieutenant and, at 17, he was accepted into West Point, the United States Military Academy for officers. When he graduated from West Point in 1928 it was as a popular but unremarkable young officer who seemed to have a knack for administration and organizing. Placed 124th out of 150 in his class, Frederick was described thus by his class book:

> He has a natural and modest personality that is bound to please. Both officers and cadets ask his advice on affairs of the Corps, knowing that they will get a practical and workable judgement … he has given invaluable aid to the Dialectic Society in all of its many activities. Whether it be managing a year book, providing the Corps with Christmas cards, decorating a ball room, arranging exhibits from outside firms, or convincing the Tactical Department that a change should be made, Fred has been asked to do it and has always done it well.[1]

In the decade after graduating, Frederick showed no signs of disabusing the notion that he was anything but a solid if unspectacular officer. He served in the Coast Artillery, the Harbor Defense Command and commanded an anti-aircraft artillery unit in California. In 1938 Frederick was sent to the Command and General Staff School at Fort Leavenworth, Kansas, on a course preparatory to becoming a staff officer.

He graduated from the school in the same year that Germany and Britain went to war, and while Europe tore itself apart Frederick took up an appointment at the Pentagon with the Operations Division of the War Department General Staff. One of his responsibilities was to make feasibility studies on reports sent to the Pentagon, and in May 1942 Frederick received a copy of Geoffrey Pyke's Project Plough.

Frederick pored over it for 12 days and then sent his report to Major General Dwight Eisenhower, chief of Operations Division. In his conclusions Frederick advised that the 'snow vehicle is not well adapted to the type of operation contemplated. It is believed that the same effect on the German war effort can be achieved by other means, the most promising of which is by subversive acts.'[2] In short, it was Frederick's recommendation that the American military establish a brigade-sized Special Forces unit to attack German targets, but not by means of snow ploughs. Eisenhower, however, rode roughshod over Frederick's recommendations, telling him that he was not going to shelve a plan that had the enthusiastic support of Winston Churchill.

The American officer initially chosen to lead Project Plough was Lieutenant Colonel H.R. Johnson. While work began on the snow plough,* Johnson met Pyke to discuss the organization of the force. Within days Johnson was ousted from command after it was decided he was 'unattuned' for the role; in reality, he and Pyke hated the sight of each other from the first moment and one of them had to go. According to Lieutenant Colonel Robert Burhans, an intelligence officer who later served in the brigade under Frederick, Eisenhower told Frederick: 'You take this Project Plough. You've been over the whole thing. You're in charge now. Let me know what you need.'

Other sources claimed subsequently that the choice of Frederick was Mountbatten's. Whatever the truth, the pair were soon on their way north to discuss the project with the Canadian Army, the outcome of which was an agreement that Canada would second some of its finest soldiers to the force, as well as provide land on which to train and snow specialists to advise on technical matters.

The only impediment to the raising of the force as far as Frederick was concerned was the continued interference of Pyke. At the end of June 1942, in a memo to Harry Hopkins, Frederick described the Englishman as being in possession of an imaginative and intellectual mind. However, he added, 'he has no knowledge of the methods or requirements for training personnel. He does not appreciate the ramifications and administrative details of creating a special

---

* The result was the T-15 Cargo Carrier, later to become the M29 Weasel, which was used by Canadian forces into the 1960s.

organisation. He appears to have an aversion to organisation and orderliness.'[3]

In early July Hopkins took Frederick's complaint, along with many others concerning Pyke, to Mountbatten who terminated Pyke's involvement with Project Plough. With Pyke back in England, Frederick was at last able to focus all his energies on raising his brigade. One of his first discoveries, as David Stirling and Junio Valerio Borghese could have told him, was that there was an innate distrust among many senior officers for any irregular force that might exist outside the parameters of normal military procedure.

Though he was able to use his influence to procure several officers to serve on his staff – notable among them being Major Orval Baldwin and Major Kenneth Wickham – Frederick was less successful in finding the men to fill his ranks. With the US Army preparing for deployment across the globe, commanding officers were not about to allow some of their most able soldiers to join a Special Forces unit. Instead Frederick organized notices to be pinned to Army bulletin boards in which he asked for volunteers to join a new unit, priority being given to 'lumberjacks, forest rangers, hunters, northwoodsmen, game wardens, prospectors and explorers'.

What Frederick got instead was commanding officers emptying their baskets of rotten apples. Soldiers with poor disciplinary records were encouraged to volunteer while men up on charges were reputed to have been given the choice of a prison sentence or volunteering for Frederick's outfit. Even the officers who stepped forward had a touch of wildness about them; the unit's Operations and Training officer was a Virginian major called John Shinberger, who kept a box of live rattlesnakes under his bed in the hope that having the reptiles in such close proximity would cure him of his phobia.

The men who did volunteer – and many had exemplary military records and simply sought adventure – were sent to the Force's training camp at Fort Harrison in Helena, Montana. By now Frederick had been made a full colonel and the unit was officially designated the 1st Special Service Force with a red spearhead as their formation patch, on which 'USA' was written horizontally and 'Canada' vertically.

On 19 July 1942 Frederick and his HQ staff were installed in Helena and men were arriving every day by road and rail. They came from all over the United States and from Canada, too, though the latter, paid by their own government and subject to their code of discipline, received lower wages than their southern comrades. The Canadians and Americans eyed each other warily at first, and there was the odd brawl with the Canadians obliged to show that they 'didn't take kindly to jokes about the King and Queen'. It was in training, however, that a mutual bond of respect was forged between the two nations.

Having divided the 1st Special Service Force into three regiments, Frederick put them through a brutal training regime; having expected a high drop-out rate, he had recruited 30 per cent more men than he needed. Each day followed a similar routine: rise at 0445hrs, then cleaning duties and breakfast by 0630hrs. At 0700hrs the men were put through a calisthenics programme and at 0800hrs they completed the 2,000m obstacle course. The rest of the day was spent on route marches, target practice, demolition courses, unarmed combat and parachute training. Two-hour lectures were held four nights a week on a broad range of subjects related to their training, and in any spare time the men went off into the hills on the 'Weasel' cargo carriers. To turn them into proficient Alpine troops, Frederick seconded a dozen Norwegian ski instructors to the force and, after six weeks' training, the men were able to complete a 30-mile cross-country march on skis carrying a full pack and a loaded rifle.

During the training Frederick flitted in and out of Fort Harrison; sometimes he would appear during a parachute drop, other times he would sit in on a lecture, and then disappear for days or weeks on end. Much of his time was spent in Washington at the Munitions Building discussing possible targets for his unit. It was suggested that his men might drop into Romania to attack the oil fields of Ploiesti, while several industrial installations in the rugged north of Italy were also mooted.

Concerned by the fact that there was no clear objective for his unit, Frederick travelled to London in the autumn of 1942 to discuss Project Plough with Mountbatten and Eisenhower (now based in Britain). He was dismayed to be met with an air of indifference to the 1st Special Service Force, even apathy in some quarters, with the Norwegians openly opposed to the idea of their country being subjected to guerrilla warfare. After a frank discussion with Mountbatten, in which the Briton was sympathetic but explained there were no other priorities, Frederick agreed to abandon Project Plough.

Frederick returned to the States deflated but defiant, and after a positive meeting with General George Marshall decided to reinvent the 1st Special Service Force as a unit capable of fighting in any terrain – not just snow. His next problem was to find a theatre in which he could show off the fighting qualities of his men, many of whom were becoming restless after months of hard training with no sign of action in sight.

At the end of November 1942 Frederick received orders to embark for New Guinea to operate against the Japanese, but 24 hours later the order was rescinded. Instead the Force underwent a course in amphibious landing tactics at the Naval Operations base in Virginia. By June 1943 Frederick was still waiting to blood the 1st Special Service Force and rumours were growing that they were bound for England to carry out raids on German-occupied France.

The rumours were wrong, however, and instead on 9 July Colonel Frederick led his 169 officers and 2,283 enlisted men on board two troopships bound for Kiska, one of the Aleutian Islands off Alaska that had been occupied by the Japanese since June 1942.

Intelligence reports indicated that there were 12,000 Japanese in well-fortified defensive positions on the island, and the Special Service Force was just one component of an Allied invasion fleet that numbered nearly 35,000 troops and included three battleships and a heavy cruiser. The Americans began landing on the night of 15 August with the 1st and 3rd regiments of the Special Service Force in the vanguard of the attack; they were braced for furious opposition but they stepped ashore in silence – the Japanese had withdrawn two weeks earlier. The invaders were relieved but staggered at the inaccuracy of their intelligence, which had also stated the island's beaches were flat and strewn with pebbles. In fact the beach was covered in huge boulders that would have been a serious obstacle to any landing under fire.

The man who came to the rescue of Frederick and his unit was Lord Louis Mountbatten. At the time that the Special Service Force was stepping ashore at Kiska, he was attending the Allied conference at Quebec, a month after the

Allies had invaded Sicily. During the conference Churchill and Roosevelt and their chiefs of staff discussed an invasion of France as well as the establishment of a front in Northern Italy. Lieutenant General Mark Clark, the commander of the US Fifth Army, approved of the idea but pleaded for more troops for his Mediterranean campaign. Remembering the Special Service Force, Mountbatten suggested that they be deployed for operations in Italy.

Two months later the Force was en route to Casablanca aboard the *Empress of Scotland*. Frederick, who had flown on ahead of his men, met them at the quayside on 5 November 1943, and together they entrained to Naples Harbour and a bivouac camp. One of the men, Lester Forrest, recalled how Frederick behaved during their stay in Naples: '[He] never blew his top except when we were sloppy, unshined shoes, bearded faces, no neckties, etc. His attitude was almost motherly at times. He would send his personal recon car to gather us up. We could see the distant firing, and hear the booms which set us to wondering as to when it was our turn.'[4]

The Force's turn came at the start of December. Blocking the Allies' advance to Rome was a section of the German Winter Line, constructed along the Camino massif with the twin peaks of Monte la Difensa and Monte la Remetanea on the right. Dug in on the mountains was the 15th Panzer Grenadiers with the Hermann Göring Division in reserve. They had resisted all attempts so far by the Allies to seize the two peaks, and inflicted on Clark's Fifth Army some 10,000 casualties by the time they pulled back to rest in the middle of November and plot their next move.

Clark planned another attempt to smash the German Winter Line and advance into the valley of the river Liri, beyond which lay Rome. Codenamed Operation *Raincoat*, the assault would begin with a heavy air and artillery bombardment followed by an attack by the British X Corps on the left and the American II Corps on the right; the 1st Special Service Force would be tasked with taking Monte la Difensa and Monte la Remetanea.

Frederick was assigned his mission on 22 November, perhaps one reason why he was 'motherly' towards his men around this time. He was confident his unit could achieve their objectives but he envisaged heavy casualties. To acquaint himself more fully with the task, Frederick took a few men and scouted Monte la Difensa under cover of darkness. Three thousand feet in height, the first third of the peak was heavily wooded, but after that it was bare crags all the way to the summit – where the Germans, in crevices and caves, were well protected from shells and bombs.

The only footpath to the top of Monte la Difensa was a rough track on the south side. On the north side was a 200ft sheer cliff, above which were six ledges each approximately 30ft in height that the Germans, and hitherto Fifth Army, deemed inaccessible. Frederick thought otherwise.

Gathering his officers around him, Frederick outlined his plan of attack: the honour of leading the assault on the mountain would go to the 600 men of the 2nd Regiment under Colonel D.D. Williamson; the 1st Regiment would be held in reserve and the 3rd Regiment would be supply carriers for their comrades in the 2nd.

Accompanied by Frederick, on the night of 2 December 1943 the Special Service Force began moving up into position under heavy rain and an artillery bombardment. The best climbers among the 2nd Regiment secured ropes on the more challenging parts of the ascent up the northern side of the mountain. At times the Germans were so close they could hear them chatting to one other. By midnight most of the men, including Frederick, had climbed noiselessly up the cliff face and were concealed among the rocky ledges. Their commander then signalled to the lead company to move forward and eliminate the German sentries with knives. This was done as planned, but as the Force edged ever-closer to the main enemy positions, which were in semi-underground bunkers on the crest of the mountain, a stray boot caused a rockfall. Suddenly a flare burst overhead, illuminating the 600 American and Canadian soldiers. One of them, Percy Crichlow, remembered: 'All hell broke loose. I dived for cover and my section, who were laboriously climbing over the ledge behind me, started to crawl into position to my left as soon as they were on the ledge in front of the topmost lump.'[5]

As the 2nd Regiment rushed forward to engage the enemy in a series of desperate hand-to-hand combats, behind them on the cliff face swarmed the 2nd Battalion of the 1st Regiment, who had been held initially in reserve. Despite the flare, the German defenders were caught off-guard by the appearance of such a large enemy force from the north side of the mountain.

Many were overwhelmed in the first rush of Special Service troops and those that emerged from their deep gun emplacements were shot dead regardless of whether their hands were raised.

Within two hours the mountain was in the hands of the 1st Special Service Force, and when dawn broke on 3 December Frederick established a forward command post on one of the ledges. From here he assessed his unit's position, deciding that until further supplies arrived it was still very vulnerable to an enemy counter-attack. The only way to transport supplies, however, was by pack mule up the rough track on the southern side, a three-hour trip from the foot of Monte la Difensa.

Frederick remained on the crest organizing the resupply, showing what one of his men later remembered as 'casual indifference' to the occasional barrage of German mortar fire, as members of the Force's 3rd Regiment embarked on the tortuous job of bringing supplies up the rough, muddy track. Removing the numerous American wounded was also a logistical nightmare, and in some cases it took eight men ten hours to remove just one stretcher case down the mountain to a point where he could be placed in a vehicle and transported to a field dressing station.

With the British X Corps having taken their objectives on the left by the morning of 4 December, Frederick switched his focus to the second peak of Monte la Remetanea, where many of the Germans on Monte la Difensa had fled 24 hours earlier in the face of the Special Service Force's attack. He dispatched a reconnaissance patrol along the ridge that connected the two mountains and the information they brought back, along with the intelligence provided by some German prisoners, convinced Frederick to storm la Remetanea without delay.

He scheduled the attack for dawn the next day, 5 December, but in the hours before dawn the Germans subjected the Special Service Force to a murderous bombardment. At the epicentre of the barrage was the 1st Regiment, who had been held in reserve during the initial attack and were now in the act of moving forward.

As they dug in as best they could, the 1st Regiment was joined by Frederick, who had left the safety of his command post to be with his men. 'I'll never forget Colonel Frederick walking by our position and telling me to keep my head down,' recalled Sergeant Allan H. Jamison. 'And here he was up in full view of the enemy himself!'[6]

The onslaught lasted for an hour, during which time the 1st Regiment was more than decimated – it lost 40 per cent of its fighting strength, forcing a 24-hour postponement of the attack on la Remetanea as Frederick reorganized his brigade. Sending out patrols to flush out the increasing number of German snipers, the colonel brought up more reserves and questioned prisoners on the exact disposition of the German defenders on the second peak. He also procured 15 cases of bourbon, 'for medicinal purposes', and ordered a slug of liquor for every man huddled on the mountainside under heavy rain and heavy mortar fire.

By midday on 5 December the German snipers on the ridge had been eliminated and Frederick decided to press on with the attack in daylight. Twenty-four hours later he sent a despatch to his second-in-command, Colonel Paul Adams, in which he said:

> Our attack to the west against hill 907 [la Remetanea] has progressed beyond the crest of 907. We are receiving much machine gun and mortar fire from several directions, principally from the draw running southwest from la Difensa, from west foothills of Maggiore and from north slopes of Camino … I shall push the attack on to the west past 907 as far as conditions of men will permit. Men are getting in bad shape from fatigue, exposure and cold. German snipers are giving us hell and it is extremely difficult to catch them. They are hidden all through the area and shoot bursts at any target. Please press relief of troops from this position as every additional day here will mean two days necessary for recuperation before next mission. They are willing and eager, but are becoming exhausted.[7]

On 7 December the Force saw the welcome sight of British troops pouring towards them after their capture of Monte Camino. The soldiers swapped stories and then at nightfall Frederick and his men began withdrawing.

In securing Monte la Difensa and Monte la Remetanea, the Special Service Force had suffered a 25 per cent casualty rate, with 532 of their number killed or wounded. Yet in accomplishing their objectives they had facilitated the Allied advance north towards Rome by dispossessing the Germans of the mountainous defensive position guarding Highway 6. Clarke Lee, a war correspondent for the Combined American Press, was effusive in his praise of the achievement, writing: 'This feat captured the imagination of the entire Fifth Army and overnight Frederick and his soldiers became almost legendary figures in a battle area where heroism was commonplace. Despite two wounds, Frederick had gone on fighting with pistol and grenade at the side of his men. The Difensa attack is destined to live in military annals because of the endurance, daring and fighting skill it involved.'[8]

The Force was not allowed long to rest and recuperate after the rigours of capturing la Difensa and la Remetanea. Withdrawn to their base at Santa Maria, they shivered in tents as the European winter intensified and men reported sick with frostbite and 'trench foot', a debilitating condition that had tortured thousands of men on the Western Front a generation earlier.

Meanwhile the Germans were still stubbornly holding on to southern Italy, fighting bitterly for every inch of land. In the Venafro sector, north of Naples, the Germans were entrenched in and around Monte Sammucro, and once more it fell to the 1st Special Service Force to dislodge the enemy and so ease the passage of the main Allied advance.

Frederick once again scouted the area personally before the attack, postponing it for 24 hours as he organized resupply lines for his men once they had taken the target. At nightfall on Christmas Eve the attack began. The 1st Regiment moved up the snow-clad mountainside in darkness, clearing Germans from foxholes and repelling small pockets of counter-attacking troops. The closer the Force got to the summit of Monte Sammucro, the more intense the fighting became. Even in the darkness German snipers were close enough to kill, and machine-gun fire and mortar fire caused further casualties. Frederick advanced with his men, tending to the wounded and encouraging the unscathed. By dawn the mountain was in the hands of the Force, although Christmas Day was spent fighting off several German counter-attacks.

From Monte Sammucro Frederick led his men to the next targets in the mountain range, Monte Radicosa and Monte Majo. The former was seized by the 2nd Regiment, now under the command of Lieutenant Colonel Bob Moore after his predecessor had been RTU'd (returned to unit) on Frederick's orders. The officer, while far from disgracing himself, had nonetheless failed to live up to Frederick's expectations and he no longer considered him fit to command.

The honour of securing Monte Majo, a key obstacle to the advance of the Fifth Army (and which was important strategically for the attack on Monte Cassino) fell to the 3rd Regiment under Colonel Edwin Walker. Having not been involved in the previous mountain assaults, the men of the 3rd Regiment were eager to prove themselves the equal of their Force comrades. Scaling a cliff almost as impressive as the one conquered by the men of the 2nd Regiment on la Difensa, the 3rd Regiment surprised the Germans on Majo and within five hours had triumphed. Furious German counter-attacks followed over the course of three days but the Special Service Force would not be moved and the attackers suffered 75 per cent casualties in their attempts to regain possession of the cold, forlorn mountain. When the photographer Robert Capa toured the battlefield a few hours later he described how '… every five yards a foxhole, in each one at least one dead soldier. Around them empty cans of C rations and faded bits of letters from home. The bodies … were blocking my path.'

In the fighting of late December and early January, the Special Service Force had suffered 75 per cent casualties, with 100 men dead or missing and a further 429 wounded or laid low with sickness. Yet still there was no respite for Frederick (who had been wounded a third time) or his men.

On 22 January 1944, the Allies landed at Anzio with the aim of outflanking Axis forces (estimated to consist of 70,000 men) on the Winter Line and expediting the capture of Rome. Crucial to the success of the operation – codenamed *Shingle* – was the speed with which the Allies moved across the marshland in the Anzio basin and into the mountains where the Germans and Italians were dug in. The initial landings caught the Germans off-guard and the Allies got ashore virtually unopposed, but within three days the Germans had reinforced their defensive positions around the beachhead with troops from the south, including a Panzer Grenadier Division and the Hermann Göring Panzer Division.

After ten days' rest the Special Service Force, its fighting strength bolstered to 1,300 men by replacements or the return from field hospitals of wounded and sick, landed at Anzio on 1 February. The Allied front line was now 32 miles wide, and the Force's mission was to hold an eight-mile stretch of its right-hand flank against any German attack to force them back into the sea. General Mark Clark had chosen the Force for this task because, as he wrote later, they were 'aggressive, fearless and well-trained'.

On 2 February the Special Service Force embarked on its first aggressive patrol across the Littoria Plain, through which ran the Mussolini Canal, and above which the Germans lurked in the mountains. The Force was soon losing men to snipers and mines, but within a week their belligerence had forced the Germans to pull back half a mile. Snipers became less of a threat, but the German artillery fire was still heavy at times. Undeterred, the Force moved beyond the canal and occupied the villages that lay between the waterway and the mountains. The village of Sabotino was renamed 'Gusville' in honour of Lieutenant Gus Heilman, whose patrol had been the first to enter. Soon Gusville became the headquarters of the 2nd Company, 1st Regiment, and it received a visit from a correspondent for *Stars and Stripes*, the US Army newspaper:

On the surface, this fantastic community appears to be just a collection of huts and tents and a few buildings; the home of cows, chickens, horses and a few pigs. But it is also home of sudden death – for Gusville is the base used by our reckless Anzio commandos whose motto is 'Killing is our business'.

Every night the Black Devils of Gusville, American and Canadian troops, steal quietly out of town, move over deep into enemy lines to kill or capture Germans. 'Black Devils' is what the Nazis call them; the Fifth Army troops call them the wild men of the beachhead … it is another spot where it is being proved that the men of the Allied nations can be fused into a deadly fighting machine. And it is being demonstrated here that these fighting men do not lose their high courage, their lighthearted spirit and their sense of humour, even under the toughest battle conditions.[9]

According to Robert Adleman and George Walton in their account of the Special Service Force, *The Devil's Brigade,* the satanic moniker originated in a diary found on the body of a dead officer from the Hermann Göring Division killed during a patrol. An entry when translated read: 'The Black Devils are all around us every time we come into the line, and we never hear them come.'

The blackness, a reference to the chalk used as camouflage by the men, wasn't the only sinister accessory of the Special Service Force men at Anzio. To further strike fear into the enemy, Frederick had some calling cards printed for his men to leave on the bodies of the German dead. Underneath the Force's red arrowhead insignia was a message in German: *Das dicke Ende kommt noch,* or 'The Worst is Yet to Come'.

Unlike the fighting on Monte la Difensa, where killing took precedence over capturing, at Anzio Frederick wanted as many Germans as possible caught for interrogation purposes. One of the most successful hauls netted 111 Germans, when a patrol led by Lieutenant George Krasevac infiltrated the enemy's front lines and surprised them as they assembled for a patrol of their own. One German officer subsequently admitted to Frederick that they had assumed the Special Service Force was a division and not a brigade.

The patrols continued throughout the early spring, with Frederick often accompanying his men. One of his fellow officers, Colonel Kenneth Wickham, recalled that his reason for doing so was to 'check the conduct of the night patrols. He had a sense of where and when he was needed. The men became aware that they would often find him in a critical area.'

After 99 days on the front line, the Force was withdrawn in May and allowed 12 days of rest. By now the unit's fighting strength was 2,000 and when they saw the arrival at their rest camp of several armoured half-tracks they guessed their role was soon to change. Sure enough, when they returned to the fray on 23 May it was as part of the VI Corps breakout from Anzio, codenamed Operation *Buffalo.*

While the main thrust was aimed at Campoleone, Velletri and Cisterna, the Special Service Force's job was to protect the right flank of the advance. The first day's objective was to seize Highway 7 to Rome, which was achieved, but some of the men advanced so quickly once across the highway that they became isolated and were caught by the retreating Germans.

One by one the Allies' aims were fulfilled and the breakout from Anzio quickened, although the Germans staged an aggressive withdrawal, bombarding the Allied units who chased them too vigorously. In one such incident the brigade suffered many casualties at Artena when they ran into a barrage of German 88mm artillery. Nonetheless on 3 June Frederick, now a brigadier general in overall command of a pathfinder task force called 'Howze', led his brigade towards Rome. He had suffered two slight wounds in the preceding days but he was determined to be at the head of his men as they entered the Eternal City. Later, in a report written at the request of the War Department to clarify the timing of the seizure of Rome, Frederick described the hours leading up to the Force being one of the very first Allied units into the Italian capital:

Early on 4 June 1944 the First Special Service Force was directed to enter the city of Rome and to secure bridges over the Tiber River. Elements of the First Special Service Force with attached elements of the 1st Armored Division proceeded toward Rome from the East, the assault force attacking along Highway 6.

At 0620 hours, 4 June 1944, the head of the assault force column passed the city limits of Rome and entered the city. This column was preceded by reconnaissance personnel who worked into the city as far as the main railroad station before returning to report their observations. This assault column consisted of 1st Armored Division vehicles on which personnel of the First Special Service Force were riding, with personnel of the First Special Service Force on foot ahead and on the flanks of the motor column.

When a portion of the assault column had entered the city, the enemy opened fire with anti-tank artillery which prevented further forward movement of the Armored Division vehicles until after the enemy defences had been neutralized. However, troops of the First Special Service Force continued on into the city in a manoeuvre to outflank the enemy defences. I can state the time of entering the city with certainty as I was in a radio vehicle near the head of the column and checked the time frequently during the advance. I definitely remember that it was 0620 hours on 4 June 1944, when the leading vehicles crossed the city limits.[10]

What Frederick omitted to include in his report was the moment he was wounded when an enemy shell exploded close to his armoured half-track, a shard of shrapnel cutting open his leg. Despite the wound, Frederick spent the afternoon of 4 June checking the bridges along the Tiber for demolition charges. At the 110m-long Margherita Bridge Frederick's patrol encountered a detachment of Germans, holding the bridge for any stragglers from the east of the city. A firefight ensured in which three Germans were killed and 12 captured, but Frederick's driver was killed and he suffered further wounds to his leg, as well as one to his arm. The wounds, the eighth and ninth that Frederick had sustained in the war, gave rise to his reputation as the 'most-shot-at-and-hit general in American history'.

While Frederick was flown back to a hospital in Anzio, his men decamped to Tor Sapienza, a suburb in the east of Rome, and from there they were sent to the far more salubrious shores of Lake Albano, 12 miles south-east of the capital. Frederick soon joined his men at the lake, albeit with an arm and a leg in plaster, and on 23 June he had them assembled for an address. To the disbelief of the Special Service Force, Frederick announced he had been posted to another command. One sergeant present said that the men 'cried like babies' when Frederick informed his men he was moving on.

Frederick had been promoted to major general (at 37 the youngest man to hold the rank in the US Army Ground Forces) and was destined for command of the 1st Airborne Task Force and a role in the invasion of southern France. Nevertheless despite the honour, he regretted the severance of a two-year bond with the Special Service Force and it pained him that he wasn't able to tell his men why he was leaving.

Having left the 1st Special Service Force, Frederick took up his new appointment and hurriedly began preparing for Operation *Dragoon*, the codename for the invasion of southern France. With the Allies struggling to break out of the Normandy beachhead, it had been decided to open a second front at the other end of the country. The task fell to the soldiers of the American VI Corps under Lieutenant General Lucian Truscott, all of whom were veterans of the bitter fighting in and around Anzio. To assist VI Corps, a new airborne division had been raised – the 1st Airborne Task Force.

With the exception of the British 2nd Independent Parachute Brigade, the Task Force was all-American, comprising the 509th Parachute Infantry Battalion, the 517th Parachute Combat Team, the 550th Glider Infantry Battalion and the 551st Parachute Infantry Battalion. In addition another unit was formed specifically for the invasion – the Provisional Troop Carrier Air Division, consisting of 450 American transport planes and 550 gliders, the aircraft that would take the Task Force into France.

To assist Frederick in his daunting task of preparing the Task Force for Operation *Dragoon*, 35 airborne staff officers were posted to his side. In a matter of weeks they had to devise the best strategy for carrying out their allotted task: to jump into the Le Muy area, a few miles inland between Cannes and Toulon on the French Mediterranean coast, and prevent German reinforcements reaching the beaches where the main landing was taking place. Facing Frederick's Task Force was the German Nineteenth Army under the command of General Hubert Weise. The Nineteenth Army contained many Eastern European volunteers who were prepared to fight to the death rather than risk capture and execution on return to their homeland.

After months of leading his men from the front, Frederick was now obliged to sit down and plan a strategy that would ensure a swift accomplishment of their task, one upon which the success or failure of the invasion might hinge. The plan he formulated was straightforward: on the night of 14 August three pathfinder teams would insert into Le Muy, carrying the latest 'Eureka' hand-held radar homing beacon system. Once on the ground they would begin transmitting on a frequency that would be picked up by the main airborne assault force and used as a guide for the British 2nd Independent Parachute Brigade, the 509th Parachute Infantry Battalion and the 517th Parachute Regimental Combat Team. Once they had dropped and seized their objectives, gliders would land at 0800hrs on 15 August (D-Day for the main invasion) with heavy weapons and fresh supplies of ammunition. Finally, on the afternoon of the 15th, the 550th Glider Infantry Battalion and the 551st Parachute Infantry Battalion would land in gliders to consolidate the expected gains made by the initial parachute assault.

The plan was executed with stunning success, resulting in the most accurate night-combat drop of the war. Eighty-five per cent of the paratroopers landed on their DZ and when the gliders landed at 0800hrs with heavy weapons and ammunition supplies, casualties were again light.

A few miles south on the landing beaches, VI Corps had established a secure bridgehead and in the afternoon of 15 August the 550th Glider Infantry Battalion and the 551st Parachute Infantry Battalion landed in their gliders without serious difficulties. Operation *Dragoon* had achieved all its aims of the first few hours and Frederick's 1st Airborne Task Force had been instrumental in securing the success of the mission. By late afternoon on 16 August, VI Corps armour linked up with the paratroopers in Le Muy and Frederick's task was complete.

At this point the British 2nd Independent Parachute Brigade was detached from the Task Force and assigned to their Eighth Army in Italy; they were replaced by the Special Service Force (now under the command of Colonel Edwin Walker) on 22 August. Frederick visited his old brigade and greeted them with the words 'I'm sure glad to see you'.

There was scant time to reacquaint themselves with one another, for the Task Force was instructed to exploit German disorganization and push east towards the Italian border. It was a memorable time for the Americans with enemy opposition light and French hospitality immense. Flowers, kisses and wine greeted the liberators in every town and village. On 24 August Frederick set up his HQ in a plush Nice hotel while his men continued on to the border and established a 60-mile north–south front along the Maritime Alps with the 1st Special Service Force at the southernmost flank by the coast.

While the war raged furiously further north in France, in the south it was all sunshine and pretty girls in what became known as the 'Champagne Campaign'. The weather closed in at the end of October, and the following month the 1st Airborne Task Force was disbanded, having achieved its purpose and the German Army now being pushed back towards Germany.

On 22 November Frederick visited the Special Service Force HQ at Menton, a French coastal town two miles from the Italian border. He issued decorations and then expressed his gratitude for all the men had done in the preceding two and a half years. Six days later the Force was pulled back to

Villeneuve-Loubet, a few miles west of Nice, and 5 December they paraded for the final time. Almost a year to the day since the 'Black Devils' had performed such heroics in seizing the supposedly impregnable Monte la Difensa, they were no more. The Canadian contingent was subsumed into their own army and the American members of the Special Service Force were transferred to various different airborne and infantry units.

✦ ✦ ✦ ✦

Frederick assumed command of the 45th Infantry Division in December 1944, leading them across the Rhine and into Germany in March 1945, where they fought their way toward Nuremburg in the closing weeks of the war in Europe. After the war Frederick returned to America, but in 1948 he was back in Europe as the commanding general of the US forces in Austria. The appointment was brief and from February 1949 to October 1950 he commanded the 4th Infantry Division at Ford Ord, California before being posted once more to Europe as chief of the joint US Military Aid Group to Greece in the aftermath of the Greek Civil War.

He didn't last long in Greece, retiring from the military in March 1952, a decision that Frederick never fully explained. According to the account given in *The Devil's Brigade*, Frederick was alleged to have incurred the wrath of a high-ranking Greek politician who demanded of the American government that Frederick be either fired or forced to retire. Not wishing to see Greece fall to the communists, the US government acquiesced and the distinguished military career of Robert Frederick came to an abrupt end. His service had seen him decorated with, among others, the Distinguished Service Cross with oak leaf cluster, the Distinguished Service Medal with oak leaf cluster, the Silver Star Medal, the Bronze Star Medal with oak leaf cluster, the French Légion d'honneur and the British DSO.

In his extraordinary career, Frederick had shattered many of the preconceptions governing the behaviour of a commanding officer in battle. He had exposed himself to enemy fire on countless times in order to lead and inspire his men, an example that didn't sit well with some of his more conservative peers, who not only objected to having Special Forces in the

US Army but also believed Frederick's conduct to be irresponsible and dangerous within the overall command structure. Ironically, however, in the same year that Frederick retired from the US military, Colonel Aaron Bank established the 10th Special Forces Group, which in time would gain global fame as 'The Green Berets'. Much of the ethos and inspiration of the Group originated in the 1st Special Service Force, with some of its wartime members recruited to its ranks.

Further fame came the way of the Special Service Force in 1968 when a film based on the book *The Devil's Brigade* was released, starring William Holden and Cliff Robertson. In the best traditions of Hollywood the film stretched the bounds of veracity at times to suit its purpose but nonetheless it helped cement the reputation of the brigade in the eyes of America. Two years after the film's release, in 1970, Frederick died in California aged 63.

Despite the many fine words that were spoken at Frederick's funeral the passing of time had dimmed the memory and weakened the impact of such eulogies. None could be compared to what the war correspondent Clarke Lee had written just after the war by way of a eulogy for the demise of the Black Devils:

It is difficult to write about Frederick's exploits without suggesting a wild-eyed composite of Sergeant York and General George (Blood and Guts) Patton. But the comparison is misleading. Frederick certainly saw as much combat as the average infantryman, and more than most, and in common with Patton, he demanded the best effort from those in his command and believed that the best way to win battles was by incessantly attacking, getting the enemy on the run and keeping him there. His military fame is founded on his own fighting record, rather than any striking of attitudes, display of showy uniforms and flashy bodyguards, or employment of a highly-coloured vocabulary.[11]

PADDY MAYNE
SPECIAL RAIDING SQUADRON

It was in South Africa that Blair 'Paddy' Mayne first left his mark on that continent. Not as a soldier, the profession in which he would later gain legendary status in North Africa, but as a rugby player of high repute.

In May 1938 Mayne sailed from Britain on board the *Stirling Castle* as a member of the British Lions rugby squad chosen to tour South Africa and Rhodesia. A recent law graduate from Queen's University Belfast, the 23-year-old Mayne was one of the youngest players in the 28-man squad but he was also one of the strongest and most athletic, a second-row forward standing 6ft 3in and weighing 16 stone who had already impressed in his three appearances for Ireland. 'He was a very quiet chap,' recalled Vivian Jenkins, the vice-captain of the Lions, 60 years later. 'He was a bit of a loner in one way but he was immensely popular on tour. At first glance you would think he wouldn't hurt a fly, but we soon discovered that when he got steamed up he would do anything.'[1]

Mayne played in 19 of the tour's 24 matches, including all three Test matches against South Africa, and though the Lions lost the series the young man from Belfast was one of the few tourists to earn the respect of their hosts. Dougie Morkel, one of the legendary figures of early South African rugby, described Mayne as 'the finest all-round forward I have ever seen and he is magnificently built for the part. In staying power he has to be seen to be believed.'[2]

Though Mayne was disciplined and controlled on the field of play, a player not known for violent excesses in an age when brawling was common, away from the pitch Mayne revealed to his Lions teammates an occasional glimpse of his dark side. Jenkins recalled an evening when Mayne and another player, a Welshman called Bunny Travers, went down to the docks in Durban with the sole intention of fighting. They got their wish and 'flattened them all', returning to the team hotel to tell their teammates all about their victory.

A few days later the squad moved north-west to Pietermaritzburg and checked into the hotel selected for them by the tour organizers. The hotel allocated the players the shabbiest rooms, reserving the best ones for some dignitaries in town for the game. Mayne was furious with their treatment, recalled Jenkins, 'and decided to stage a one-man protest ... he proceeded to break everything in the room, the bed, the wardrobe, the drawers, he broke the whole bloody lot, and then piled it in a heap in the middle'.[3]

The hotel owner was apoplectic on discovering the vandalism and Mayne was summoned to a meeting with Jock Hartley, manager of the tour party, in the hotel garden. Whatever was said, Mayne took it badly, judging that the room had got what it deserved. When the tourists assembled after lunch to take the bus, Mayne was missing. He reappeared three days later, just in time to help the Lions beat Natal 15-11, a game in which he was described by one South African newspaper as 'the outstanding forward'. Eventually Mayne disclosed to Jenkins, an experienced and talented full-back whom the Irishman admired and respected, details of his three-day escapade. Having found a bar in which to drown his sorrows, Mayne had got talking to a local farmer, then 'the two of them had a few drinks and decided to go on a bit of a thrash. They had ridden on horseback to a village where a dance was being held. They rode straight into the hall, across the dance floor and then back out again, chased by several irate villagers.'[4]

✦ ✦ ✦ ✦

Mayne was in Belfast when war broke out in 1939. He had joined a firm of solicitors, George Maclaine and Company, and divided his time between the legal profession and the rugby field. He won three more caps for Ireland in that year's Five Nations Championship, and in the same month as he played against Wales in what would turn out to be his last international match, Mayne enlisted in the Territorial Army, in an anti-aircraft battery of the Royal Artillery. In light of his subsequent actions, Mayne's decision to choose such a passive unit was a startling one, though perhaps the intelligent Irishman foresaw that the early stages of the war would be defensive.

But the months of 'Phoney War' following the declaration of hostilities between Britain and Germany on 3 September left Mayne bored and frustrated, so with no aircraft to shoot down he decided to transfer to the infantry, enlisting in the Royal Ulster Rifles in April 1940. Two months later Mayne was on the move again, this time volunteering for Britain's first Special Forces unit, the idea of which sprang from Winston Churchill himself. 'We have always set our faces against this idea but ... there ought to be at least 20,000 storm troops or "Leopards" drawn from existing units,'[5]

Churchill instructed his chiefs of staff in a memo. The name 'Leopards' was subsequently ditched in favour of 'commandos', after the irregular Afrikaner units that had caused the British Army such strife during the Boer War.

The volunteers were organized into five commando 'battalions' – Nos 1, 6, 7, 8 and 11, with the latter better known as Scottish Commando on account of its ranks being filled from the Scottish regiments. The men of 11 Commando assembled in the Borders town of Galashiels under the command of Lieuenant-Colonel Dick Pedder, among them Mayne and a fresh-faced lieutenant from the Gordon Highlanders called Bill Fraser.

Lieutenant Mayne – now known to one and all as 'Paddy' – and his new comrades were posted to the Isle of Arran where they underwent rigorous training during the autumn months. One of the privates, Jimmy Storie, remembered that Mayne was 'a rough Irishman and liked plenty of go. He was happy doing that and he didn't like sitting around. In Arran he was known to sit on his bed and shoot the glass panes out of the window with his revolver.'[6]

In January 1941 it was decided to send three commando battalions to the Middle East to carry out raids against Italy's stretched lines of communications along the North African coast, as well as targets in the Mediterranean and Balkans. The battalions selected were 7 Commando, 8 Commando and 11 Commando. They arrived at Geneifa, Egypt, on 7 March and within 48 hours they were being addressed by General Archibald Wavell, Commander-in-Chief Middle East Forces. From now on they would be known as 'Layforce', under the command of Colonel Bob Laycock; the name 'commando' banished for fear of alerting the enemy to their presence in North Africa, particularly now that a German expeditionary force, the Afrika Korps, had recently arrived to reinforce the ailing Italian Army.

For six weeks 11 Commando idled away their time, the men growing ever more restless, before they were sent to Cyprus in anticipation of a German invasion at the end of April. But the Nazis never came and the soldiers took out their frustration on the one-shilling bottles of Cyprian wine. Mayne landed himself in trouble when he threatened the owner of a nightclub with his revolver in a dispute over the bar bill – behaviour that didn't endear him to his commanding officer, Geoffrey Keyes, son of Sir Roger, Director of Combined Operations, and a man with whom the Irishman shared a mutual antipathy.

11 Commando eventually saw action in June, not against the Germans but against the Vichy French forces in Syria. Fearing that the airfields in Syria would be used by the Axis forces to attack Allied positions in Egypt, Churchill ordered Wavell to seize them from the French before they could be handed over to the Germans. The 7th Australian Division were given the task, with 11 Commando charged with making a seaborne landing at the river Litani, which flowed south through Syria before debouching into the Mediterranean Sea. 11 Commando was to secure a bridgehead in the face of the strongly fortified position on the northern bank of the river.

The commandos accomplished their mission but at the cost of 45 officers and men killed and a further 84 wounded. Mayne not only emerged unscathed from his first action, but distinguished himself as cool and courageous, an officer with initiative and the ability to make correct decisions quickly in the heat of battle.

Yet in spite of 11 Commando's admirable performance at the Litani, within days the men were informed that Layforce was being disbanded. Some returned to their parent unit and others wound up at the Middle East Commando depot waiting for a decision on their future from Middle East Headquarters (MEHQ). Mayne went to the depot with a vague notion of travelling to China to teach guerrilla warfare to the Chinese Nationalist Army in their fight against Japan, but that was before he received a visit from David Stirling.

Stirling persuaded Mayne to join his new venture, provisionally entitled L Detachment of the Special Air Service Brigade, with the Irishman the last of the six officers to be recruited to the nascent Special Forces unit. Among the others were two of Mayne's fellow officers from 11 Commando, Bill Fraser and a southern Irishman called Eoin McGonigal, as well as an ascetic Welshman by the name of Jock Lewes.

One of the 60 men recruited to L Detachment in the summer of 1941 was Reg Seekings, a Fenman who would serve alongside Mayne for the duration of the war. He recalled that 'David and Paddy had a respect for each other's abilities' although socially they were opposites. Stirling was debonair and charming, imbued with the easygoing confidence of the privileged and a man with the necessary airs and graces to open doors among Cairo's polite society. Mayne was not a man given to small talk. Though fiercely intelligent and charming when he chose to be, he could be volatile, pugnacious and brusque to the point of downright rudeness. Much of this was due to his shyness and the self-consciousness he felt over his mammoth size. 'His appearance was a bit over-awing and he had a very powerful presence but his big trouble was he couldn't live with his size and strength,' reflected Seekings.[7] This was particularly true with the opposite sex, a species he never learned to handle. Seekings remembered Mayne referring to himself as an 'ugly brute', a description not recognized by his peers. Vivian Jenkins said he was 'magnificent-looking' and during the 1938 Lions tour he was much in demand among the young women of South Africa. But unable to relate to women, Mayne recoiled from their subtle advances and masked his dissatisfaction in bouts of heavy drinking. Exceptionally devoted to his mother, Mayne also grew up with an almost sanctified view of women, and men who served under him soon discovered a surefire way to incur his wrath. 'He understood people who got drunk, that was fair enough, but what he couldn't bear were louts and bad manners,' remembered John Randall, who joined the SAS in 1944. 'He hated bad language and objected to rude comments about women, and if you didn't abide by those rules you were liable to be thumped and thumped bloody hard.'[8]

As L Detachment took shape in the late summer and early autumn of 1941 the men saw more of Mayne than they did of Stirling and Jock Lewes – the three men credited as the driving force behind the SAS. Stirling was spending a lot of time in Cairo, using his charm to wheedle what he wanted for his unit, while Lewes was devising his eponymous bomb that would prove so destructive on future desert raids. Mayne oversaw a lot of the physical training and in a force of outstandingly fit young men he stood out for his strength and stamina.

In November 1941 L Detachment embarked on its inaugural mission, a raid that was to be executed against the backdrop of Operation *Crusader*. The aim of the Eighth Army offensive was to retake the eastern coastal regions of Libya (an area known as Cyrenaica) and seize the Libyan airfields from the Axis forces, thus allowing the RAF to increase their supplies to Malta, the

Mediterranean island that was of such strategic importance to the British. But General Erwin Rommel also prized Malta and was busy finalizing his own plans for an offensive; he intended his Afrika Korps to drive the British east, take possession of the airfields and prevent the RAF reaching Malta with vital supplies. In addition, the fewer British planes there were to attack German shipping in the Mediterranean, the more vessels would reach North African ports with the supplies he needed to win the Desert War.

On 17 November, L Detachment's task was to infiltrate between these two vast opposing armies and attack the Axis airfields at Gazala and Tmimi in eastern Libya at midnight. With Stirling in overall command of the 54-man operation, Mayne was put in charge of sections three and four with Jock Lewes commanding sections one and two. None of the raiders, however, met with success and Mayne was one of only 21 men to return from the disastrous operation. The rest were either killed or captured, victims of a violent desert storm that scuppered the Detachment's chances of success from the moment they jumped from their Bombay aircraft.

Undeterred, Stirling changed tack and enlisted the help of the Long Range Desert Group (LRDG). Parachuting was too hazardous and unreliable a means of infiltration; in future L Detachment would reach their target in vehicles driven by the LRDG. The final approach would be made on foot and once the raid had been carried out, the men would make for a pre-arranged rendezvous point with the LRDG.

L Detachment set up base at Jalo Oasis, an old fort set among palm trees and pools of water in the deep interior of the Libyan Desert. On 8 December Stirling, Mayne and nine other men boarded seven Chevrolet trucks driven by the LRDG and embarked for Sirte, a coastal town 350 miles to the north-west (and the birthplace of Colonel Muammar Gaddafi). Once within range of the target Stirling split the raiding party, taking Sergeant Jimmy Brough to attack the airfield at Sirte, while instructing Mayne and the remaining men to hit the neighbouring strip at Tamet.

Stirling had no luck at Sirte, but at Tamet Mayne wreaked a whirlwind of destruction. Not only were 24 Axis aircraft destroyed using the innovative Lewes bombs, but Mayne attacked a pilots' mess and killed several enemy airmen with small-arms fire and hand grenades. Two weeks later Mayne returned and destroyed a further 27 aircraft, most of which had arrived just 24 hours earlier to replace those machines blown up a fortnight before.

Tamet airfield was dubbed 'Paddy's Own' in recognition of the 51 aircraft destroyed by the big Ulsterman, and by the end of 1941 Mayne was acknowledged as the most effective operator in L Detachment. Malcolm Pleydell, a shrewd and thoughtful doctor who became the unit's medical officer in 1942, enjoyed analyzing Mayne. On the one hand Mayne could be erudite and garrulous when the mood took him, talking rugby or discussing his love of literature. But then there was the other side, the side Vivian Jenkins glimpsed a few years earlier in South Africa. 'This sort of fighting was in his blood,' wrote Pleydell of Mayne. 'There was no give or take about his method of warfare, and he was out to kill when the opportunity presented itself. There was no question of sparing an enemy – this was war, and war meant killing.'[9]

Ultimately, Pleydell was relieved to be on the same side as Mayne, not just because of his martial prowess but for the way he led his men. 'Paddy was very courageous but he was also cautious and careful, and he never took unnecessary risks,' recalled Pleydell. 'He was a good leader of men and respected by all, even though he was essentially a bit of a loner who was happy in his own company. I remember the first time I was with him on operations going up towards Qara Matruh and we saw two ME 110s. Everyone jumped out of the vehicles and hid behind boulders. Well, I just followed everyone else until they disappeared. Paddy later told me that the most important thing to do if you spotted enemy planes in the desert was to be as still as possible. Get behind any cover or just lie on the floor and don't move. Movement is what will catch the pilot's eye.'[10]

Another of his men, Corporal Sid Payne, who served under Mayne from 1942 to 1945, endorsed Pleydell's opinion: 'Paddy loved the war but had a charmed life. I've seen him walking down and fire going on all around him, and he never ducked. He wasn't reckless ... he would look at an op[eration] and if he thought it was impossible he wouldn't do it. He was a very careful man and wouldn't take unnecessary risks.'[11]

Mayne's sangfroid under fire was legendary, but another vital component in his character that served him well as a soldier was his reaction time. Rugby wasn't the only sport Mayne excelled at; he was a fine golfer and swimmer, and as a student at Queen's he had won the Irish Universities Heavyweight Boxing Championship. For such a big man Mayne was astonishingly nimble on his feet, and compared to the average soldier his incredibly quick reflexes gave him a split-second longer to size up a situation and react accordingly. In short, Mayne's physique and temperament made him ideal for the guerrilla warfare he was waging against the Axis forces in North Africa.

In the spring of 1942 the Desert War had become a static stalemate after the fluidity of the preceding months. The British were busy strengthening their defensive positions at Gazala while Rommel was augmenting his thinly stretched supply lines after his successful counter-attack that had resulted in the recapture of the Libyan port of Benghazi and the eastward retreat of the British forces.

In March Stirling proposed to MEHQ a series of raids on Axis airfields in the Benghazi area as well as an attack on shipping in the port itself. Given the authority to proceed, Stirling and his men re-established base at Siwa Oasis in western Egypt, and on 15 March a raiding party departed on the 400-mile mission to Benghazi. Close to their target area the party split up to attack a string of airfields, with Mayne leading Graham Rose, Bob Bennett and Jock Byrne towards Berka Satellite airfield. Byrne later described what happened:

> Carefully crossing the road in darkness we crept onto the airfield, almost at once coming across two German sentries who were standing together smoking near an anti-aircraft gun. Rose removed the cover from the barrel of the gun so that I could stuff a [Lewes] bomb into it after first squeezing the time pencil. Later, under some trees, we discovered the first of a series of bomb dumps which were dug in and covered by tarpaulins. Wasting no time we began placing our bombs, passing rapidly from dump to dump. It was dark and there was no one about. Soon afterwards Paddy decided to search for the aircraft with Bob, leaving Rose and myself to continue laying bombs in the dumps, which we found at regular intervals.[12]

As well as the anti-aircraft gun and bomb dumps, the raiders accounted for 15 aircraft. Throughout the weeks that followed the unit continued to attack

Axis airfields, increasing their overall tally of destroyed aircraft to 143 in six months, of which Mayne was responsible for well over half.

By now L Detachment had been considerably expanded; Stirling was a major, Mayne a captain, and both wore the ribbon of the Distinguished Service Order. Elsewhere the news was bad. In June the Germans were on the move east across the desert, capturing the port of Tobruk and advancing ever-closer to Egypt. The Royal Navy began pulling out of Alexandria and at Cairo British staff officers burned papers in expectation of a German conquest. But the Axis surge was stopped by the Eighth Army at El Alamein and once more the Desert War became inert, ideal conditions for L Detachment to recommence operations.

At Mayne's suggestion it was decided to change the unit's *modus operandi*. No longer would they rely on the LRDG (or the 'Long Range Taxi Group' as they were affectionately known); instead they would be self-sufficient. 'Capt. Mayne suggested to Major Stirling that jeeps should be provided,' recalled Captain George Jellicoe, a recent addition to L Detachment. Stirling embraced the idea wholeheartedly and procured 15 American jeeps, known as Willie Bantams, and fitted them with a dozen Vickers K machine guns, capable of firing 1,200 rounds per minute. Stirling also managed to prise from the grasp of the LRDG Mike Sadler, a brilliant desert navigator who had worked with L Detachment on several previous occasions. He and Mayne were to become staunch comrades in the years to follow, and by the end of the war few men knew the Irishman as well as the softly-spoken Englishman who shared Mayne's fondness for practical jokes.

There was no doubt that Mayne enjoyed the first jeep attack carried out by L Detachment on 26 July, though in that he wasn't alone. The target was Sidi Haneish, an airfield approximately 30 miles east-south-east of Mersa Matruh, and the outcome was a savage triumph for Stirling and his men. Having driven on to the airfield at night in two columns, the jeeps unleashed a tornado of fire that destroyed or damaged 30 aircraft. British casualties were two dead. One of the men on the Sidi Haneish raid was Johnny Cooper, one of the original members of L Detachment from its formation a year earlier. He said of Mayne:

I never saw him scared. He hadn't the same sort of fear the rest of us had. You can never really get into a person that deeply but he was as near as you can get to being fearless. He didn't have any problem about his own safety, and it seemed that he accepted death was part of the job and if it happened, then it happened.[13]

By October 1942 L Detachment had been expanded to regimental status and was known now as 1 Special Air Service (1SAS), comprising 29 officers and 572 other ranks in four squadrons. Mayne, now a major, led A Squadron into the interior of the Libyan Desert in October, where they passed a fruitful three weeks cutting railway lines and attacking vehicle convoys in an area between Tobruk and Matruh. Following the commencement of the Eighth Army offensive at El Alamein, Mayne and his men began attacking the retreating Axis forces. In his subsequent report on their activities Mayne described some of their successes:

About the 24th October the railway was blown up at Fuka, mined east of Piccadilly and blown up further to the west. A convoy was attacked on the Siwa track and Italian prisoners were taken.

A similar operation, not located, took place about the 26th October.

On the night 29th/30th October, the railway line was blown up in nine places north [actually north-west] of Sidi Aziz over a stretch a quarter of a mile long.

The main and looplines at Niswel el Suf were blown up on the 31st October; and fifteen Italians and five Germans were captured. The same patrol also destroyed four machine guns, one W/T installation and three trucks.

On 29 November, A Squadron was joined at their remote base at Bir Zelten by Stirling and his B Squadron. Stirling briefed Mayne on forthcoming operations: A Squadron would attack enemy transport between Sirte and El Agheila while he and his men would head 200 miles west and harry the retreating Germans around Tripoli. With the military objectives clear, Stirling and Mayne joined their men in a sing-song around a campfire, and Malcolm

Pleydell watched as 'Paddy, with his bushy beard and massive shoulders ... [started] giving way to the mood of the moment and joining in with his strange unmusical singing to each song in turn'.[14]

A squadron inflicted further damage on the increasingly ragged Axis forces before returning to Egypt in the first week of January 1943. Mayne and his men enjoyed a spot of leave, a repose ruined for Mayne by news from home informing him that his father had died. A month later he received another blow, this one felt by the whole of the regiment, when it was confirmed that a B Squadron patrol led by Stirling had been captured during their attempt to link up with First Army in Tunisia.

Stirling's capture couldn't have come at a worse time for 1SAS. The Desert War was all but won and the regiment was facing an uncertain future regarding deployment. Stirling had been contemplating operating in the mountains of the Caucasus (hence the reason Mayne and A Squadron had in late January undergone a ski course at the British Army Mountain Warfare training centre in the Lebanon) but like many of his best ideas he kept them in his head rather than in a file. One recent arrival to the SAS, Lieutenant Peter Davis, was sure that 'the regiment would now be disbanded since it no longer had Stirling's powerful personality to hold it together'.

Yet Mayne's own personality was nothing if not powerful; he just lacked Stirling's charm as well as his social standing. Perhaps some people who didn't know Mayne well, who were unaware he was a graduate of law from Queen's University, were deceived by his bear-like physique and gruff manner into believing he was all brawn and no brain. Anthony Greville-Bell wasn't one of them. The young cavalry officer (who would win a DSO in 1943 serving with 2SAS before commanding a squadron in Malaya) had a great respect for Mayne and reflected that his impatience with dithering staff officers was his Achilles heel. 'Paddy was useless with dealing with senior officers because if they did something to annoy him he threatened to punch their noses. He wasn't the right man to command the regiment really but who else could you put in charge when he was there because he was so outstanding ... the epitome of an SAS officer.'[15]

With the SAS no longer required in North Africa, Mayne oversaw the restructuring of the regiment. 1SAS was reorganized into two squadrons: Mayne took command of the Special Raiding Squadron (SRS), while the remaining half of the regiment was reconstituted into the Special Boat Squadron (SBS) under the command of George Jellicoe.

Mayne divided his force of approximately 280 men into three troops – 1, 2 and 3 Troops – and took them off to Palestine where they underwent several weeks of punishing training in preparation for their next operation – wherever that might be. Mayne proved himself a brutal commanding officer, setting exacting standards in all aspects of training and demanding they be met. He divided the three troops into two equal sub-sections and these were then further sub-divided into three-man squads of specialists: Bren gunners, riflemen and rifle bombers. In addition, to each troop was assigned a mortar section, an engineers' section and a signallers' section. 'Each sub-section was a highly efficient little fighting unit, capable of providing its own support in many of the usual situations which one expects to meet in battle,' wrote Davis, who had discovered that Mayne was not only a brilliant soldier, but was also an astute judge of character. All the time in Palestine Mayne was 'silently watching with those sharp, penetrating eyes of his ... making a mental picture for future reference of the individual, inner character of everyone he observed'.[16]

No man that Mayne deemed unsuitable lasted long. Johnny Cooper recalled that 'if a soldier wasn't doing his job properly he wouldn't tolerate it, that man would be RTU'd. He was quite ruthless in getting rid of those soldiers he felt let down the regiment.' It wasn't only in training that Mayne expected his men to follow his example. Sid Payne, who had joined the SAS at the end of 1942, recalled one time in Palestine when a fellow soldier rushed into their tent one evening with a warning to make themselves scarce. 'He said "Out, quick, Paddy's looking for someone to booze with", so we all shot out the tent. He was like that, looking for someone to booze with. He was a hard drinker, he'd fill a tumbler half full of whisky and expected everyone to be the same.'[17] On one occasion Johnny Wiseman had the misfortune to be caught in Mayne's bacchanalian net, and soon wished he hadn't: 'We were in the mess and I said something that upset him so he threw me on the ground,' he remembered. 'At this stage we all had beards and he was a big chap and he put his knees on my arms and called for a razor. Then without water and soap he shaved off half my beard. He was as drunk as a lord.'[18]

The training in Palestine was hard, but it was effective, too, and when the Special Raiding Squadron went into action for the first time they accomplished their task with conspicuous success. The mission had been the elimination of a coastal gun battery at Capo Murro di Porco (Cape of the Pig's Snout) on the south-eastern tip of Sicily on 10 July 1943. It was impressed upon Mayne and his men that it was imperative that the battery was destroyed without delay, as the main British invasion fleet would be sitting ducks if the guns remained operating. The SRS suffered just one fatality, but two days later when they landed in assault craft at the port of Augusta (erstwhile base of Junio Valerio Borghese's Italian naval commandos of the Tenth Light Flotilla), resistance was stiffer. Here they encountered not Italian defenders such as those at Murro di Porco, but hardened fighters from the Hermann Göring Division.

As the SRS scrambled up the beach and sought refuge among the narrow streets of Augusta, Mayne stepped serenely ashore. 'He had one hand in his pocket, his cuffs – as was his habit – turned back and behind him trotted his signaller,' remembered Bill Deakins, one of the unit's explosives experts. 'It was never done out of bravado but simply to give the men confidence.'[19]

Mayne's self-possession was on display two months later when the SRS took part in the invasion of Italy. Tasked with seizing the seaside resort of Bagnara, on the southern tip of Italy, the SRS approached the beach in the early hours of 4 September. The assault craft landed and the doors opened, but still there was no incoming fire. Did that mean the pristine white sand was laced with mines? 'No one knew if the beach was mined or not,' remembered Alf Dignum, a signaller in the SRS. 'Paddy was first up the beach, walking all the way, and by the time we'd followed him up there was still only one set of footprints!'[20]

Such had been the speed and stealth of the SRS landing at Bagnara that the Germans were taken utterly by surprise. Those in the town surrendered, while their comrades in the hills above fought on for 24 hours before withdrawing under fire from a Royal Navy cruiser.

The SRS pulled back to Gallico and enjoyed some well-earned R&R, during which time they heard of the Italian armistice. The men celebrated with wine and song and Davis remembered how Mayne 'would lean back, glass in hand, like some Roman emperor watching his gladiators prove their worth in the arena'.

The following month the SRS proved their worth during the ferocious battle for Termoli, an Adriatic port 20 miles above the spur of Italy's boot. The object of the assault, carried out in conjunction with 3 Commando and 40 Royal Marine Commando, was to secure Termoli for the 78th Division; thereby hastening Fifth Army's progress towards Naples along the road that led from Termoli to Campobasso, approximately 40 miles south. The raiders came ashore shortly before dawn on 3 October and by dusk Termoli was in their hands, for the loss of just one man. But the Germans didn't intend to cede Termoli without a fight and on 5 October, as elements of the 78th Division began advancing inland, the 16th Panzer Division counter-attacked. The 78th fell back in confusion, and it was left to the SRS and commandos to halt the German attack. Casualties were heavy, and in one devastating incident a cluster of shells landed in a side street just as a section of SRS were boarding lorries to reinforce a threatened sector. Eighteen men were blown to bits.

Mayne participated in little of the fighting in and around Termoli during the 48 hours it took to halt and then repel the German counter-attack; instead the Irishman showed his skill as a battle commander, deploying his three troops as and when they were needed to bolster creaking flanks or to fill gaps in the line vacated by fleeing British infantrymen. Then at dawn on 6 October the 38th Irish Brigade landed, along with four Sherman tanks, and the Germans fell back for good.

The SRS had triumphed, but at a heavy price. Of the 207 men who landed at Termoli, 21 were dead, 24 wounded and 23 were in captivity. Four days after the battle the men received a visit from General Miles Dempsey, commander of XIII Corps, under whose auspices the SRS had been operating. In his address Dempsey told the SRS: 'In all my military career –

and in my time I have commanded many units – I have never yet met a unit in which I had such confidence as I have in yours.' He then listed six reasons why he held the squadron in such high esteem: the training, their discipline, fitness, their confidence, their planning and lastly 'you have the right spirit, which I hope you will pass on to those who may join you in the future.'[21] It was a glowing endorsement, not just of the Special Raiding Squadron but also of Paddy Mayne and all the principles he had drilled into his men in the preceding nine months.

The SRS reverted to 1SAS upon its return to Britain in January 1944 and Mayne, now with a Bar to his DSO after his exemplary leadership in Italy, was under the command of Brigadier-General Roderick McLeod. The SAS Brigade of approximately 2,500 men included 2SAS, two French regiments (the 3rd and 4th) and 5SAS, comprising a squadron of Belgian paratroopers.

Now that 1SAS was to consist of four squadrons, each of 12 officers and 109 other ranks (in addition there was a squadron HQ comprising two Troops), Mayne's priority was to expand the 200 men of the SRS into a full-blown regiment so that they would be ready for the expected Allied invasion of France. He was allocated a car and undertook a great deal of 'arduous motoring' as he scoured the country's barracks and depots in search of suitable recruits to the regiment. Other officers and men heard of the recruitment drive and presented themselves at Darvel, 1SAS's base in south-west Scotland. One such soldier was a signals officer, Lieutenant John Randall:

> I joined the regiment on the same day as Fraser McLuskey [the regiment's chaplain who won a Military Cross in 1944] and we were both marched into see Paddy Mayne. I don't know if he was all that keen to have either a signals officer or a padre. Fortunately this was on a Thursday and on the Saturday there was an inter-squadron rugger match. I must have acquitted myself rather well on the wing because from then on I always had a good relationship with Paddy. From the very day I joined the regiment Mayne

always appeared to be the man in charge. He had a very physical presence. He didn't shout and yell, he had a quiet voice but when he spoke you knew jolly well he meant what he said. He said he expected officers to work hard at being good soldiers and expected them to behave as gentlemen. We admired him and we always felt that he would never commit any member of the regiment to an operation he felt didn't have at least a 50/50 chance of succeeding and he would never ever commit to an operation that he wouldn't be prepared to undertake himself. With a leader like that you had the basis for a fantastic regiment and that's what we were.[22]

New recruits, officers and men alike were exposed to the SAS's brutal training regime designed to weed out the weak and the lazy. Everyone, even veterans of the desert, had to undergo a parachute course at Ringway, Manchester, and there were lessons in explosives, firearms, unarmed combat and map work. There were frequent field exercises in the countryside surrounding Darvel, with the men jumping from an aircraft and then laying dummy charges on selected targets, and at Kilmarnock railway depot they learned all about the most effective way of blowing a train off the tracks.

Mayne had been wary from the start of Roderick McLeod's appointment as brigadier of the SAS Brigade. He was a soldier with no previous experience of the SAS and Mayne feared he would see them as an adjunct to the Parachute Regiment, to be used in large airborne operations at the expense of their more specialized skills. His concerns were justified when, on 25 March 1944, McLeod wrote to Mayne outlining what he expected of the SAS in the impending invasion of France: 'Infiltration will be by land, sea or air according to circumstances, and training in all methods will be carried out.' Four days later Supreme Headquarters Allied Expeditionary Force (SHAEF) issued the SAS Brigade with its operational instructions for the invasion. Thirty-six hours before the main invasion fleet began landing, the SAS were to parachute into Normandy between the landing beaches and the three Panzer divisions in reserve, and prevent those reserves from reinforcing the front line. It was, as David Stirling wrote later, 'bloody suicidal … it would have been quite ineffective and marvellous opportunities would have been totally missed'.

Mayne was said to have been dismayed by the instructions, but it was David Stirling's brother, Bill, who argued against the mission in his capacity as commanding officer of 2SAS. Why Mayne took a back seat is not known, although the two may have agreed that Bill Stirling's words would carry more clout with the staff officers at SHAEF than Mayne's. Whatever the reason, Stirling did indeed bring about a change of orders (although he resigned anyway) and it was agreed that the SAS Brigade would carry out 43 missions in France. With the exception of one operation – *Titanic* (involving a six-man party dropping into Normandy a few hours ahead of the main invasion fleet to spread confusion with dummy parachutes) – all missions were to occur deep behind enemy lines with the objective of impeding German forces as they headed north to prevent an Allied breakout from the landing beaches.

SAS parties parachuted into central France throughout June and Mayne followed their progress from his headquarters. Daily messages were transmitted from the signallers in France, allowing Mayne to assess the situation on the ground, and organize resupplies by air if necessary. Jeeps were soon being dropped by parachute to the SAS raiders, along with fresh arms and ammunitions, additional clothing (the summer of 1944 was exceptionally wet in France) and luxuries such as cigarettes and chocolate. He also instructed Regimental Sergeant Major Rose to send letters to the families of all the men in France, reassuring them that their son/brother/husband was fine, but temporarily unavailable.

On 7 August Mayne parachuted into France along with Mike Sadler and two other SAS soldiers. The original intention had been to drop east of Orléans, where a party of men from D Squadron were engaged on Operation *Gain*, to inform them of their impending role in a new mission codenamed *Transfigure*. *Transfigure* would involve both D Squadron and Bill Fraser's A Squadron, acting as reconnaissance troops for a major Allied offensive aimed at crushing German resistance west of the Rhine. (*Transfigure* was never put into operation because of the American breakout from the Cotentin Peninsula that began in late July.)

Mayne had to reorganize his plans when D Squadron's camp was overrun by Germans, and so he inserted further south, among the dark forests of the

Morvan, west of the city of Dijon, where A Squadron were operating under Bill Fraser. Mayne didn't stay long to enjoy the hospitality of A Squadron. Taking a jeep, he set off across northern France to check on the progress of the other various SAS operations. By now the Allied breakout from Normandy was quickening. By the end of the month Paris was liberated and the Germans were falling back towards Belgium.

In total the SAS Brigade was estimated to have killed 7,733 German soldiers during operations in France, as well as accounting for 740 motorized vehicles, seven trains and 29 locomotives, in addition to the 400 air strikes provided by their intelligence. In return 330 of their number had been killed, wounded or were missing. General Dwight Eisenhower, Supreme Allied Commander in Europe, expressed his gratitude in a letter to Brigadier McLeod in which he asked him to pass on his 'congratulations to all ranks of the Special Air Service Brigade on the contribution which they have made to the success of the Allied Expeditionary Force'.

Mayne's reward, other than receiving such high praise for his men from the Supreme Allied Commander, was a second Bar to his DSO. The citation described his role in organizing his troops in France during August and concluded:

> During the next few weeks he successfully penetrated the German and American lines in a jeep on four occasions in order to lead parties of reinforcements. It was entirely due to Lt-Col Mayne's fine leadership and example, and his utter disregard of danger that the unit was able to achieve such striking success.[23]

Apart from a sojourn in Brussels in the early winter of 1944 (where C Squadron was employed on counter-intelligence work), Mayne was in England as the war in Europe approached its climax. The SAS Brigade had a new brigadier in 'Mad Mike' Calvert, recently returned from Burma where he had performed fine work with Orde Wingate's Chindits. There was talk of 1SAS being deployed to the Far East once Germany had been beaten, as well as the possibility of an operation in Norway.

But there was still work to be completed in Germany. On 18 March a combined force of 1SAS and 2SAS (codenamed 'Frankforce' after Brian

Franks, CO of the 2SAS contingent) departed the regimental HQ of Hylands House in Essex, destined for the Rhine. However, Mayne remained in England, preparing B and C squadrons for their imminent entry into the Third Reich. David Danger, Mayne's signaller, remembered that in time-honoured fashion Mayne ensured that once the day's business concluded the pleasure began. 'We had these parties at Hylands with Paddy and he had a Shillelagh, which he banged and the party would start, and you didn't leave until you asked Paddy and if he didn't like it you had to stay there and drink. There were some wild parties.'[24]

Yet despite his uncompromising attitudes to drinking and training, Mayne could be compassionate if the mood took him, particularly to his younger soldiers whom he regarded as surrogate sons. One of them, 20-year-old Bob Francis, had fallen in love with a French girl during operations in France in September 1944. The pair became engaged and the Frenchwoman came to London where she found a job working for the French food ministry. Knowing that the regiment was shortly to resume operations, Francis asked Mayne if he could have a couple of days' leave with his fiancée. Mayne gave Francis a week.

> Then Paddy asked 'where are you going to stay?' I said I had no idea. He said 'I have friends who have a hotel'. He wrote the name of this hotel in Queen Anne's Gate and told me to go there and he said we'd be well taken care of. Then he asked if I had any money. When I replied 'a little bit', he reached into his pocket and gave me £10. I'd never seen such a sum... Anyway we were at the hotel for three or four days and when I went to pay the bill the two ladies who were running the hotel said 'There's no bill, Blair has said it's to be charged to him.' That was on top of the £10 he gave me.[25]

On another occasion Lieutenant Denis Wainman, a young officer who joined the regiment in late 1944, arrived at Hylands from his parachute course to find the place deserted except for Mayne. His CO explained that the regiment was somewhere north on a training exercise, one which Mayne was shortly to go and inspect. The pair drove up together during which time Wainman saw another side of Mayne: 'We took it in turns to drive and we stopped at some place for a drink and Paddy said "The trouble is that any place I'm at, if there's a dance or anything, I have to be there as the colonel. There are all these majors there with their wives and it's all very difficult. So now I'm going to take my crowns off." So he went in to this bar as a Second Lt and we had a beer and talked... They've said all sorts of things about Paddy down the years and yes he was a tough character but he was also very gentle and very intelligent.'[26]

On 6 April Mayne led B and C squadrons on what was to be the regiment's last operation of the war. It was codenamed *Howard*, and their role was to carry out reconnaissance patrols for the 4th Canadian Armoured Division as they pushed into northern Germany towards the medieval city of Oldenburg. It was a dangerous, dirty mission, the SAS pitted against the fanatical dregs of the Nazi regime, most often teenage members of the Hitler Youth, but sometimes also professional soldiers defending their homeland. One such confrontation unfolded on 10 April as the two squadrons continued towards Oldenburg.

Mayne was travelling with C Squadron, while B Squadron was commanded by Major Dick Bond, a relatively inexperienced SAS officer. David Danger was in the back of Mayne's jeep, alongside a gramophone and a stack of Irish discs.

On the front of the jeep there was a big loudspeaker and when we went across [to Germany] we used to play his records on this thing, and all the troops that were parked by the side of the road waved and sang. Paddy had the idea that he was going to harangue the German forces through this loudspeaker and call on them to surrender, and I was to operate this thing and play various Irish tunes if necessary... I was the one who got the message over the radio that the rest of the squadron had run into an ambush and one of the officers had been killed. Paddy asked what was happening and when I told him he threw me off the jeep and set off down the road.[27]

What happened next remained a bone of contention for many years among those members of 1SAS present. On arriving at the scene, Mayne discovered that Bond and his driver were dead and a number of soldiers were pinned down in a ditch. The fire was coming from the woods to their right and from a group of farm buildings between the lane and the woods.

Mayne's response demonstrated that even after five years of fighting he had lost none of his destructive energy. First he ran across the open field to the outhouses, scoping out the German sniper believed to be concealed therein. Satisfied that he knew his position, Mayne returned to the column and took a Bren gun from a jeep. Mayne and another soldier, Billy Hull, then doubled back to the buildings and together flushed out and killed the sniper. Back on the track Mayne jumped into the driving seat of a jeep and, with Lieutenant John Scott manning the twin Vickers in the back, roared off up the track, past the stranded men and towards a crossroads. Now within sight of the Germans in the woods, the vehicle came under heavy small-arms fire, but Mayne nonchalantly swung the jeep around at the crossroads and sped back with Scott pumping bullets into the trees. He repeated the procedure until the enemy fire subsided, and only then did he stop to pick up the men from the ditch.

Mayne was put forward for the Victoria Cross and few doubted he would receive it, a fitting finale to what had been a spectacular war. The citation for the award, signed by Brigadier Calvert, Major General Vokes of the 4th Canadian Armoured Division and Field Marshal Bernard Montgomery, 21st Army Group, stated: 'There is little doubt that Mayne's exceptional personal courage and leadership saved the lives of many men and greatly helped the Allied advance on Berlin.'

Three months later, however, the award was downgraded to a DSO, ostensibly because Mayne had not acted alone but with Scott. This was a specious line, one that could be contradicted by dozens of other VCs. In all likelihood the decision to deny Mayne the VC was one purely born of spite by senior staff officers. Not only did they view the SAS as a bunch of renegade irregulars, besmirching the reputation of the British Army, but Mayne was an uncouth Irishman, prone to heavy drinking and insubordination.

It was not a view shared by King George VI. When he presented Mayne with his fourth DSO at Buckingham Palace he asked why it was that the VC had 'so strangely eluded him'. Mayne was said to have replied: 'I served to my best my Lord, my King and Queen and no one can take that honour away from me.'[28]

The ambush that cost the lives of Bond and his driver, a Czech Jew called Mikhael Levinsohn, was the last great adventure of Paddy Mayne's war. There were further skirmishes during Operation *Howard* but the 4th Canadian Armoured Division was finding the going tough and their advance had been reduced to a crawl; the SAS were reassigned to the 2nd Canadian Division further north towards Esenz on the North Sea. But they still took casualties and as late as 29 April, Mayne sent a signal to A and D squadrons who were pushing up towards the Baltic Sea port of Lubeck, informing them: 'Squadron now plodding along through bog and rain on their feet. Tpr. Kent killed by mine. Nobody very happy.'

Mayne must also have been contemplating his own future. Germany was on its knees and word had just reached him of David Stirling's release from captivity. Mayne had led 1SAS for two and a half years and now faced the prospect of handing the reins back to Stirling. To compound his uncertainty, there was still no clear role for the SAS after the end of the war in Europe, and Mayne feared the brigade might be misused by SHAEF as it nearly had been prior to D-Day. He expressed his concerns to Brigadier Calvert, far more of a soldier's soldier than Roderick McLeod, and received the cabled reply: 'Understand your worries. You are quite right to raise them… Hope can put you on good wicket soon as possible.'

Mayne celebrated VE-Day, 8 May 1945, in Brussels, and the next day his two squadrons were reunited with A and D squadrons, at Poperinghe, 70 miles west. The next day the regiment was shipped back to England and within the week were on the move once more, this time flying to Bergen in Norway, together with 2SAS, to organize the disarming of 300,000 Germans. It was an enjoyable summer for the 760 SAS men in Norway; there was little trouble from the Germans and a lot of hospitality from the locals, particularly the young women. The only ugly incident involved a large contingent of SAS soldiers and some so-called Norwegian militia fighters dubbed the 'Grey Shadows', derided by the British on account of the fact that they'd spent most of the war hiding in Sweden. Now back in Norway they took exception to the SAS and a mass brawl ensued – what came to be known as the 'Battle of Bergen' – by the city's ornamental lake.

Many of the SAS officers joined in the fray, though whether Mayne flexed his muscles wasn't recorded. If he didn't, he did nothing to stop the fighting, and according to Lieutenant Peter Weaver, for most of his stay in Bergen Mayne 'held court in the mess on the top floor of a large building ... there still seemed to be a plentiful supply of free champagne available'.[29]

Brigadier Mike Calvert had now arrived in Bergen, and for a few weeks two of the greatest Special Forces soldiers of World War II were in tandem. Alas, there was no opportunity to fight the enemy, so instead they took on one another. But between the 5ft 8in Calvert and 6ft 3in Mayne there was only ever going to be one winner, as Calvert stated in his memoirs: 'We had a particularly hilarious guest night in the mess,' he wrote. 'At one stage during the evening Lieutenant-Colonel Paddy Mayne, a giant of a man who played rugger for Ireland and won no less than four DSOs, had heaved me over his shoulder; my forehead came into contact with a fender and I ended up with two huge black eyes.'[30]

The next day Calvert had a meeting with Lieutenant-General de Boer, commanding officer of the Germans in Bergen, at which de Boer's aide-de-camp (ADC) sniggered at the brigadier's injuries. Calvert's own ADC, Major Roy Farran, an outstanding officer in 2SAS, took offence at this slight from his opposite number, and gave the German two black eyes of his own as a punishment for his impertinence.

Back in Britain, meanwhile, it appeared the SAS Brigade might be sent to the Far East, although Mayne wasn't involved in the discussions. Instead David Stirling, released from captivity in April 1945, and Calvert lunched with Winston Churchill to discuss the possibility of the SAS operating in China to sever the Japanese supply line to Malaya. On 5 August, Field Marshal William Slim, commander of the British Fourteenth Army, wrote to

Calvert promising he would consider the proposal. However, the next day the United States dropped the first of two atomic bombs on Japan and within a fortnight the war in the Far East was over.

Mayne left Norway ahead of his regiment and arrived back in Essex unannounced. Major Johnny Wiseman had been left in charge of Hylands House but was living just outside the base with his new wife. 'I got a message telling me to hurry back to the mess as the colonel had turned up from Norway and he was in a hell of a mood.'

Mayne was furious to discover that Wiseman, who had carried out his administration duties unfailingly, had nonetheless chosen to live outside the camp. In his eyes it was a betrayal of the regiment. Wiseman tried to reason with Mayne – after all, the pair had fought together for three years and Wiseman had been decorated with a Military Cross on Mayne's recommendation – but the Irishman believed there had been a breach of trust. Wiseman was sacked on the spot. Mayne also tried to have him reduced in rank from major to captain but the War Office refused to oblige.

On 25 August the two SAS regiments sailed from Norway for Britain and soon the Brigade was being dismantled. First to go were the Belgians, returned to their own army on 21 September, followed by the two regiments of French SAS on 1 October. There was no reprieve for 1SAS and 2SAS, even though General Miles Dempsey, commander of the Second Army, wrote in a letter to Calvert: 'I always enjoyed having detachments of the SAS in Second Army, and their work was always up to the standard one expects of them. I wish I had been able to see more of them.'[31]

✦ ✦ ✦ ✦

On 1 October, 1SAS paraded for the final time at Hylands House in front of Brigadier Calvert and the following month, having tied up all the loose administrative ends, Mayne left the British Army as one of the most decorated soldiers in its history. He did not return to Northern Ireland and the firm of solicitors for which he had briefly worked before the outbreak of war; after six years of adventure that would have been far too dull. Instead

Mayne signed on for a two-year expedition to Antarctica with the Falkland Islands Dependencies Survey, along with two other former 1SAS officers – Mike Sadler and John Tonkin.

The survey's objective was as much political as it was scientific, the aim being to establish a number of bases in the Antarctic region in the face of claims from Argentina and Chile. Mayne flew by air, arriving in Montevideo, Uruguay, before his fellow expedition members who came by sea. Left to his own devices for a few days Mayne drank a lot and began keeping a journal, a feature of which was references to bouts of acute pain.

Mayne had suffered an injury to his back at some point during the war, although he concealed his suffering from his comrades. When exactly the injury occurred is not known, but it might well have been during that first fateful L Detachment raid in November 1941 when the unit parachuted into a gale-force storm. The pain intensified when the expedition left Uruguay for the Falklands in January 1946 and when they arrived in Port Stanley, Mayne was examined by two doctors, who 'talked of paralysis and serious trouble, so I am going home. It is still hurting me quite a bit. I think the movement of the ship causes a lot of the trouble.'[32]

Mayne arrived home in Northern Ireland in March 1946, preceded by several articles in the local press heralding the return of their prodigious son. The theme was uniform: Colonel Mayne, war hero and bravest of the brave, is coming back to Belfast. Such unwanted attention would become the bane of Mayne's life.

In April he was appointed Secretary of the Incorporated Law Society of Northern Ireland, and he was enrolled in the Belfast Arts Club, the golf club and the sailing club. Although his back injury prevented him from resuming his rugby career, the 31-year-old Mayne was a regular spectator at matches in the Province. He moved back into the family home in Newtownards and bought a red Riley Roadster, a sports car that was soon a regular sight on the road between Belfast and Newtownards, ten miles to the east of the city.

But beneath the surface Mayne struggled to reconcile himself to the banality of civilian life after six years of thrilling adventure. There was also the psychological fallout from his war service. Like most men of his generation,

Mayne was loathe to admit that the horrors of combat might have scarred him mentally. It was an era of the 'stiff upper lip' and there was no such thing as Post-Traumatic Stress Disorder (PTSD). Yet evidence points to Mayne having suffered from such a condition in the years after the war. He would lose his temper for the most trivial of reasons, he had trouble sleeping and he turned increasingly to alcohol. Mayne had always liked a drop or two – one commando colleague recalled that he could drink a bottle of whisky without getting a glow on – but back in Northern Ireland his excesses took on a sinister tone. These culminated in an explosive incident in 1952.

In Dublin on a February weekend to watch Ireland in the Five Nations rugby championship, Mayne endeavoured to find the Old Belvedere rugby club. He was in his cups and in need of further refreshment, but instead of knocking on the door of the clubhouse he banged on the door of Senator Quirke, a Dublin senator.

The senator's son answered the door and when Mayne was informed he had the wrong house, a fracas ensued, with the veteran soldier refusing to accept his mistake. Not surprisingly the senator's son came off worse, and it took several bystanders to subdue Mayne as the police were called. Mayne pled guilty to assault and his solicitor told the court that his client's 'conduct on this occasion was entirely repugnant to his normal behaviour'. The court fined Mayne a total of £25 but the real damage was done in the press reports of the incident on both sides of the border.

In January 1955 Mayne turned 40 and there were signs he was putting the wild days to bed. The previous year he had invested in a poultry house, employing a breeder full-time to develop the business. His mother was diagnosed with Parkinson's disease and he and his sisters spent many hours at her side. Then, 11 days before Christmas in 1955, Mayne went out for a few drinks with friends. He was returning home at 4am, speeding through the narrow streets of Newtownards when he clipped the back of a parked lorry and smashed into a telegraph pole.

Four months after his death a tribute to Mayne appeared in *Mars and Minerva*, the regimental journal of the Special Air Service. It had far more resonance than any of the hyperbole that appeared in the national press in the days and weeks after the tragedy:

The gift of leadership and the ability to inspire complete devotion and loyalty were his to an exceptional degree. In spite of his great physical strength, he was no 'strong arm' man. In the many operations in which he personally took part, and in those he planned for others, the same meticulous care and attention to detail was applied by him. He seemed to know instinctively exactly what the enemy's reaction would be to the devastating raids he carried out far behind the enemy lines, and was able to give his orders accordingly.[33]

RALPH BAGNOLD
LONG RANGE DESERT GROUP

Major Ralph Bagnold sat before the General Officer Commander-in-Chief Middle East. He watched nervously as Sir Archibald Wavell picked up the note that Bagnold had sent him half an hour earlier outlining why, in his view, it was imperative to explore the interior of the Libyan Desert. Wavell fixed his one good eye on the man in front of him. 'Tell me about this,' he said.

It was 23 June 1940, 13 days after Italy's declaration of war on Britain, an act of belligerence that had ominous implications for His Majesty's forces in Egypt and their control of the Suez Canal. Italy might launch an attack from Libya in the west or come from the south, from Eritrea and Ethiopia, and across the Sudan. Faced with such a dire situation, Wavell's eyes had lit up when Bagnold's note landed on his desk.

The 44-year-old Bagnold explained that 'we ought to have some mobile ground scouting force, even a very small scouting force, to be able to penetrate the desert to the west of Egypt, to see what was going on.'

'What if you find the Italians are not doing anything in the interior?' retorted Wavell.

Bagnold thought for a moment: 'How about some piracy on the high desert?'

Wavell grinned, then asked Bagnold if he could be ready to start operations in six weeks.

'Yes,' said Bagnold, 'provided...'

'Yes, I know, there'll be opposition and delay,' interjected Wavell, picking up a small bell on his desk.

Major General Arthur Smith, Wavell's Chief of Staff, entered the room at the sound of the bell and was instructed to type up an order in his superior's name: 'I wish that any request by Major Bagnold in person should be met instantly and without question.'[1]

✦ ✦ ✦ ✦

Ralph Bagnold was born in Plymouth in April 1896, the son of a lieutenant-colonel in the Royal Engineers. Upon the outbreak of World War I Bagnold was commissioned into his father's old regiment as a second lieutenant, serving on the Western Front and rising to the rank of captain. In a conflict unprecedented in its carnage, Bagnold's greatest achievement was to simply survive Ypres, the Somme and Passchendaele. He didn't have a particularly 'good' war, with a Mention in Despatches the only recognition for his three years of active service.

In 1919 Bagnold – still just 23 – went up to Cambridge to read Engineering, and upon completion of his studies he resumed his military career with the 5th Division Signal Company, then serving in Ireland. In 1926 Bagnold was posted to Egypt and it was as part of his research into his new posting that he read the work of Dr Alois Musil, a Czech scholar and explorer who, in the late 19th and early 20th centuries, travelled across 13,000 miles of Arabian desert by camel. The fruits of his endeavours were more than 50 books (several of which were lavishly illustrated with maps) and 1,000 articles for various academic and scientific journals. Not all of those who read his work were admirers. T.E. Lawrence, better known as Lawrence of Arabia, the British officer who helped foment the Arab revolt against the Ottoman Empire in World War I, expressed his views on a Musil book about North Arabia in an undated letter to Bagnold sometime in the 1920s: 'It is difficult to read because Dr Musil is not anxious to convey more than the facts of his observations,' wrote Lawrence in reply to a letter from Bagnold. 'Arabia has been fortunate in attracting so far people who travelled in it, rather than people anxious only to map it. Musil's map seems to me wasted because he does not distinguish between the part which is observed and the part which is hearsay.'[2]

The extent of the correspondence between Bagnold and Lawrence in the 1920s is unknown, but it seems likely that the young army officer would have sought the famed explorer's advice before embarking on his first expedition in October 1927. Now a major in the Signals, Bagnold led six men on a 400-mile journey from Cairo to Siwa Oasis in the west under the auspices of the Frontier Districts Administration of the Egyptian Ministry of War. They travelled in three Model T Ford cars, carrying 42 gallons of petrol and enough food to last ten days. The objective of the expedition was to map some of the interior of the north-east Sahara known as the Libyan Desert, which was 'roughly the size and shape of India'. Hitherto only the Egyptian side of the desert had been subjected to the cartographers' handiwork and it was Bagnold's aim to explore the Libyan side. In the subsequent account of the expedition Bagnold wrote:

In the first fifty miles … horizon followed pebbly horizon interminably – no features visible that were not multiplied in every direction as in a hall of mirrors – no living plant or even insect. The gnarled black trunks of forest trees that lie about for many hundred miles only increase the sense of utter lack of life, for they have ages ago been turned to stone. Their broken splinters, mingled with the flints, tinkled on one another steely hard under our wheels. Sometimes the logs lie singly for several miles, sometimes in tumbled heaps; perhaps the vast debris of some flood that swept over north east Africa long ago.[3]

At sunset on the first day of their adventure, they hunkered down behind a low bank 100 miles from the Nile and dined on tinned food, boiled in water that was then used to make a pot of tea. The next day the explorers encountered the Ramak Dunes and also saw faint vehicle tracks that Bagnold surmised to be those of the British Light Car Patrols (LCP), the desert force of World War I that had patrolled the Egyptian border against German-backed Senussi tribesmen.

For the next two days they negotiated as best they could the desert terrain, often forced to make tedious detours to circumvent towering razor-backed sand dunes as they searched for the ancient camel track that would guide them across the Sabbakha, a river of rock salt. Away in the distance the explorers saw the 1,000ft-high cliffs that 'separate for over five hundred miles the coastal plateau of north east Africa from the low-lying inner desert here far below sea level'.

Eventually they found the camel track and Bagnold could feel the ground soften under the wheels of their vehicles. Looking around him he could understand why the ancient Greeks had believed 'this Libyan land was the home of the petrifying Gorgons'. He continued:

It was a painful crossing. The cars creaked and groaned as each wheel climbed independently and fell over the cracked waves of upthrust salt. For nearly an hour we crawled across at walking pace, past here and there the bones of camels who had fallen broken-legged by the way. Halfway we passed a brine pool edged with snowy crystals and translucent rose-pink salt boulders. The rough road twisted down the cliff face. Below, it ran out into the stuffy low-lying hollow for a dozen miles of soft sand followed by interminable meadows of salt with coarse grass and stunted palms.[4]

Having crossed the Sabbakha, the explorers found themselves in a thick palm forest among which were damp gardens of oranges and pomegranates. Bagnold wrote of the thrill in knowing that Alexander the Great must once have passed this way en route to Siwa to have himself proclaimed a God (in approximately 332 BC). On reaching Siwa they bathed and visited the nearby village of Aghormi, where they bought bread and dates at the market, replenished their supplies and enjoyed a cup of coffee. They returned by a different route, heading north from Siwa to the coastal road and coming back to Cairo via towns that would, in a few years' time, be of great strategic importance to the British Army: Sidi Barrani, Mersa Matruh and El Daba.

The five-day expedition whetted Bagnold's appetite for more desert adventures and he returned to the desert in 1930, penetrating as far south as the Jebel Uweinat. In September 1932 Bagnold headed an eight-strong team that embarked from Cairo to explore 'the whole of the north-west portion of the Anglo-Egyptian Sudan up to the border of French Equatoria' while making notes on geology, archaeology and vegetation. Over two months, their four vehicles traversed 5,000 miles of desert in an adventure that was serialized in *The Daily Telegraph*. In his articles Bagnold described discovering remote oases, forgotten camel tracks and, in the shade under a little overhanging cliff, they stumbled upon some cave paintings of 'little red figures of men, some of whom carried bows and were wearing a plumed headdress. There were red animals, too, mostly giraffe, which belong to a very different climate from this now lifeless wilderness.'[5]

In the mid-1930s Bagnold spent what he later described as five years 'spent happily in research laboratories in the Alps and in London clubs'. It was an absurdly modest appraisal of a period of Bagnold's life when he dedicated himself to scientific research. The fruit of Bagnold's labour was published in the book, *Libyan Sands: Travels in a Dead World* and a paper entitled *The Physics of Blown Sand and Desert Dunes*. In the latter he wrote:

In 1929 and 1930, during my weeks of travel over the lifeless sand sea in North Africa, I became fascinated by the vast scale of organisation of the dunes and how a strong wind could cause the whole dune surface to flow, scouring sand from under one's feet. Here, where there existed no animals, vegetation or rain to interfere with sand movements, the dunes seemed to behave like living things. How was it that they kept their precise shape while marching interminably downwind? How was it they insisted on repairing any damage done to their individual shapes?... No satisfactory answers to these questions existed. Indeed, no-one had investigated the physics of blown sand. So here was a new field, I thought, one that could be explored at home in England under laboratory-controlled conditions.[6]

More than 75 years later, *The Physics of Blown Sand and Desert Dunes* remains a classic reference for desert geologists.

In 1938 Benito Mussolini's fascist Italy ruled Libya in the north and Ethiopia, Eritrea and Somalia to the east, and the perceptive Bagnold knew that he had ambitions to add Egypt and its precious Suez Canal to his African Empire. Six years after his last expedition, Bagnold, now retired from the army, was back in the Libyan Desert. Although he described his experiences in a 1,700-word article for the *American Scientist* journal (for which he was paid $40 and commended by the editor for his crisp prose) with particular focus on the geology, archaeology and vegetation discoveries, there is little doubt Bagnold and his fellow British explorers were also reconnoitring the region ahead of the war he knew was looming.

Less than a year after the expedition, Bagnold was recalled to the colours. Bagnold underwent a signals refresher course at Bulford and on 26 August 1939 – a week before the outbreak of war – he was appointed commanding officer of the East Africa Signals stationed in Kenya. On 28 September 1939 Bagnold sailed on the *Franconia* for East Africa, but a week later the *Franconia* accidentally collided with another vessel. It caused a change in his schedule that would take his army career in a dramatic direction. The *Franconia* put in at Malta and Bagnold transferred to the *Empress*; now, instead of going to East Africa, he sailed for Port Said. Immediately Bagnold cabled the War Office asking to remain in Egypt, as he knew the region far better than East Africa. On 16 October he was granted permission to join 7th Armoured Division (later immortalized in the North African campaign as the 'Desert Rats') as a signals officer in Mersa Matruh, one of the coastal towns he had passed through in 1928.

The news was well received by the English-language *Egyptian Gazette*. In its mischievous 'Day In Day Out' gossip column, detailing the comings and goings of British military personnel in Cairo, it commented on Bagnold's posting: 'Major Bagnold's presence in Egypt at this time seems a reassuring indication that one of the cardinal errors of 1914–18 is not to be repeated. During that war, if a man had made a name for himself as an explorer of Egyptian deserts, he would almost certainly have been sent to Jamaica to report on the possibilities of increasing rum production … nowadays, of course, everything is done much better.'[7]

Once at Mersa Matruh, Bagnold soon gauged the precarious situation confronting the British. Italy's Marshal Rodolfo Graziani was estimated to have around half a million troops at his disposal, a force far superior to the 50,000 men under Wavell's command. There were Italian garrisons at Kufra and Uweinat in the south-east of the country, the latter close to the Egyptian and Sudanese borders. It was imperative, in Bagnold's view, that the British learned the disposition of the Italian forces; there was the very real likelihood that the enemy might strike east and seize the Nile and then Cairo when, as was inevitable, war erupted between Britain and Italy. 'I began to wonder why we had no other separate force with a range of action proportionate to the vast size of the interior,' he wrote. 'No one knew what surprise campaigns might be in store for us. 500 miles of the inland frontier was now left entirely unpatrolled, guarded only by the supposedly impassable Sand Sea.'[8]

Bagnold was dismayed to find that the only map in the possession of the British was a 'reprinted sheet dated 1915 on which the interior of Libya was an almost medieval guesswork'. However, he was pleased to see that some of his recommendations to the British Army in the wake of his pre-war expeditions had been put into practice.

First there was the Bagnold sun compass. In his first expedition into the Western Desert Bagnold had discovered that the magnetic compass was unreliable because of the metal in their vehicles, resulting in the impractical necessity for the men to take a bearing some distance from their vehicle. 'It was quite hopeless for long distance travel,' reflected Bagnold, who put his mind to devising an alternative means of navigation. His invention, which was subsequently manufactured by Watts & Co of London, was a sun compass, a modification of the sundial, which gave true bearings and not magnetic ones. On the rotating dial, which was fixed to the front of the vehicle, was a pointer that the driver lined up with an object on the horizon and then followed as he drove, ensuring that the pin's shadow was on the pointer. It was not perfect, and allowances had to be made for the variation of the sun's azimuth, but by adjusting the bearing every 20 minutes, it was possible to navigate with confidence.

At night Bagnold had navigated with a theodolite, using the stars as his guide, much as a sailor relied on a sextant, and this too had been adopted by the British Army. They were also using sand channels, 5ft-long sheets of steel that slid under the rear wheels of trucks and jeeps for support on the sand, and Bagnold's method of water conservation had been implemented. Having discovered that vital water was lost in the desert when radiators boiled over and blew water off through the overflow, Bagnold came up with an ingenious solution for his vehicles: 'Instead of having a free overflow pipe we led the water into a can half full of water on the side of the car so it would condense in the can. When that began to boil too it would spurt boiling water over the driver who would have to stop. All we had to do was turn into wind, wait for perhaps a minute, there'd be a gurgling noise, and all the water would be sucked back into the radiator, which was full to the brim.'[9]

Fearful that the British in Egypt could be outmanoeuvred by the Italian forces in Libya, Bagnold drafted a memo for Middle East Headquarters (MEHQ) in which he suggested that some American trucks (he had great faith in American vehicles, having used them on his previous desert expeditions) should be acquired and used to reconnoitre the Egyptian side of the Western Desert. General Percy Hobart, commander of the 7th Armoured Division, approved of the idea but told Bagnold: 'I know what will happen;

David Stirling, the founder of the SAS, photographed here with the Winged Dagger badge on his cap. The famous winged dagger and SAS motto 'Who Dares Wins' came about as a result of a competition between the men. (Topfoto)

Paddy Mayne (far right) with David Stirling on his right. The pair had contrasting personalities but together they complemented one another to devastating effect. (Courtesy of John Robertson)

1SAS rugby team photographed before one of their matches. Paddy Mayne, a former Ireland international rugby player, is pictured second from left in the middle row. (Author's Collection)

Anders Lassen, Special Boat Squadron, pictured at Lake Commachio, Italy, on 8 April 1945. (Imperial War Museum, HU 2125)

Colonel Edson Raff, known affectionately as 'Little Caesar' to his men, is pictured here with Eleanor Roosevelt during a visit to England. Not long after this photo was taken, Raff led his men into North-Africa as part of Operation Torch.(Corbis)

Evans Carlson, US military observer, pictured here with Mao Zedong, leader of the resistance against the Japanese in China, in 1940. (Getty Images)

Brigadier General Robert Frederick, centre, establishes his command post just outside of Rome on 4 June 1944. Frederick was popular with his men, always leading from the front. However, as a result of this, he would become the most wounded American general of the war. (NARA)

Frederick receives the town flag of Le Muy, France, on 17 August 1944 after his task force liberated the town following Operation *Dragoon*. (NARA)

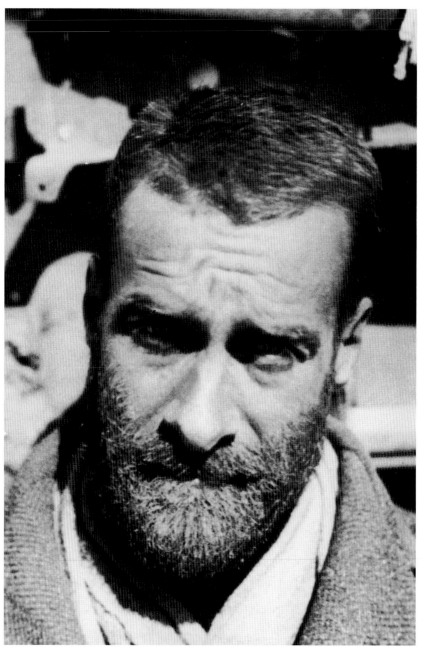

Major Ralph Bagnold, founder and first commander of the Long Range Desert Group, pictured here *c*.1930. (Getty Images)

Ex-commando and Italian Fascist leader, Prince
Valerio Borghese pictured here after the war in
1946. (Getty Images)

Friedrich von der Heydte,
commander of the Fallschirmjäger,
and recipient of the Iron Cross.
(Topfoto)

Adrian von Fölkersam (centre) pictured in Budapest with Otto Skorzeny (left).
(Bundesarchive Bild 102I-680-8283A-30A)

Orde Wingate, leader of the Chindits, in discussion with officers in the jungle along the Burmese border with India during his guerrilla campaign against Japanese troops in the area, 1943. (Getty Images)

Colonel Charles Hunter (centre), commander of the 'Merrill's Maruaders' commando unit, pictured here in Burma with American general Joseph Stilwell (left) in 1944. (Getty Images)

they'll call it a matter of high policy and pigeon-hole it.' Hobart was right, and though Bagnold submitted his idea again in January 1940, it received the same response. Bagnold could do nothing but vent his frustration in private at the blinkeredness of much of MEHQ, writing: 'The Cairo staff, rarely venturing beyond the cultivation, had long been a little frightened of the desert which they did not understand ... they had always discouraged any desire among officers to get to know it. For there was risk; and casualties incurred in peacetime had unpleasant consequences for those in charge ... all British Cairo grew anxious lest a man might die or a government vehicle have to be written off.'[10]

So in the spring of 1940 – instead of patrolling the Western Desert and plotting the disposition of the Italian troops who, while still officially at peace with Britain, were openly pro-German – Bagnold was appointed to the signal staff of General Archibald Wavell, Commander-in-Chief Middle East Command, and despatched 'across the snows of Anatolia and Thrace (Turkish regions in the Balkans) collecting technical details about telegraphs and telephone'.

Increasingly resigned to a war in the quiet backwaters of the conflict, Bagnold's military career was saved by events thousands of miles away in Western Europe, with the German occupation of the Low Countries in May 1940 and the Italian declaration of war on Britain the following month. A direct consequence of the declaration was that because Italy controlled the Mediterranean and Red Sea sea routes, British forces in the Middle East were now cut off from their comrades in Europe. In addition, the collapse of France and the establishment of a puppet government under Marshal Pétain deprived General Wavell of a whole army corps of Syrian troops.

There was another threat, too, one that only Bagnold really understood. It came from Kufra in the heart of the Libyan Desert, and could lead to the fall of Egypt and the Sudan. Kufra was an isolated post in the south-east of Libya. Surrounded on three sides by depressions, it was of strategic importance because it served as an air base for Italian East Africa, and also because its topographical location commanded outstanding views of the land traffic.

Had Bagnold been authorized to carry out reconnaissance patrols of the Libyan Desert nine months earlier, he would have known the exact strength of the large Italian garrison at Kufra. 'A well timed raid by a party say 2,000 strong could sever temporarily our only land connection between Egypt and Khartoum,' wrote Bagnold. 'With submarines to obstruct the alternative Red Sea route, this interruption might vitally affect the delicate and precarious adjustment of our pitiful resources between the two theatres of war [North Africa and Western Europe].'[11]

On 19 June 1940, Bagnold submitted his memo for a third time, and this time it was noticed. Four days later he was sat in front of Wavell who, at the end of their meeting, rang his little bell and instructed his chief of staff to give Bagnold every available assistance in assembling his new unit – provisionally called the Long Range Patrol. Time was of the essence, for the British expected the Italians to launch a major offensive by the end of August at the very latest. But Bagnold had been fine-tuning his original memo for months and knew exactly how he envisaged the force. As he later explained there would be three patrols, 'every vehicle of which, with a crew of three and a machine gun, was to carry its own supplies of food and water for 3 weeks, and its own petrol for 2,500 miles of travel across average soft desert surface – equivalent in petrol consumption to some 2,400 miles of road. By the use of 30-cwt [30-hundredweight] trucks there would be a small margin of load-carrying capacity in each. This margin, if multiplied by a large enough number of trucks would enable the patrol to carry a wireless set, navigating and other equipment, medical stores, spare parts and further tools, and would also allow extra petrol to be carried for another truck mounting a 2-pdr gun with its ammunition, and a light pilot car for the commander.'[12]

One of the first tasks facing Bagnold was to requisition enough reliable vehicles capable of covering in excess of 2,500 miles without breaking down. The British Army possessed no such thing so Bagnold turned to the commercial Chevrolet 30cwt (30-hundredweight), and 33 were purchased from the Egyptian Army or from vehicle dealers in Cairo. Sun compasses, sand channels, radios and medical supplies were begged, borrowed or stolen in the weeks following the unit's formation. So were the Arab headdresses and leather sandals that replaced the army-issue leather boots and service dress caps.

As to who to recruit to his fledging enterprise, Bagnold was well aware that the merciless hinterland of the Western Desert could make or break a man. He contacted some of his old colleagues who had accompanied him on previous expeditions into the desert, and before long Bill Kennedy Shaw, Pat Clayton, Teddy Mitford, and Rupert Harding-Newman had joined him in Cairo. Bagnold overcame the fact that Kennedy Shaw and Clayton were civilians by having them commissioned into the Intelligence Corps.

Bagnold designated his patrols R, T and W (the letters chosen at random) with each one comprising two officers and 30 men. Each patrol was armed with nine Lewis light machine guns of World War I-vintage, two Vickers machine guns, a Bofors light anti-aircraft gun and an assortment of small arms. Within each patrol there would be two gunners, two navigators, one fitter, one mechanic, 11 drivers, ten machine gunners, one wireless operator and one medic. Despite the emphasis on drivers and gunners, Bagnold insisted that every man recruited to his force must be proficient in both skills.

With most of his officers boasting a considerable knowledge of the desert, Bagnold now needed to find a small cadre of men with the right temperament to join his Long Range Patrol. 'They should be resourceful, alert, intelligent and possessed of a sense of responsibility, and emphasis should be laid on these qualities rather than on mere toughness. The Long Range Patrol is a complicated technical mechanism in which a breakdown might spell disaster even though no enemy is encountered.'[13]

In Bagnold's view the average British soldier was 'apt to be wasteful' when it came to looking after equipment, so when he learned that there was a New Zealand division under Brigadier Puttock idle in Egypt he paid them a visit. Though the Kiwis had arrived safely in North Africa, the supply ship with all their arms and ammunition had been sunk en route, so they were unemployed until further supplies arrived. Bagnold was given permission to recruit the small number of New Zealanders needed to fully complement the Long Range Patrol, and subsequently he was never given any cause to regret the chain of circumstances that led to his visit to the New Zealand division. 'They made an impressive party by English standards,' reflected Bagnold. 'Tougher and more weather-beaten in looks, a sturdy basis of sheep farmers leavened by technicians, property owners and professional men including a few Maoris.'[14]

Bagnold tried to make training as realistic as possible, with the New Zealanders being particularly schooled in desert driving. The Kiwis were quick learners, and before long they were covering 150 miles in fully loaded trucks. Flag signals were deployed to help patrols travel in strict formation, and Kennedy Shaw had the task of instructing the men in desert navigation using the sun compass. They progressed from training only in the day to travelling at night using the theodolite and the stars, and Bagnold was astonished when the New Zealanders had mastered the art of navigating at night within a week.

Bagnold explained to his Long Range Patrol that their purpose was primarily reconnaissance and that they were to discover what the Italians were up to in their desert forts behind the Great Sand Sea, the natural barrier roughly the size of Ireland that stretches from Siwa Oasis, in the north-west of Egypt, almost as far south as Sudan. When informed of their role, commented Bagnold, the Kiwis were 'quietly thrilled'.

In August the Long Range Patrol embarked on their first mission. It was led by Pat Clayton, a pre-war desert explorer who had spent nearly 20 years with the Egyptian Survey Department. Clayton led a reconnaissance of the Jalo–Kufra track used by the Italians in Benghazi (a port on the northern coastline of Libya) to resupply their garrisons at Kufra and Uweinat. Having driven east into Libya, Clayton's two-vehicle patrol watched the track for three days but observed no enemy vehicles. But it wasn't a wasted expedition. Clayton returned to Egypt, having penetrated 600 miles from his base into enemy territory, with two important details. Firstly, Clayton had noted that enemy aircraft rarely detected sand-coloured vehicles in the desert as long as they were stationary. Secondly, he had discovered a route that crossed first the Egyptian Sand Sea and then, once inside Libya, the Kalansho Sand Sea. The two seas were in fact connected further north to form, as Bagnold later described, 'an irregular horseshoe' shape in the south. Clayton had pioneered a route across the two Sand Seas that would become the point of entry into Libya for future patrols.

The Egyptian Sand Sea is a breathtaking phenomenon. One Long Range Patrol officer, Michael Crichton-Stuart, never forgot his first sight of the sea:

'The parallel lines of dunes run almost north and south, rising to some 500 feet in the centre of the Sand Sea. Packed and shaped by the prevailing wind over thousands of years, this Sand Sea compares in shape and form with a great Atlantic swell; long rollers, crested here and there, with great troughs between. It is utterly lifeless, without a blade of grass or a stone to break the monotony of sand and sky.'[15]

On 27 August 1940 Bagnold and his 80 men were inspected by General Wavell, and on 5 September Bagnold led the Long Range Patrol in its entirety into Libya on the trail blazed a month earlier by Clayton. He was delighted with the way the New Zealanders adapted to their unfamiliar surroundings and they were soon averaging 30 miles a day as they pierced the interior of the Libyan Desert. Soon the force split, with R Patrol under 2nd Lieutenant Don Steele, a Kiwi, returning to their base at Siwa to resupply, while Teddy Mitford's W Patrol reconnoitred north towards Kufra and T Patrol under Pat Clayton went south as far as the border with Chad.

Bagnold gave orders that the daily water allowance was one gallon per man, a fragile defence against a brutal midday sun. Teddy Mitford wrote in his diary: 'On this and the three preceding days there were a number of cases of heat stroke among the men. It was remarkable to notice in the shade of almost every stone a dead or dying bird.'[16]

The three patrols returned to Cairo with little to report. Whatever Marshal Graziani was doing at his headquarters in Sidi Barrani, his troops were nowhere to be seen in the Libyan Desert. The news conveyed to General Headquarters (GHQ) Cairo by the Long Range Patrol prompted Wavell to amend the unit's operational instructions in October. No longer were they to carry out reconnaissance missions; instead they were to go on the offensive and, as Bagnold later wrote, 'stir up trouble in any part of Libya we liked, with the object of drawing off as much enemy transport and troops as possible from the coastal front to defend their remote and useless inland garrisons'.[17]

The Long Range Patrol relished their opportunity to be more pugnacious. While some patrols mined roads, others blew up bomb dumps or attacked isolated desert outposts manned by bored Italians. Just as Wavell had hoped, Graziani diverted troops from the coastal regions into the interior to escort supply columns and reinforce outposts.

On 1 October Wavell wrote to Bagnold to express his gratitude for the work accomplished by his unit in the three months since its formation. He said:

Dear Bagnold

I should like to convey to the officers and other ranks under your command my congratulations and appreciation of the successful results of the recent patrols carried out by your unit in central Libya.

I am aware of the extreme physical difficulties which had to be overcome, particularly the intense heat. That your operation, involving as it did 150,000 track miles, has been brought to so successful a conclusion indicates a standard of efficiency in preparation and execution, of which you, your officers and men may justly be proud.

A full report of your exploits has already been telegraphed to the War Office and I wish you all the best of luck in your continued operations in which you will be making an important contribution towards keeping Italian forces in back areas on the alert and adding to the anxieties and difficulties of our enemy.[18]

In early December 1940 the Long Range Patrol, having proved its worth, was expanded, with three new patrols; 'G' Patrol, drawn from the 3rd Battalion Coldstream Guards and the 2nd Battalion Scots Guards; 'Y' Patrol comprised Yeomanry recruited from the 1st Cavalry Division in Palestine; and 'S' Patrol was made up of South Rhodesians. Simultaneously the three original New Zealand patrols were reduced to two with some of their number required to return to their regiments. It was Bagnold's proud boast that 'including the men on headquarters more than 50 different regiments are now represented in L.R.D.G.'. The initials stood for 'Long Range Desert Group', the new name of the unit that by the end of the war would be a byword for efficiency, resourcefulness and courage.

Emboldened by the expansion of his unit, Bagnold planned the LRDG's most audacious operation to date, an attack against Murzuk, a well-defended Italian fort set among palm trees with an airfield close by, approximately 1,500 miles west of Cairo. As Bagnold noted, the fort 'was far beyond our self-contained range but a raid on it seemed possible geographically if we could get some extra supplies from the French Army in Chad'. No one in Cairo knew whose side the French forces in Chad were on. Other French dependencies had declared for the Vichy regime, but from Chad there had been no announcement. Bagnold and Wavell thought that an invitation for the French to support a daring raid might be just the sort of escapade to rally them to Britain's cause.

Bagnold flew to Chad and met the commander of the French troops, Colonel Jean Colonna d'Ornano, a tall red-headed officer, who demanded to know the purpose of Bagnold's visit. 'I told him frankly what I wanted – petrol, rations and water,' recalled Bagnold of the meeting. D'Ornano agreed to cooperate but with a caveat. 'I'll do all you ask but on one condition,' he told Bagnold. 'You take me with you to Murzuk with one of my junior officers and one NCO and we fly the French flag alongside yours.'[19]

The LRDG raiders, consisting of T and G patrols under the overall command of Pat Clayton, rendezvoused with the French near Tazerbo, 350 miles east of Murzuk, on 4 January 1941. As promised D'Ornano had delivered the supplies requested by Bagnold, and the Frenchman and nine of his men were seconded to the LRDG as they struck out west toward Murzuk. On 11 January they stopped for lunch just a few miles from Murzuk, and then the force divided, with Clayton's T Patrol going off to attack the airfield while G Patrol targeted the fort. Michael Crichton-Stuart recalled that as they neared the garrison they passed a lone cyclist: 'This gentleman, who proved to be the Postmaster, was added to the party with his bicycle. As the convoy approached the fort, above the main central tower of which the Italian flag flew proudly, the Guard turned out. We were rather sorry for them, but they probably never knew what hit them.'

In the maelstrom of fire that followed, the LRDG lost two men (including Colonel D'Ornano) and suffered several casualties, but the damage inflicted on the Italians was far worse. The main block of the fort was destroyed by a withering mortar barrage, and the garrison commander had the misfortune to return from lunch midway through the onslaught. Neither his staff car nor the escort vehicle made it through the fort's gates.

Clayton arrived at the fort having wreaked havoc on the airfield, destroying three light bombers, a sizeable fuel dump and killing or capturing all of the 20 guards. Now he ordered the LRDG to withdraw into the vastness of the desert before the inevitable aerial reinforcements arrived from Hon, a large Italian air base 250 miles to the north-east. The LRDG paused to bury their dead five miles to the north of Murzuk, while the French contingent asked permission to slit the throats of their prisoners. Clayton turned down the proposal and the next day the unit headed toward Chad, overrunning a small outpost at Traghen as they went.

The British had been right to court the French in Chad. Even though D'Ornano was dead, his successor, General Leclerc, formed an effective alliance with the LRDG. Guided by T and G patrols (the latter composed of former Guardsmen under the command of Captain Michael Crichton-Stuart), a Free French force captured Kufra on 1 March 1941, but the success was a rarity for the Allies in what was an otherwise wretched few months. Rommel had arrived in North Africa on 12 February, and by the end of April the Afrika Korps had pushed back the Allies' Western Desert Force (later known as Eighth Army) to the Egyptian frontier. The Mediterranean port of Tobruk was the sole remaining British possession in Cyrenaica.

In February 1941 Major Guy Prendergast, a good friend of Bagnold's who had accompanied him on his expeditions of 1927 and 1932, joined the LRDG as its second-in-command. An experienced pilot who had also explored the desert by aircraft, one of Prendergast's early initiatives was to form the unit's own air force, consisting of two single-engine monoplanes made by the Western Aircraft Cooperation of Ohio (WACO) and bought from their private owners in Cairo. The aircraft, which were piloted by Prendergast and a New Zealander called Barker, were used to keep in regular contact with MEHQ in Cairo and with the patrols scattered across the desert.

With Kufra now in Allied hands, Bagnold moved the LRDG headquarters there from Cairo, a distance of 800 miles. The drawback to the relocation was that MEHQ instructed Bagnold to establish a permanent garrison there until such a time when the Sudan Defence Force could take over. It was a short-sighted decision and one that resulted in a frustrating summer in general for Bagnold and the LRDG, who were not by training or temperament a static garrison force.

At Kufra, Bagnold schooled his men in some of the more primitive ways of the desert such as how to eat a desert snail by sucking him out of its shell, and how to bathe without water. The latter intrigued the men, as Les Sullivan, an LRDG fitter, recalled: 'He taught us to bath in the sand. He said that washing does not get you clean because we don't normally get dirty. He reckoned you washed and bathed to get rid of dead cells of skin. So in deep desert we bathed in the sand. We were not allowed water to wash, shower or clean teeth. All water was very precious and was necessary for cooking and drinking and so that was rationed.'[20]

Rations (which were packed in wooden petrol cases when the LRDG was on a patrol) were considered of the utmost importance by Bagnold and he issued his unit with a sample menu (with recipes) based on the food available. This consisted of:

Breakfast suggestions
Porridge (no milk or sugar)
Fried bacon with oatmeal fritter
Bacon and oatmeal cake
Bacon stuffed with cooked oatmeal
Bacon with oatmeal chuppatties

Tiffin
Lentil soup
Various sandwich spreads on biscuits
Cheese and oatmeal savoury
Cheese and oatmeal cake
Oatmeal and date cookies

Dinner
Stewed mutton with dumplings
Meat pudding

Each man was allowed six pints of water a day with one issued at breakfast, two in the evening as tea and one at midday with lime juice. The outstanding two pints were drawn by the men in the evening and were used to fill water bottles for the following day. 'The men,' wrote Bagnold, 'are trained to use their water bottles during the day at their own discretion for sipping from time to time to moisten their lips.'[21]

Fortunately, while Bagnold's patrols were on garrison duty at Kufra, G and Y patrols were operating out of Siwa Oasis 400 miles to the north, and they spent May and June of 1941 reconnoitring the enemy troops' positions in eastern Libya. The versatility of the LRDG was evident in July when, under the command of Jake Easonsmith, the two patrols displayed the full range of their desert skills. Writing shortly after the war, Bagnold described it thus:

> It was decided to carry out reconnaissance with small parties into the southern foothills of the Gebel Akhdar with the object of getting some idea of the enemy's dispositions in this area, 300 miles behind his front line, and also making contact with friendly Arabs. Easonsmith carried out a number of such journeys, dropping native agents and in some cases British officers on the outskirts of the Gebel and picking them up a few days later when their tasks had been completed. In addition he was able to collect a number of our troops who had been sheltering with the Arabs in Cyrenaica [eastern Libya] since our withdrawal in the Spring [of 1941]. On one occasion information had been received that a Free French pilot was hiding up near a well in enemy territory and a patrol was sent off to try and pick him up. They located the well but could see nothing of the pilot and were about to leave when a head appeared out of a dry cistern almost under their feet. This was in fact the pilot who had been reluctant to announce himself earlier as he thought that the party of bearded and dishevelled ruffians could not possibly be British troops. In an interval between two such trips Easonsmith, working behind but nearer to the enemy's front line, successfully shot up a large Italian MT [Motorized Transport] repair section.[22]

In July 1941 the Sudan Defence Force arrived at Kufra to relieve Bagnold and the rest of the LRDG, which were then able to resume their offensive operations against the Axis forces, conducting invaluable reconnaissance in the Sirte desert inland from the Libyan coast. One patrol ventured to within 40 miles of the Axis-held port of Benghazi, bringing back invaluable information for MEHQ which was in the throes of planning a large offensive for November, codenamed Operation *Crusader.*

Since February 1941 the Germans had been arriving in North Africa to fight alongside their Italian allies, but despite the presence of the Afrika Korps, no unit comparable to the LRDG emerged on their side during the Desert War. Only once did the Germans attempt a mission behind British lines, a sortie led by a pre-war desert explorer named Count Ladislaus de Almásy, who was Hungarian-born and British-educated. But he discovered that most of the Germans under his command lacked the initiative and self-sufficiency to survive the desert.

Bagnold and Almásy had bumped into each other in the Middle East before the war and they did so again in 1951, when the Count told his British acquaintance 'a strange story of an interview he had with Rommel in 1942. If true it throws a curious light on Rommel's attitude even at that relatively early date. Poor Almasy. With his knowledge of the interior and of how to travel in it he must have longed to do what my people were doing. But Rommel was no Wavell and he was kept on a tight rein.'[23]

There were other reasons, of course, as to why Rommel didn't raise a unit similar to the LRDG – notably constant fuel constraints and the fact that the British military installations were less remote and better guarded – but ultimately it was because the German mentality was not as individualistic, adventurous or innovative as its British counterpart.

But the British top brass could at times be just as narrow in its outlook as the Germans. In August 1941 Bagnold was promoted to colonel and recalled to Cairo to take up a desk job at GHQ. It was a decision that infuriated many of the LRDG, who knew their leader as 'Baggy'. 'He was a great lad and the worst thing that happened to him was that he got promoted and put into GHQ Cairo,' recalled Les Sullivan. 'He used to get his own back by any trouble we got into in Cairo – and we often did get in trouble, getting arrested by Redcaps [Military Police] – then we would phone GHQ and he would get us out of where the Redcaps were holding us.'[24]

On one occasion, remembered Sullivan, some members of the ex-Guards G Patrol recently returned from 'Up the Blue' (the slang for the desert) misbehaved in the restaurant/bar Groppis, one of the most glamorous in Cairo. The outraged owner of Groppis sent a letter to GHQ demanding compensation for what he claimed was £6,000 worth of damage. As the LRDG were blamed, the letter ended up on Bagnold's desk. 'He wrote to Groppis and said in flowery language that it was dreadful, etc, and we can't have it,' remembered Sullivan. 'He said "I enclose a cheque for £6,000 and in future Groppis is out of bounds to all ranks." He sent it off and in no time it was back again with a note [from the owner] saying "Please don't make Groppis out of bounds and here's the cheque. I'll pay!"'[25]

With Bagnold in Cairo, command of the LRDG fell to Major Guy Prendergast, who proved himself a more than capable replacement in leading the unit during its role in *Crusader*, the purpose of which was to rid Cyrenaica of the Afrika Korps. The LRDG's initial task in the operation was to infiltrate enemy lines and observe and report their troop movements and reactions to the main British advance. But on 24 November, six days after the start of the offensive, the LRDG was ordered to attack 'with the utmost vigour enemy communications wherever they offered suitable targets'.

For the next few weeks the LRDG operated as guerrilla fighters, attacking German and Italian targets in three areas – the coastal road north of Agedabia; the Barce to Maraua road and the Tmimi to Gazala road. One of the most brazen strikes was made by Y Patrol under the command of Captain David Lloyd-Owen, who in broad daylight attacked an Italian fort at El Ezzeiat, killing two enemy soldiers and capturing a further ten. Five weeks later and 500 miles away, Lloyd-Owen assaulted another fort in Tripolitania and the night after ambushed an Italian convoy on the coast road near Tmimi, killing 11 soldiers.

Lloyd-Owen had joined the LRDG from The Queen's Royal Regiment just before Bagnold relinquished command of the unit, but in that short space of time he was able to gauge something of his leader's character. Writing in his memoirs, *Providence Their Guide*, Lloyd-Owen said:

He had such a shrewd understanding of the capabilities and limitations of human nature that he knew that he would only get the best out of it by devoted attention to what I described as the four fundamentals essential to successful desert travel, which are also the secret if any small behind-the-lines force is to triumph.

These four tenets are: the most careful and detailed planning, first-class equipment, a sound and simple communications system and a human element of rare quality. Ralph Bagnold had learnt these things the hard way in his pre-war desert ventures, and he was not the sort of man to forget them when it came to applying them to war. It was his teaching of the men who served with him in the Long Range Desert Group that made us ever mindful of every minor detail in order to ensure success.[26]

It was Lloyd-Owen who was partly responsible for expanding the role of the LRDG in North Africa still further from December 1941 onwards. On the night of 16/17 November a small force of British paratroopers under the command of Captain David Stirling jumped into Libya, intent on attacking five enemy landing strips. But bad weather thwarted their designs and the mission was aborted with heavy casualties. Lloyd-Owen's patrol rescued some of the survivors, including Stirling, and it was the start of a partnership that was to prove immensely profitable for the British and hugely damaging for the Axis. The force was L Detachment of the Special Air Service, and one of its number from the early days recalled the esteem in which they held the LRDG. 'After a while we started to call them the Long Range Taxi Service,' recalled Jeff Du Vivier, 'but it was a joke the LRDG took well. They knew how much we respected them.'[27]

The SAS weren't alone in their respect for the LRDG. Throughout their operational life in the North African desert – which continued up until March 1943, when the advance of the American First Army from the west and the British Eighth Army from the east trapped Axis forces in a small pocket of Tunisia – the LRDG won plaudits for their pluck and professionalism.

Throughout the battle of El Alamein in autumn 1942, the LRDG carried out invaluable reconnaissance patrols on the German forces, as well as laying mines and strafing enemy transport columns. Y Patrol, for example, spent several perilous days concealed near Marble Arch, 600 miles west of El Alamein, reporting on the Axis army as it fled towards Tunisia. Between

30 October and 10 November 1942, the number of enemy vehicles heading west each day rose from 100 to 3,500. At times the retreating Germans pulled off the road and rested, their lorries and tanks a matter of yards from the hidden LRDG patrol.

In his report on their exploits during this period, the British Army's director of military intelligence in Cairo wrote: 'Not only is the standard of accuracy and observation exceptionally high but the Patrols are familiar with the most recent illustration of enemy vehicles and weapons… Without their reports we should frequently have been in doubt as to the enemy's intentions, when knowledge of them was all important.'[28]

In the final two years of World War II, the LRDG served with distinction in the Aegean and the Balkans. But the desert is where their indelible legacy remains. 'Never during our peace-time travels had we imagined that war could ever reach the enormous empty solitudes of the inner desert, walled off as it has always been by sheer distance, by lack of water and by impassable seas of huge dunes,' Bagnold recalled in 1945. The success of the LRDG owed much to their courage and resourcefulness; but just as important was the maverick spirit fostered by Ralph Bagnold – daring to venture where others feared to tread.

✦ ✦ ✦ ✦

Bagnold was far from being from the same warrior caste as Blair Mayne or Anders Lassen, and he was the antithesis of the 'Gung Ho' guerrilla fighter Evans Carlson. Bagnold was a scientist first and a soldier second, and it was to his first love that he returned in 1944. Having retired from the army that year aged 48, with the honorary rank of brigadier and the Order of the British Empire (OBE) for his work in raising the LRDG, Bagnold married a year after the war ended and for the rest of his life devoted himself to his scientific studies. Among the papers he authored were 'Motion of waves in shallow water', published by the Royal Society of London in 1946, 'The sand formations in southern Arabia', published by *The Geographical Journal* in 1951 and 'Flow resistance in sinuous or irregular channels', published by the United States Geological Survey in 1960. His work was recognized with a string of awards, including the Founders' Gold Medal of the Royal Geographical Society, the Wollaston Medal of the Geological Society of London and the Penrose Gold Medal of the Geological Society of America. In 1977, in his 82nd year, Bagnold gave the keynote address at a NASA conference on the desert landscapes of Earth and Mars, and his work *The Physics of Blown Sand* was an important reference for NASA scientists in studying sand dunes on Mars.

Bagnold died on 28 May 1990, aged 94, and his considerable collection of private papers relating to his scientific and military work were donated by his family to the Churchill Archives in Cambridge. Among Bagnold's war correspondence was the draft of a letter he sent to Archibald Wavell in January 1945, just a few months after he had retired from the army. In the letter Bagnold thanked Wavell for his role in giving life to the Long Range Desert Group five years earlier. 'I shall never forget your friendly encouragement in 1940/41,' wrote Bagnold.

Bagnold was aware that the gratitude was mutual, and perhaps the belated letter was a response – now that he had more time on his hands – to an official despatch issued by General Wavell in October 1941, after he had been replaced by General Claude Auchinleck as Commander-in-Chief of British forces in the Middle East. In the despatch Wavell declared:

> I should like to bring to notice a small body of men who for a year past have done inconspicuous but invaluable work, the Long Range Desert Group. It was formed under Major (now Colonel) R.A. Bagnold in July 1940, to reconnoitre the great Libyan desert on the Western borders of Egypt and the Sudan. Operating in small independent columns, the Group has penetrated in to nearly every part of desert Libya, an area comparable in size with that of India.
>
> Not only have patrols brought back much information but they have attacked enemy forces, captured personnel, destroyed transport and grounded aircraft as far as 800 miles inside hostile territory. They have protected Egypt and the Sudan from any possibility of raids and have caused the enemy, in a lively apprehension of their activities, to tie up considerable forces in the defence of distant outposts.

Their journeys across vast regions of unexplored desert have entailed the crossing of physical obstacles and the endurance of extreme temperatures, both of which a year ago would have been deemed impossible. Their exploits have been achieved only by careful organisation and a very high standard of enterprise, discipline, mechanical maintenance and desert navigation.[29]

JUNIO VALERIO BORGHESE

TENTH LIGHT FLOTILLA

At the time of his death in August 1974 Junio Valerio Borghese was known throughout Italy as 'The Black Prince'. Such was his notoriety that he was denied full military honours and a full funeral ceremony at his burial in the Basilica de Santa Maria Maggiore. Instead Italian riot police looked on as a small crowd of Borghese's followers cried 'Italia, Italia, Fascisi, Fascisi!'[1]

It was an ignoble end to a life that had begun 68 years earlier in Rome. Junio Valerio came into the world the son of an Italian aristocrat from the illustrious Borghese family, and among his Tuscan antecedents were one pope (Paul V), three Italian cardinals and Pauline Bonaparte, younger sister of Napoleon.

From an early age Junio Valerio was marked out as a future naval officer and in 1922 he enrolled in the Naval Academy in Livorno, a port city on the Tyrrhenian Sea. Seven years later Borghese entered the Italian Navy and by the time he was 27 he was a submarine commander.

He was also an ardent follower of Benito Mussolini, the fascist Italian dictator who had come to power in the same year Borghese entered the naval academy. When Italy's military forces invaded Ethiopia and, in May 1936, proclaimed the country to be part of Italian East Africa, Borghese described it as 'a victory actually achieved by a people fighting in unison for its right to live'.

A few weeks after the subjugation of Ethiopia, Mussolini turned his attention to the civil war raging in Spain, offering General Franco the use of his forces. In all, an estimated 75,000 Italians fought for the Nationalists during the Spanish Civil War, and Borghese was one of them. He was part of the Submarine Legion (*Sottomarini Legionari*) and commanded the *Iride* during hostilities.

When Italy entered World War II in June 1940, Lieutenant Borghese had just turned 34 and was in command of the submarine *Vettor Pisani*, an old vessel that he recalled had many 'wheezy whims'. A month later the *Pisani* took part in the naval battle of Calabria (known to the Italians as the battle of Punta Stilo) in the waters of Calabria at the toe of Italy. The outcome was inconclusive, although one consequence was that the *Pisani* was withdrawn from active service after Borghese complained to his superiors of the number of leaks she sprang.

Along with two other Italian naval officers, Borghese was sent on a commanders course in submarine warfare at Memel on the Baltic. The course was run by the German Navy and specialized in teaching operations against the British Atlantic convoys. For nearly two weeks Borghese served on U-boats, observing the crews at work and concluding that in terms of skill and proficiency there was little difference between German submariners and their Italian counterparts. It was a theme that featured heavily in Borghese's memoirs, perhaps an indication that during the war he had encountered more than once the stereotypical view of the Italian Navy – as expressed by Admiral Sir Andrew Cunningham, Commander-in-Chief of the British Mediterranean Fleet 1939–43, when he declared a 'healthy contempt' for his adversary. In his memoirs entitled *Sea Devils*, Borghese praised 'the heroism of which Italians are capable when properly led, with due attention paid to their physical and spiritual needs'.

Upon his return to Italy in August 1940, Borghese was appointed commander of the *Scire*, a 620-ton submarine with a crew of 50. The vessel, along with the submarine *Gondar*, had been adapted into an 'assault craft transport' with three steel cylinders welded on deck (one forward and two aft), all with the same pressure resistance as the submarine. In these cylinders the secret weapon of the Italian Navy would be transported – the two-man torpedoes into which so much energy had been channelled in the years preceding the outbreak of war.

✦ ✦ ✦ ✦

The Italian Navy were the pioneers of naval sabotage in the 20th century. In October 1918, with Italy fighting alongside Britain, France and the United States against Germany, Sub-Lieutenant Raffaele Paolucci and naval engineer Major Raffaele Rossetti embarked on a mission to attack the battleship *Viribus Unitis*, pride of the Austro-Hungarian fleet, at anchor in the Croatian harbour of Pula.

Pooling their innovative resources, the pair modified an unexploded German torpedo so it could be piloted by them underwater at a speed of three to four miles per hour, powered by two propellers driven by compressed air. They set out from Venice just weeks before the end of the war on the torpedo boat and when they were within range of Pula, Rossetti and Paolucci boarded their human torpedo and slipped beneath the harbour's defences. They planted a mine on the hull of *Viribus Unitis* that exploded at dawn on 1 November, sending the ship to the bottom of the sea.

Though World War I ended less than three weeks later, the Italian Navy had glimpsed the potential of human torpedoes, and in the years after the war they were at the forefront of developing the new weapon. Two engineer officers, sub-lieutenants Teseo Tesei and Elios Toschi, spent years working on the prototype until in the words of the latter they had produced a weapon which 'in size and shape [is] very similar to a torpedo but is in reality a miniature submarine with entirely novel features, electrical propulsion and a steering wheel similar to that of an aeroplane ... equipped with a long-range underwater breathing gear, the operators will be able, without any connection with the surface, to breathe and navigate under water at any depths up to thirty metres and carry a powerful explosive charge into an enemy harbour.'[2]

Initial tests proved satisfactory and in 1936 the pair were authorized to oversee the construction of several more such weapons. Meanwhile the nucleus of what would become the Tenth Light Flotilla was established at La Spezia, on the north-west coast of Italy, under the charge of Commander Catalano Gonzaga.

Simultaneously, another naval sabotage unit was being formed using a different form of attack craft. It was Duke Amedeo of Aosta's idea to attack British shipping using fast, lightweight speedboats with explosives packed into the bow. The pilot, having circumvented the harbour defences, would set course for his target and jump clear in the seconds before the speedboat exploded.

Not long after the formation of the two units, however, the Italian naval command decided to abandon both projects. With the war against Ethiopia concluded, and with resources being directed towards assisting the Nationalists in the Spanish Civil War, the top brass saw no need to channel time, effort and money into two sabotage units. Though Borghese had yet to join the saboteurs, he wrote later that the decision was in part motivated by a distaste for innovation among certain senior officers, a distrust that others such as David Stirling, Evans Carlson and Orde Wingate had also encountered during their military careers.

'A new invention inevitably provokes reaction, distrust and scepticism,' wrote Borghese. 'There were the conservatives: guns alone, in the future, as in the past, could decide the question of naval superiority; what could two men, immersed in chilly water and the darkness of night, do against the insuperable defensive measures taken by a fleet at anchor at a naval base?'[3]

For two years the sabotage units were in abeyance until, in 1938, with war in Europe seeming evermore likely, they were reconstituted as the First Light Flotilla under the command of Commander Paolo Aloisi. By the time Britain and France declared war on Germany in September 1939, the Italian Navy was building 12 human torpedoes; Admiral Cavagnari, chief of the naval staff, had been won over by a documentary film on their capabilities.

At the beginning of 1940 Borghese encountered the First Light Flotilla for the first time when he was asked to pilot the submarine *Ametista* on the first full practice run with the human torpedoes. They put to sea in the Gulf of La Spezia with three of the weapons lashed to the deck of the submarine; the aim of the exercise was for three two-man crews to slip undetected into the Italian naval base on the island of Tino and place dummy charges on the cruiser *Quarto*. Two of the human torpedoes failed to reach their target, but the third succeeded in mining the keel of the *Quarto* without being seen by her crew or any other Italian sailor in the harbour.

The exercise made a deep impression upon Borghese. Having specialized in underwater weapons and being a submarine commander, he could see with lucidity how effective in war the new weapon could be. He labelled the explosive motorboat an 'assault weapon' and described the human torpedo as an 'insidious weapon', one that required its operator to possess a different temperament to the former:

Impetuosity is as necessary to the one as a cool head to the other; the former concentrates his whole store of energy in an action of a few seconds, while the latter must economise it for hours and hours; the former is all nerves and the other must not have any; the former defies, in a single supreme instant, an enemy who faces him and whom he can see; the latter, submerged in the utter darkness of the nocturnal depths of the sea, is guided on his blind course by the luminous dials of his instruments

181

and becomes aware of his target only when his bare hands touch the mighty keel of the enemy vessel; the former, finally, is the infantryman who, exposed to a hostile barrage, leaps from a trench to the attack with grenade or bayonet; the latter is the pioneer making his way through enemy lines, overcoming all obstacles, surrounded by snares and perils, entrusted to an extremely vulnerable apparatus, and protected from the paralysing chill of the waters only by a thin rubber diving suit.[4]

What all volunteers to the First Light Flotilla shared, however, was a devotion to Italy and a willingness to die for their country. It was made plain to all potential recruits that capture was almost inevitable on any given mission and death was a strong probability. Despite the bleak outlook, there was no shortage of volunteers of all ranks.

On 1 September 1940 a training centre was established at San Leopoldo, near the naval academy at Livorno, and Borghese helped weed out those men who were deemed unsuitable. The first practical test involved all recruits undertaking a divers course using underwater breathing apparatus. While they learned the rudiments of diving, the volunteers were also being assessed psychologically. Once they were cleared as sufficiently devoted to their country, the men were questioned as to their motives in volunteering. 'Financial reverses, for instance, or disappointment in love, or family quarrels were valid reasons for turning down an applicant,' recalled Borghese.

If they passed this selection criteria, the would-be recruit received a rigorous medical examination and a final interview with commanding officer Angelo Belloni, in charge of the training base. Only then was the sailor accepted into the First Light Flotilla and sent to either the surface craft unit or the underwater division.

The former trained at La Speziai, while the latter were posted to Bocca del Serchio, situated at the mouth of the river Serchio in northern Italy and bordering the San Rossore estate of King Victor Emmanuel. Here they became even more proficient as divers, while also learning how to pilot the human torpedoes, how to navigate underwater and how to place explosives on enemy ships in the pitch blackness of a night mission.

One of the men accepted as a pilot of a human torpedo in 1940 was Petty Officer Emilio Bianchi. More than 50 years later he recalled life at the Bocca di Serchio. 'Training was quite hard, actually very hard. In the middle of winter we would dive at 9:00pm and spend the whole night drilling and diving with our "pigs" [the nickname given by the men to the torpedoes]. Training was very challenging and exhausting, and only our enthusiasm allowed us to carry on.'[5]

It was decided on one occasion that Bianchi and his comrades would launch a dummy attack against their own naval base at La Spezia (where their assault craft colleagues were training). 'We could not alert the sentries of our operation, so the attack was carried out in complete secret and with the risk of getting shot by our own soldiers,' recalled Bianchi. They set out from the island of Tino, at the westernmost end of the Gulf of La Spezia, and negotiated the double defence lines near Punta Santa Maria without being observed. 'To bypass the defences, we had special tools [industrial wire cutters and pneumatic jacks] which would allow us to break the net without too much effort,' remembered Bianchi. With only a limited supply of oxygen in their breathing apparatus it was vital that the pilots of the torpedoes expended as little energy as possible in their approach to the target, which in this case was the battleship *Giulio Cesare*. 'The most difficult aspect was the fact that we had to operate at a depth of 45 feet in a very dark night, and therefore we were practically blind and had to be in perfect sync with our teammate. Once the charge was attached to the keel of the 'friendly' ship, the drill was not quite over. Due to the secrecy of our activities, we had to escape from the base as if we were the enemy.'[6]

The successful completion of the exercise encouraged the Italian Navy to expand the unit. Its name was changed from the First Light Flotilla to the Tenth Light Flotilla and the assault craft unit was designated the 'Surface Division', under the command of Lieutenant-Commander Giorgio Giobbe. The human torpedo unit was christened the 'Underwater Division' and Borghese was appointed its commanding officer, an appointment which would run in tandem with his command of the submarine *Scire*. A 'Sub-aquatic Research Centre' was also founded under the command of Angelo Belloni, the purpose of which was to examine how humans could best function underwater for long periods, while naval engineer Major Mario Masciulli was appointed to develop the underwater weapons research at La Spezia.

In addition, the Tenth Light Flotilla made use of some of Italy's finest manufacturers to further enhance their capabilities, including Pirelli, which helped in the manufacture of breathing sets and rubber suits, and the engine design company C.A.B.I., (Cattaneo Applicazione Brevetti Industriali) which worked on the actual torpedo.

The human torpedoes used by the Tenth Light Flotilla were modelled on that invented by Raffaele Paolucci and Major Raffaele Rossetti in 1918. It was 22ft (6.7m) in length and 21in (53cm) in diameter. The pilot, always an officer, sat at the front steering the torpedo, while the other crew member was at the rear. Their feet were secured by stirrups and a windscreen provided a breakwater enabling the pilot to steer the torpedo using the instrument panel consisting of 'a depth gauge, a magnetic compass, a voltmeter, an ampere meter, a manometer for registering pressure in the trimming tanks and a spirit-level. The control instruments were all luminous so as to allow them to be read at night under water.'[7]

At the front of the torpedo, in the 71in (1.8m)-long 'pig's snout' was 661lb (300kg) of explosives. A clutch by the pilot allowed him to detach the warhead from the rest of the torpedo. Behind the warhead was the fore trimming tank, then the accumulator battery ('of 30 elements with tension capacity of 60 volts'), the electric motor, the stern trimming tank and finally the propeller shaft with rudders attached to the propeller. The second crew member sat above the electric motor with his back resting against a trunk containing a tool kit, among which were 'compressed air net-lifters and net cutters, scissors, the kind of clamps called "sergeants", used in attacking the keels of enemy ships, plenty of rope, also required for this operation and coiled round a billet of wood'. The maximum speed of the 'pig' was 2.5mph, with the pilot using a flywheel connected to a rheostat with four different speeds. Like the original model of 1918, the rudder was based on the same principle as the *cloche* system of early aircraft.

The operators of a human torpedo were given a special diving suit made of rubber, which left only the head and hands uncovered. Emilio Bianchi described it thus:

We wore heavy wool clothing, somewhat similar to long johns, from feet to torso, and sweaters on top. We then wore a waterproof diver suit. Actually it was waterproof only in theory since often water came pouring in because the suit was very delicate and anything sharp would tear it up. It was made out of rubberized canvas and it had the unpleasant feature of wrinkling up at a depth of 30 feet or more. This action created a pliers-like motion, which would grab your skin and whip it. Once out of the water at the end of a drill, it looked like we had been flagellated. On the head we wore a hood lined in wool, but water seeped in, causing terrible cramps, but then the water inside the hood would warm up and the pain would go away.[8]

Their oxygen supply, enough for six hours, was carried on their backs in bottles and passed through a flexible, corrugated tube into a rubber breathing bag. The divers exhaled through the same tube, and the air was 'expelled into a canister of soda lime crystals for detaining and absorbing the carbon dioxide produced by respiration'.

Borghese worked his men hard during the winter of 1940 but he also ensured they made the most of their free time. He encouraged sports, organized wild boar hunts and – despite his own strident fascist views – refused to allow the discussion of politics. He also forbade the men to bring women back to the base. But most of the time, when the men weren't in the water, they studied reconnaissance photos of British naval bases in Malta, Alexandria and Gibraltar, until they knew their way round every harbour defence from memory.

A few of the recruits died during the training, usually drowned, while others were dismissed by Borghese if he believed them unfit for the type of missions he knew awaited. Those that remained, however – men such as Emilio Bianchi and his pilot, Sub-Lieutenant Luigi Durand de la Penne – were considered by Borghese as outstanding examples of Italian seamen. In attempting to explain why the men of the Tenth Light Flotilla were a cut above their peers, Borghese wrote:

It was not ambition: they evaded, even in their hearts, all personal distinction and were embarrassed by decorations and praise; it was not the hope of wealth, they had no reward for what they did; it was not professional promotion, which was easier to achieve from a desk in the Ministry than on active service; and it was not even the common human vanity to which the distinction of being pointed out as the heroes of such exceptional undertakings might appeal, for death stood across the chosen path, and what was the use of being pointed at after death? It was one faith alone that inspired them … they felt it their duty to devote themselves entirely to the service of their country without any kind of reservation.[9]

Gibraltar in the autumn of 1940 was a prime target for Borghese and the Underwater Division of the Tenth Light Flotilla. The peninsula was the headquarters of the British fleet in the western Mediterranean as well as an important supply base and a vital junction for merchant shipping from North America and Southern Africa. In addition, Gibraltar was too far from Italy to allow the Italian air force to launch attacks.

On 21 October the *Scire* departed from La Spezia bound for Gibraltar. Eight days later the submarine was in the Straits. Now Borghese was required to demonstrate great skill in manoeuvring the *Scire* into a suitable position from which to launch the three 'pigs'. He needed to be close enough to the harbour to give the pilots every chance of reaching their targets, but not too close to run the risk of being detected by patrolling British anti-submarine boats equipped with hydrophones. Borghese also had to submerge to the sea bed so that the operators could safely pull the 'pigs' from the cylinders strapped to the deck of the submarine. This had to be done at a depth of at least 50ft, otherwise a British vessel could inadvertently collide with them.

Borghese chose as his drop point the far end of the Bay of Algeciras, where the river Guadarranque debouches into the sea. The two drawbacks with this location were that it necessitated sailing past Gibraltar itself, as well as going headlong into the prevailing current. Nonetheless Borghese dived to a depth of 230ft and, on the evening of 29 October, stole into the bay. It was an excruciating passage north with everyone on board the *Scire* conscious that on the surface above there were British vessels on the lookout for enemy submarines.

'The silence aboard became absolute,' recalled Borghese. 'We were now at our closest to Gibraltar, only about two miles off. Everyone was wearing rope soles, the metal switch-keys of out instruments were wrapped in cloth, all machinery aboard not essential to the progress of the submarine was stopped. Every possible precaution was taken to prevent the watchful enemy, so close now, from becoming aware of our presence.'[10]

At 0130hrs on 30 October the *Scire* was in position, less than 400 yards from the Spanish coast and three miles from Gibraltar Harbour. The 'pig' operators made their final preparations for exiting the submarine, while Borghese received a communiqué from the Supreme Naval Command confirming that two British battleships were in the harbour. At 0200hrs Borghese surfaced and the three two-man crews passed out of the escape hatch and pulled their craft from the canisters before boarding them. Immediately the *Scire* dived and negotiated her way back through the Bay of Algeciras and out into the open sea. The three crews were on their own, with instructions to swim ashore to Spain and make contact with a waiting Italian agent once their mission was complete.

One of the crews was piloted by Sub-Lieutenant Luigi Durand de la Penne with Petty Officer Emilio Bianchi as his assistant. The pair had retrieved their 'pig' from its canister on the port quarter and found it to be in working order despite its arduous journey from La Spezia. Climbing into position, the pair surfaced and soon realized that the compass was jammed. De la Penne decided to continue with the mission, even though it would mean navigating by the lights of Gibraltar Harbour three miles to their south with de la Penne keeping his head just above the water line. 'After some delays, we were able to reach the military port where some British boats were dropping depth charges all around [presumably because the British had picked up suspicious sounds with their anti-submarine listening devices], but without giving us too much trouble,'[11] recalled Bianchi, who had lost contact with the other two crews immediately after departing the *Scire*.

De la Penne thought it prudent to submerge until the British patrol boats had passed, so the torpedo dropped to a depth of 50ft and continued its slow progress towards Gibraltar with the crew navigating blind. Subsequent events were disputed by de la Penne and Bianchi; the former wrote in his operational report that an explosion from a British depth charge caused the 'pig' to stop, but Bianchi said years later (laughing at the memory) that 'it was an internal explosion probably due to gases formed inside the battery compartment just under my bottom that caused the motor to seize up'.[12]

De la Penne struggled with the controls for a few moments and then abandoned the craft as it descended to the sea bed. Bianchi remained at his post: 'I should remind you that our breathing apparatuses did not allow us to descend more than 45 feet, while reaching 90 feet was absolutely forbidden,' he recalled. 'My craft kept going down and, in checking the depth gauge, I noticed that it was stuck at about 90 feet. At this point, the craft touched the bottom and stopped ... if the depth of the sea had been any greater I would have surely died.'[13]

Bianchi opened the tool kit container, but the effort required to fix the 'pig' was too great at that depth and he 'felt the initial symptoms of dizziness and gave up'. Surfacing, Bianchi found de la Penne and together the pair swam to the Spanish shore, having first sunk their breathing apparatus as instructed by Borghese. After two hours in the water they scrambled ashore at 0530hrs, whereupon they removed their diving suits and buried them in the sand. Two hours later they met the Italian agent at the rendezvous point.

Once back in Italy, de la Penne and Bianchi learned that neither of the other two crews had been successful due to faults with the 'pigs' and that two of their number were now in British hands. Yet despite the ultimate failure of the mission, Borghese (awarded the Italian Gold Medal for his part) was encouraged by certain aspects of the raid. It had been proved possible to sail into the Bay of Algeciras, right past Gibraltar, without detection, and the British defences had been found to be far from impregnable. It was clear that the 'pig' operators were adversely affected from having to spend days cooped up in the submarine prior to launching their torpedoes and in future Borghese decided they would join them just prior to a raid. But his most pressing concern was to discover the causes of the three pigs' malfunctions and rectify them as soon as possible.

While the Underwater Division of the Tenth Light Flotilla returned to its base at Bocca di Serchio, the Surface Division began preparing for an attack against British shipping at anchor in Souda Bay, on the north-west coast of Crete. The raid was carried out in March 1941 by six E-boats packed with explosives, and the results were spectacular. As well as the sinking of the cruiser *York*, three merchant vessels were sunk or badly damaged at the cost of six pilots captured. Disturbed by the manner of the audacious attack, the British officially blamed the sinking on German aircraft, but behind the scenes the Admiralty ordered an urgent investigation into the raid in a desperate effort to prevent future assaults.

Satisfied that the shortcomings that had bedevilled the attack on Gibraltar in October had been remedied, Borghese ordered a new mission against the British base in May 1941. The submarine *Scire* sailed from the Mediterranean to the Atlantic, arriving at Cadiz on 23 May. There it took on board the operators of the 'pigs', all of whom were fresh and fit, having been spared the voyage in the *Scire*. Three days later Borghese piloted the submarine past Gibraltar to the northern end of Algeciras Bay and the three crews embarked upon their mission. A last-minute intelligence report from the Italian Supreme Command had informed the saboteurs that there were no Royal Navy ships at anchor in Gibraltar, but there were plenty of merchant vessels waiting to be sunk.

But once more fate was unkind to the Italians. The first crew aborted their attempt almost immediately after leaving the submarine when they realisedd their vessel was damaged. On the second 'pig' one of the men got into difficulties with his breathing apparatus, and the third 'pig' inexplicably sank just as the crew were preparing to attach the warhead to the hull of a British ship. It was a bitter disappointment for Borghese and his men, the only saving grace the fact that all six men evaded capture and eventually returned to Bocca di Serchio.

However, the grief Borghese felt at this failure was eclipsed in May, when the Surface Division struck Malta, attacking targets in La Valletta Harbour and the bay of Marsa Muscetto. Encouraged by their success at Souda Bay, another 17 E-boats had set out to ram British vessels, but both attacks failed disastrously. The Surface Division was all but wiped out, with 15 men dead, 18 taken prisoner and ten E-boats sunk or captured.

Among the dead were Lieutenant-Commander Giorgio Giobbe, leader of the Surface Division, and Commanding Officer Vittorio Moccagatta, in overall command of the Tenth Light Flotilla. Borghese was promoted to lieutenant-commander and placed in temporary charge of the Flotilla and his first act was to appoint Salvatore Todaro as the new CO of the Surface Division. Then Borghese set about restoring morale to a unit reeling after the failure at Gibraltar and the catastrophe at Malta.

> I subjected the veteran pilots of the Serchio, who were anxious to renew their former experiments with greater chances of success, and the recruits who had since been coming in, full of the enthusiasm of neophytes, to exercises of the most concentrated, thorough and rigorous description. The object was to put them in a condition to overcome the difficulties which had in the previous operations prevented successful action.[14]

As well as intensifying and improving training methods, Borghese liaised with several naval departments to produce some innovations for the unit; acoustic and incendiary mines were developed to spread in harbour entrances, as was the 'bug', a 6.6lb (3kg) explosive device in a small circular casing that could be clamped to the hull of ships and set off using a timer. These 'bugs' would be carried in a shoulder pouch by frogmen, part of a new unit of 'assault swimmers'. Each frogman would wear 'long, rubber fins which gave him greater speed during approach and enabled him to swim and to dive without using his arms', and a luminous compass strapped to the wrist.

By late September 1941 Borghese judged his unit ready to recommence operations and he decided once more to attack Gibraltar. Despite the fact that they encountered sterner defences in light of their previous visits (including noiseless patrol boats that dropped depth charges at regular intervals at the entrance to the harbour), the Italians managed to sink three British ships: the naval tanker *Denby Dale*, the merchant ship *Durham* and the tanker *Fiona Shaw*.

The news of the mission was greeted with acclaim in Italy, with the six operators receiving the Silver Medal and Borghese being promoted to commander for his success 'in bringing back his submarine and its crew to the base, despite the difficulties due to determined pursuit by the enemy and to navigation underwater driven to the limit of human endurance'. King Victor Emmanuel paid a visit to the base of the Underwater Division, bringing with him a wild boar from his estate for the men, and telling Borghese that he knew well the problems caused by the currents off Gibraltar because he had fished there many times.

The Italians had first attempted to raid the harbour at Alexandria in August 1940. On that occasion, however, as the submarine *Iride* and torpedo boat *Calipso* approached the Egyptian port, they were spotted by a British aircraft returning from a bombing mission. The pilot alerted his command and within minutes three Swordfish torpedo-bombers from the aircraft carrier *Eagle* attacked the Italian raiders, sinking the *Iride*.

Eighteen months later, in December 1941, Borghese decided it was time to return to Alexandria with the 'pigs' in the hope of inflicting more damage on a navy reeling from the loss of the aircraft carrier *Ark Royal* (sunk by a German U-boat on 13 November off Gibraltar) and the battleship *Barham* (which had met a similar fate 12 days later with the loss of 841 men).

The loss of the *Barham* reduced the number of British battleships in the Mediterranean fleet to two, and so the remaining ships, *Queen Elizabeth* and *Valiant*, were ordered into the anchorage at Alexandria. Borghese planned the attack meticulously, studying dozens of air reconnaissance photographs and acquainting himself with every harbour defence deployed by the British. Although he had his men train relentlessly for the raid, in the conditions that best replicated those they were likely to encounter in Alexandria, Borghese told none of the operators the actual target; secrecy was paramount if the mission was to have any chance of success.

The men chosen for the mission stood little chance of escaping once they had planted their explosives, so Borghese gathered them together to ask for volunteers, saying: 'Now, boys, we want three crews for an operation in the very near future. All I can tell you about it is that it differs from Gibraltar operations in the fact that return from it is extremely problematical. Is there anyone who would like to take part in it?' Every one of the men raised their hands, so it was left to Borghese to select the six operators. Those chosen, he recalled, were 'the pick of the bunch' and included Luigi Durand de la Penne and Emilio Bianchi.

On 3 December the *Scire* left La Spezia with its crew still ignorant of their destination. The operators travelled separately by aircraft, rendezvousing with the submarine on the Aegean island of Leros on the 12th, although they were quartered on land as if they were nothing to do with the *Scire*. Borghese briefed the men the following day, updating them on weather reports, harbour defences and showing them the very latest aerial photos of Alexandria.

Admiral Biancheri, Commander-in-Chief of the Aegean naval sector, arrived on Leros and requested a demonstration of the human torpedoes of which he had heard so much. Borghese looked at him in disbelief and flatly refused in case British spies were present on the island.

The *Scire* left Leros on 14 December and proceeded south, submerged during the day and surfacing only at night to charge the batteries and circulate some fresh air inside the vessel. Borghese was faced with the challenge of depositing the raiders within striking distance of their targets while avoiding the considerable British defences: as well as a minefield 20 miles north-west of the harbour, there were 180ft-deep anti-submarine nets six miles from Alexandria, plus detector cables and other mines in scattered positions.

Not only were these obstacles to be surmounted, but it was crucial to the success of the mission that the human torpedoes were launched at the precise point calculated; any discrepancy would irreparably damage their chances of accomplishing their task, for they had limited amounts of oxygen. Navigating in such a situation, reflected Borghese, required 'the exactitude of a draughtsman working with compass and ruler'. He had to take into account the drifting caused by strong underwater currents and the necessity of travelling for long periods underwater at a great depth.

While Borghese and the crew of the *Scire* piloted the vessel towards Alexandria, the six operators reposed and reserved their energy for the imminent challenge. De la Penne slept for most of the time, waking only to eat copious amounts of fruit cake, and Emilio Bianchi was equally relaxed. 'In Alexandria, thanks to our secret service and scouts, we knew perfectly where the battleships were and how to operate,' he recalled of his state of mind prior to the mission. 'We just had to repeat what we had done during our drills.'[15]

On 18 December Borghese received an intelligence report confirming that the *Valiant* and *Queen Elizabeth* were still at anchor in Alexandria. On the same day he wrote in his log that they were 'continually regulating our movements in accordance with the rise of the seabed, till at 1840 hours, we found ourselves at the pre-arranged point, 1.3 miles by 356 [degrees] from the lighthouse at the west mole of the commercial harbour of Alexandria at a depth of 15 metres'.

Using his periscope to check the coast was clear, once it was dark Borghese surfaced so that he could emerge onto the coning tower. From his position he was able to identify some of Alexandria's more prominent buildings and confirm that, after 16 hours of blind navigation, they were at the exact pre-arranged point. When the three crews were in their suits and ready to set sail in the 'pigs', Borghese wished them luck and watched as first Captain Antonio Marceglia and Petty Officer Spartaco Schergat departed, followed in quick succession by Captain Vincenzo Martellotta and Petty Officer Mario Marino in the second 'pig' and de la Penne and Bianchi in the third. With the three crews on their way towards the harbour, Borghese dived and began the long journey back to Italy.

Immediately after leaving the *Scire*, the three 'pigs' had a stroke of good fortune when three British destroyers hove into view. The harbour's net gates opened and the guide lights went on, allowing the raiders to slip unseen into Alexandria ahead of the enemy vessels. Though the three torpedoes had lost one another in the black water, each knew their own orders: de la Penne and Bianchi were to attack the *Valiant*, Marceglia and Schergat the *Queen Elizabeth* and Martellotta and Marino a loaded oil tanker.

De la Penne and Bianchi soon saw ahead of them the huge hull of the 32,000-ton battleship. Encountering its protective anti-torpedo netting, Bianchi cut their way through it, and they approached their target. But the exertion of dealing with the netting had exhausted Bianchi to such an extent that he fainted, slipping from the 'pig' and floating to the surface. Regaining consciousness, he clung to a floating buoy out of sight of the British sentries patrolling the deck of the *Valiant*.

Under the surface, de la Penne had noticed the disappearance of Bianchi but his more pressing concern was for the 'pig', which for some reason had dropped like a stone to the sea bed. Diving down to investigate, de la Penne discovered that a steel wire had snagged the propeller, and despite his best efforts he was unable to restart the motor. De la Penne was faced with a stark choice: either abort the mission or try to drag the 'pig' a few yards so that it was directly beneath the hull of the *Valiant*. He decided on the latter, as Borghese recounted in his memoirs:

With all his strength, panting and sweating, he dragged at the craft; his goggles became obscured and the mud he was stirring up prevented his reading the compass. His breath began to come in great gasps and it became difficult to breathe at all through the mask, but he stuck to it and made progress. He could hear close above him the noises made aboard the ship, especially the sound of an alternating pump, which he used to find his direction. After 40 minutes of superhuman effort, making a few inches at every pull, he at last bumped his head against the hull. He made a cursory survey of the position: he seemed to be at about the middle of the ship, an excellent spot for causing maximum damage.[16]

In fact the torpedo was underneath the *Valiant*'s port bulge, abreast A turret, and close to the turret's shell room and magazine. It was a little after 0300hrs and de la Penne set the fuse on the warhead to explode at 0500hrs. Once he had surfaced de la Penne found Bianchi clinging to the mooring buoy at the bow of the *Valiant*. They were soon spotted by British sentries above and as the pair waited to be picked up they listened to the guards 'talking contemptuously about Italians. I called Bianchi's attention to the probability that in a few hours they would have changed their minds'.[17]

At 0330hrs a British patrol boat appeared and the two Italians were hauled on board. The officer in command asked them a few rudimentary questions and on the way to shore 'expressed ironical sympathy with their lack of success'. De la Penne and Bianchi said nothing, and after a brief interrogation conducted in Italian the pair were returned to the *Valiant* where the ship's captain, Charles Morgan, was more appreciative of their mission. He wanted to know where they had placed the charge. De la Penne and Bianchi refused to cooperate, so an armed escort placed them in a hold not far from A turret. They were well treated, given a tot of rum and a cigarette, and encouraged to disclose the whereabouts of the charge. Bianchi curled up and went to sleep while de la Penne kept one eye on his watch. At 0450hrs he told his guards he wished to speak to Captain Morgan. In his operational report on the incident de la Penne described subsequent events:

I was taken aft into his presence. I told him that in a few minutes his ship would blow up, that there was nothing he could do about it and that, if he wished, he could still get his crew into a place of safety. He again asked me where I had placed the charge and as I did not reply he had me escorted back into the hold. As we went along I heard the loudspeakers giving orders to abandon ship, as the vessel had been attacked by Italians, and saw people running aft … a few minutes passed (they were infernal ones for me: would the explosion take place?) and then it came. The vessel reared with extreme violence. All the lights went out and the hold became filled with smoke.[18]

The charge had exploded under the port bulge, holing an area some 60ft by 30ft and causing extensive flooding in several compartments and some electrical damage. De la Penne and Bianchi were taken up on deck, from where they saw the ship begin to list to port some four or five degrees. The two Italians turned their gaze towards the *Queen Elizabeth* just a few hundred yards away. They could see startled sailors standing in her bows watching the drama on the *Valiant*. Suddenly a great explosion rent the air and the *Queen Elizabeth* 'rose a few inches out of the water and fragments of iron and other objects flew out of her funnel, mixed with oil, which even reached the deck of the *Valiant*, splashing everyone of us standing on her stern.'

The *Queen Elizabeth* had been blown up by Marceglia and Schergat in a flawless act of sabotage. Having cut through the anti-submarine net, the pair attached a loop-line from one bilge keel to the other, and fixed their warhead on the line so that it was suspended 5ft beneath the hull of the battleship. It exploded under the 'B' boiler room, devastating the ship's double-bottom structure and inflicting damage to a section of the ship measuring 190ft by 60ft. Compartment by compartment the vessel began flooding up to the main deck level, until eventually the *Queen Elizabeth* sank to the bottom of Alexandria Harbour.

As a frantic manhunt ensued for the two saboteurs, Marceglia and Schergat swam ashore, slipped off their diving suits and posed as French sailors. The evasion plan required all six operators to rendezvous with an Italian submarine that was lying ten miles offshore from Rosetta, the men having to first steal a boat to make the pick-up point.

Marceglia and Schergat made their way to the railway station where they took a train to Rosetta, 40 miles east of Alexandria. They spent the night in a cheap hotel and the next evening made their way towards the harbour with the intention of stealing a boat. Here their luck ran out and they were stopped by an Egyptian patrol. Identified as Italians, the two saboteurs were handed over to the British.

The last two saboteurs, Martellotta and Marino, successfully destroyed a 16,000-ton oil tanker called the *Sagona* to complete a night of devastating triumph for the Tenth Light Flotilla, although Borghese himself, sailing back towards Italy, would have to wait more than a week to hear the news. For 39 hours the *Scire* remained submerged before surfacing and making for Leros, and from there Borghese piloted the vessel to La Spezia. After covering 3,500 miles in 22 days at sea, he arrived home on 29 December. Waiting to welcome them ashore was Admiral Bacci with a telegram from Admiral Riccardi, Under-Secretary of State for the Navy, commending Borghese and his crew for their part in a highly successful mission.

The sinking of the *Queen Elizabeth*, which took 18 months to raise and repair, and the damage to the *Valiant* was a grave setback for the British fleet in the East Mediterranean, even if the Royal Navy pretended otherwise. It denied Italian claims of the *Valiant* having suffered a similar fate to that of the *Queen Elizabeth* and to prove it, released photos to the press of the ship at anchor at Alexandria. What the photographs carried by the British papers didn't show, however, was the extensive damage that de la Penne and Bianchi's torpedo had caused to the *Valiant* below the waterline. It was another year before the battleship was able to resume operations. 'For the first (and last) time in the course of the war,' wrote Borghese, 'the Italian Navy achieved crushing superiority and dominated the Mediterranean; it could therefore resume, with practical immunity, supplies to the armies overseas and carry out transport of the German Afrika Korps to Libya, thus causing the defeat, a few months later, of the British Army which was driven out of Cyrenaica.'[19]

Despite his satisfaction with the attack on Alexandria, Borghese was astounded to discover that his superiors were not going to exploit the success to its maximum advantage; with the British fleet all but out of action, a large-scale assault on the island of Malta – for so long a thorn in the side of the Axis – would almost certainly have succeeded. Borghese later divided the blame at this missed opportunity between the hesitancy of the Italian general staff and the refusal of the German High Command to supply the fuel for aircraft and warships.

Bianchi, who along with his five fellow saboteurs was sent to a prisoner-of-war camp, agreed with the sentiments of his commander concerning Malta. 'The island was exhausted, we could have taken it with little risk, but we never got there,' he reflected years later. The six saboteurs were all conferred with the Gold Medal upon their return from captivity and in an act of high irony, de la Penne received his decoration from the new chief of the Allied naval mission to Italy – none other than Captain Charles Morgan, erstwhile commander of the *Valiant*.

Borghese received the Military Order of Savoy for his role in the attacks on Alexandria Harbour, the citation praising his 'great technical competence and shrewdness … and cool determination'. What delighted Borghese even more, however, though he didn't hear of it for a long time after, was the speech given by Winston Churchill to a secret session of the House of Commons on 23 April 1942. It was the British Prime Minister's grave duty to inform the House about the details of the attack:

> Extreme precautions have been taken for some time past against the varieties of human torpedo or one-man submarine entering our harbours. Not only are nets and other obstructions used but underwater charges are exploded at irregular intervals in the fairway. None the less these men had penetrated the harbour. Four hours later explosions occurred in the bottoms of the *Valiant* and the *Queen Elizabeth*, produced by limpet bombs [*sic*] fixed with extraordinary courage and ingenuity, the effect of which was to blow large holes in the bottoms of both ships and to flood several compartments, thus putting them both out of action for many months.[20]

Thrilled at the success of the attacks on Alexandria, the Italian admiralty instructed Borghese to relinquish command of the submarine *Scire* and focus

all his efforts on leading the Underwater Division of the Tenth Light Flotilla.*
Borghese formulated a brazen plan to return to Alexandria and finish what
they'd started in December, by destroying the *Valiant* and *Queen Elizabeth* as
the two vessels lay in the large repair dock. The date of the attack was set for
May 1942, and as in the previous mission a submarine, the *Ambra*, sailed
from La Spezia to Leros where it took on board the six operators.

Although the saboteurs were deposited close to the target the attack failed;
the British defences had been strengthened considerably in the wake of the
previous assault with 'searchlights, star-shells, aircraft and cruising patrol
vessels' sweeping the harbour continuously. In addition the operators lacked
the experience of their predecessors, who had been, as Borghese described
them, the 'pick of the bunch'. Finally, the captain of the submarine *Ambra* was
an inferior pilot to Borghese and was at least a mile west of the pre-arranged
drop-off point. All in all it was a dispiriting mission with none of the
saboteurs getting close to their target. Borghese knew he must look for fresh
ideas with which to disrupt British shipping.

Borghese's skills and *savoir faire* were now much in demand and he was
invited to Berlin in the summer of 1942 to discuss widening his scope of
operations from the Mediterranean to the Atlantic and beyond. An attack on
New York was mooted, as was a raid against British targets in Freetown,
Sierra Leone. From Berlin Borghese travelled to Paris, where he met Admiral
Dönitz, Commander-in-Chief of the German submarine fleet at his
headquarters in the Bois de Boulogne, and he then headed south to the
German submarine base at the Atlantic port of Bordeaux. Despite being well
received by the German submariners, Borghese struggled to impress upon
them the potential of human torpedoes. This, he wrote, was because they
were not 'suited to the German military mind, since they demanded, in
addition to skill in the water and seamanlike qualities, conspicuous gifts of
personal initiative and individual enterprise'.

Borghese had another reason for visiting Bordeaux, other than to meet
and greet his German allies, and that was to test a new craft in which he

---

* In its first mission without Borghese the *Scire* was sunk by a British torpedo-boat off Haifa with
the loss of all hands.

harboured high hopes of success. It was a pocket two-man submarine, weighing 12 tons and carrying two torpedoes, that would be launched against targets in North America. His original intention had been for a German U-boat to carry the mini-submarine across the Atlantic in a specially adapted 'pouch', but in Bordeaux Borghese carried out several tests that convinced him the most practical method of transportation was for the U-boat to carry the mini-submarine in a bed on its deck. 'An important step forward had been taken on the road to the realization of our plans for the future, which was certainly on the audacious side,' wrote Borghese of his time at Bordeaux.

Back in Italy, Borghese turned his thoughts once more to Gibraltar. The port was now busier than ever, with a huge flow of shipping coming in and out of the harbour, so much so that many merchant supply ships were anchored outside the harbour defences in the bay of Algeciras. Using a false name, Borghese rented a cottage on the north coast of the bay, a little over two miles from Gibraltar, but on Spanish territory. A Spanish woman moved in and soon she was joined by her husband, an Italian naval officer, as well as a team of 12 assault swimmers from the Tenth Light Flotilla. From the front room of the cottage the men observed the Allied steamers at anchor in the bay and formulated their plan of attack. On the night of 13 July 1942 the dozen frogmen crept from the cottage to the sea and swam out to the supply ships, where charges were laid against four vessels. Though none were sunk in the resultant explosions, all required a considerable period in the repair yards. Two months later another attack was carried out by three frogmen and this time the 1,787-ton steamer *Raven's Point* was sunk.

By early 1943 the tide of the war in North Africa had turned against the Axis, and Italy in particular was under threat from the Allies. Ethiopia had been lost and Mussolini's forces had been thrown out of North Africa, retreating towards Tunisia before withdrawing across the Mediterranean to Italy. The Italian Navy no longer ruled the waves in the region and British air assaults had forced them to sail north to the safe haven of La Spezia and Genoa. 'The Tenth [Light Flotilla] therefore had to bear the burden of developing such offensive activity as, in the naval sphere, might be suggested by circumstances,' remembered Borghese. On 8 May 1943 three 'pigs' attacked merchant vessels in Gibraltar and achieved the sinking of three supply ships totalling 20,000 tons. It was another daring act by Borghese's men but he knew in the great scheme of things such destruction was but a minor inconvenience to the dominant Allies.

Shortly afterwards the Tenth Light Flotilla, both the Underwater and Surface Divisions, was withdrawn to Sicily to await the inevitable invasion. When it began on 10 July, the Surface Division carried out numerous ambushes on Allied shipping, but again they were of little consequence other than to prove the courageous defiance of the motorboat crews. As if in acknowledgement of the impending defeat, the Italian Admiralty awarded the Tenth a Gold Medal for its work of the previous three years. The citation included the passage:

> In numerous undertakings of great daring, in contempt of all danger, against difficulties of every kind, created as much by natural conditions as by the effectiveness of defensive installations at the harbours, the gallant men of the assault divisions of the Navy, trained and directed by the Tenth Light Flotilla, have contrived to reach the enemy in the secure retreats of fortified harbours, sinking two battleships, two cruisers [in reality one cruiser, *York*], a destroyer and a large number of steamers, totalling more than 100,000 tons.[21]

The citation, however, was the unit's epitaph, for although a lone frogman named Luigi Ferraro carried out a bold solo mission in Alexandretta Harbour, Turkey, in July 1943, sinking the 7,000-ton *Orion*, Italy was invaded on 3 September and five days later declared an armistice with the Allies.

With Mussolini held captive by his fellow Italians at Gran Sasso in the mountains of Abruzzo (although he was freed on 12 September by a daring German commando operation led by Otto Skorzeny), Borghese despaired of the internecine warfare erupting among his fellow Italians, writing that 'the atmosphere of defeat and betrayal was everywhere'. It was still Borghese's intention to launch a mini-submarine raid against New York, an attack planned for December 1943, but on the evening of 8 September, at the Tenth's base in La Spezia, he heard by radio the declaration of an armistice.

✦ ✦ ✦ ✦

Still a committed fascist, Borghese joined the Repubblica di Salò (Republic of Salo), founded on 23 September as a state of southern Europe led by Mussolini and loyal to Germany. He took with him those men of the Tenth Light Flotilla who shared his political views,* and although there were no further human torpedo attacks, they fought alongside the Nazis for the rest of the war.

Borghese formed a close friendship with Otto Skorzeny, the German Special Forces commander, who had led the daring mission in September 1943 to liberate Mussolini from the Campo Imperatore Hotel on top of the Gran Sasso mountain in central Italy. Borghese was one of the few Italians that Skorzeny respected, writing in his wartime memoirs that he was 'the model of what an officer should be'. On one occasion in 1944 the pair discussed the likely outcome for Europe if the Allies triumphed and Borghese's comments left a deep impression on Skorzeny: 'In this war,' Borghese explained, 'Europe, the real Europe, is fighting against Asia. If Germany fails, the true core of Europe will disappear and so I and my men are prepared to stand at your [Germany's] side to the bitter end and fight on at the gates of Berlin, if need be. The Western Allies, who are now helping to overthrow Germany, will bitterly regret their action.'[22]

It was during the final year of the war that Borghese earned his grim sobriquet 'The Black Prince'. As the Germans and fascist Italians were pushed relentlessly northwards up Italy towards the Austrian border, they were subjected to hit-and-run attacks from partisans. Borghese's response to these raids was brutal, involving torture and execution, not just of captured partisans but of those villagers suspected of involvement.

The Tenth Light Flotilla was officially disbanded on 26 April 1945, although by then Borghese had already taken steps to ensure he did not meet summary justice at the hands of the partisans. An agent from the American Office of Strategic Services, James Angleton, took him into custody and

---

* Luigi Durand de la Penne was not one of them. On release from prison he chose to fight against the Germans, while Emilio Bianchi's health was so poor that he took no further active part in the war.

spirited him to Rome. Subsequent reports allege that the Americans were interested in developing Borghese's naval guerrilla warfare for use against the Japanese but the rapid conclusion of the war in the Pacific cancelled such a partnership.

When Borghese was finally brought before a court, friends in high places ensured that the majority of charges against him were dropped or dismissed. On 17 February 1949 he was found guilty of collaborating with the Germans and of involvement in the deaths of eight partisans, yet he was immediately freed as part of a general amnesty, and on account of his war record prior to September 1943.

But if the Italian authorities had hoped such clemency would result in Borghese drifting quietly off to some backwater, they were mistaken. He joined the Italian Social Movement and in 1951 became its chairman. In the 1960s Borghese founded the Italian National Front and in 1970 planned a coup d'état to end what he saw as the country's descent into left-wing anarchy. The uprising – said at the time to involve 4,000 men under the command of the former submariner – failed and Borghese fled to Spain and sought exile under General Franco.

Few in Italy, save for a few fascists, mourned the death of Borghese four years later. This, after all, was the Black Prince, a vicious slayer of partisans and a man who fought alongside the Nazis until the bitter end. Yet the post-war vilification of Borghese has obscured the fact that for three years this Italian aristocrat was not only a brilliant submarine commander but the bold and innovative leader of the Tenth Light Flotilla, the first naval Special Forces unit.

BARON VON DER HEYDTE

FALLSCHIRMJÄGER

From an early age Friedrich August Freiherr von der Heydte despised the Nazi Party, a dislike that was mutual. Reichsmarschall Hermann Göring, commander of the German Luftwaffe, mocked his devout Catholicism by referring to him as the 'Rosary Paratrooper'.[1] Such was the level of antipathy between von der Heydte and the German National Socialist party that had he not been such an outstanding soldier, one of their few great Special Forces leaders, he might well have faced a Nazi firing squad long before the end of the war.

✦ ✦ ✦ ✦

Von der Heydte was a scion of the Bavarian aristocracy, born in Munich on 30 March 1907. His father, a Freiherr (the equivalent of a British baron) had served in the Royal Bavarian Army and his mother was of French origin. Both were devout Catholics, a piety that their son inherited, and which was nurtured when he enrolled at the Munich Catholic school. However, World War I – during which Friedrich was a pageboy to the Royal Court of the House of Wittelsbach – destroyed all hope the von der Heydtes held of young Friedrich enjoying the privileged life of a nobleman, and with the abolition of the German monarchy following the end of the conflict Friedrich von der Heydte enlisted in the army as an officer cadet in the 18th Cavalry Regiment.

In 1927 von der Heydte enrolled at Innsbruck University to read law and economics, his studies sponsored by the military as his indigent family could not afford the fees. In his adolescence it had been Communism against which the politically aware von der Heydte had railed but, on moving to Berlin after completing his bachelor's degree, he found a new enemy – the National Socialists. His time at Berlin University was marked by several confrontations with the emerging Nazis, confrontations that frequently ended in fistfights as von der Heydte defended his liberal views.

Disgusted with the rise of Adolf Hitler and the Nazis, von der Heydte left Berlin for Vienna where he became a student at the Austrian Consular Academy. In 1934, a year after Hitler had become Chancellor of Germany, von der Heydte took out Austrian citizenship and in 1935 he spent some time studying in Holland. However, the same year he was recalled to the army as the German military began a programme of secret expansion. Despite being known to the Gestapo as an anti-fascist, von der Heydte escaped the purge of officers deemed to lack the 'revolutionary spirit' that Hitler wanted in his armed forces.

By late 1937 von der Heydte's cavalry regiment had been formed into an anti-tank unit, much to his chagrin as he loved horses, and two years later, after attending an officers course at the War Academy, he was appointed commander of the 246th Anti-tank Battalion of the 246th Infantry Division, and he led his men first into Poland and then westwards through the Low Countries where he was awarded the Iron Cross, 1st Class.

On 1 August 1940, von der Heydte transferred to the Airborne Corps, the *Fallschirmjäger*, and, on successfully completing Jump School in October, was appointed to command of 1st Battalion, 3rd Parachute Regiment. Six months later, in April 1941, the regiment was growing increasingly frustrated at its lack of action. The 600 men of the regiment had just completed a six-week training course and were desperate to be blooded now that the German military machine was on the move once more, attacking Yugoslavia and Greece.

Like von der Heydte, many were former infantrymen who had volunteered to become paratroopers, motivated either by idealism, ambition or adventure. 'The idealists were by far the most difficult to handle,' recalled von der Heydte in his memoirs.

> 'Quite a lot of them, who had been in the Hitler Youth and were saturated with national slogans, failed when they came to recognize that a soldier's trade is rough and that in time of war enthusiasm has value only when paired with knowledge, endurance, toughness and self control. Many times in the course of the war did I see a soldier lose his nerve and go literally mad under the pressure of heavy combat. And in all these cases the type of man who broke to pieces under the inexorably gruesome hardness of a soldier's war was the fundamentally soft idealist.'[2]

The ambitious volunteers also presented problems, reflected von der Heydte, because their desire to better themselves as individuals often impaired their *esprit de corps*. The best sort of volunteer were the adventurers, men like von der Heydte, who 'had jumped easily into life and [who] found it worth living for, whatever it brought along, provided that it did not become monotonous'.[3]

Towards the end of April a rumour passed among von der Heydte's men that General Kurt Student, commanding officer of the German Airborne Corps, had been summoned to see Hermann Göring to receive operational orders for an imminent mission for his troops. A few days later von der Heydte learned that there had indeed been substance to the rumours – his battalion, the entire regiment, was to break camp and entrain for an unknown destination.

Von der Heydte and his men travelled through Hungary, Romania and Bulgaria until they reached the Mediterranean Sea at Salonika. They established a camp to the east of an airfield near the village of Topolia, and the next day, on 16 May 1941, von der Heydte attended a meeting hosted by Student at the Hotel Grande Bretagne in Athens. The first thing von der Heydte saw when he entered the room was a large map of Crete on the wall. Then, 'in a quiet but clear and slightly vibrant voice General Student explained the plan of attack. It was his own, personal plan. He had devised it, had struggled against heavy opposition for its acceptance and had worked out all the details.'[4]

Crete had been in Allied hands since the previous autumn, when they had garrisoned the island (which measures 160 miles from east to west) following Italy's attack on Greece. Situated in the Mediterranean, equidistant between Athens and the Egyptian coast, the island's airstrip allowed British bombers to attack the Romanian oil fields that were vital to the German war effort, while its harbours were a haven for the Royal Navy from where they could attack German supply ships.

Student had indeed argued vociferously for the plan to be accepted at a time when the German High Command was focused on the impending invasion of Russia (which would begin on 22 June 1941). Eventually he won his case and was authorized to go ahead and plan Operation *Mercury*, the first airborne invasion in military history.

Von der Heydte and his fellow officers listened intently as Student unveiled his plan for the seizure of Crete. Simultaneously, the island would be attacked at four different locations with the Assault Regiment, commanded by Brigadier General Eugen Meindl dropping to the west and securing the airfield at Maleme. The 2nd Regiment, led by Captain Hans Wiedemann, was tasked with occupying the town of Rethymnon and its adjoining airfield, and the 1st Regiment under Major Erich Walther would jump into Gournes in the north and capture Heraklion.

Von der Heydte's 3rd Regiment, under the command of Colonel Richard Heidrich and reinforced by a parachute-engineer battalion, had the town of Chania on the north-west coast of Crete as its objective. Commanding the 1st Battalion, von der Heydte's mission was to jump into the Agya Penitentiary, a flat and exposed plain, and secure the road that led from Chania to Suda, further east along the coast. Meanwhile the 2nd Battalion under Major Helmut Derpa was to land east of the Agya Penitentiary and oust the British from the high ground at Galatas, south-west of Chania. The mission of the 3rd Battalion under Major Ludwig Heilmann was to go in first and capture the Alikianou to Chania road, around which were fruit plantations that sloped down from the coastal heights to the Agya Penitentiary.

Once Student had explained the plan, he handed over to his intelligence officer, who confidently asserted that the island was defended by two or three weak Greek divisions, and a 'British force of divisional strength consisting mainly of Dominion troops (New Zealanders) under command of the well-known General Freyberg'. The intelligence officer added that the local population was believed to be 'sympathetic' to a German invasion, and in fact there already existed an underground network of pro-German resistance fighters who would identity themselves during the landing by uttering the codeword 'Major Bock'.

On the evening of 16 May, von der Heydte treated his orderly, 18-year-old Willi Riese, to a meal in a small Athens taverna and the teenager listened rapt as his commanding officer 'told him the history of Athens, of the battles against the Persians, of the war with Sparta, and of the heroic fight against Philip of Macedonia'.

When they returned to battalion headquarters, von der Heydte found his men enjoying bottles of beer and cognac that had been issued on his orders. The paratroopers were in high spirits, talking of girls and escapades, and it occurred to von der Heydte that he alone felt oppressed as he recalled another tale from the past. 'Somehow,' he wrote later, 'I could not help recalling the youths who had been sent to Crete every nine years to die in sacrifice to the Minotaur.'[5]

On the evening of 19 May, the 120 men of von der Heydte's 1st Battalion began preparing for their historic airborne operation. One of them was the former heavyweight boxing champion of the world, Max Schmeling, who at 35 was one of the oldest members of the battalion. Schmeling had held the world heavyweight title between 1930 and 1932 but as a paratrooper he was unremarkable, although von der Heydte employed his physical strength to good effect as leader of his mortar section.

Now, on the eve of battle, Schmeling was sent to see von der Heydte by the battalion medical officer because he was suffering from severe diarrhoea. 'He was in a quandary,' remembered von der Heydte, 'because if he reported sick it might be assumed that he was trying to shirk, and this he did not wish to do under any circumstances. So I advised him, as I think any battalion commander would have done in a similar situation, to tie his waterproof jumping suit especially tightly from behind and to fly and jump with the rest of us.'[6]

At 0400hrs on 20 May, the battalion began taking off from Tanagra in Greece. Von der Heydte was one of the few men on board his transport who had seen action and knew what awaited them in Crete. The rest, the idealists, adventurers and ambitious young men that comprised the 1st Battalion were blithely indifferent and anticipated an easy occupation to go with those of the Norway, Denmark and the Low Countries. Before long the men were all singing the 'Song of the Paratroops':

Fly on this day against the enemy!
Into the 'planes, into the 'planes!
Comrade, there is no going back!

Von der Heydte and his men of the 1st Battalion dropped into Crete unopposed on the morning of 20 May. As he floated down to earth, von der Heydte had identified the village of Alikianou, and landed, only narrowly avoiding a large reservoir and a fig tree. He looked at his watch – 0715hrs –

and then dug out a guide book to Crete that he had bought from a stall in Athens to see if the buildings he could see in the distance were those of a prison. Satisfied that they were, von der Heydte began advancing down the dusty white road that led from Alikianou to Chania. 'Psychologists may ponder whence that sense of power and courage is derived once a parachutist has gained terra firma after a successful jump,' wrote von der Heydte later. 'It is a sensation almost of intoxication. He feels himself a match for any man and ready to take on anything that comes along.'[7]

Von der Heydte quickly assembled his battalion and began to attack the enemy positions on the high ground overlooking Chania. The 2nd and 3rd companies advanced up the lower slopes of Great Castle Hill, supported by a machine-gun platoon, but were met by heavy British resistance. Going to ground in an olive-tree orchard, the paratroopers worked their way upwards and into the Cladiso Valley.

Von der Heydte set up a command post in a deep gully at 1030hrs and began receiving conflicting reports from his company commanders that indicated the British had established a strong line of defence. Two British artillery pieces situated in an olive grove had been neutralized after fierce hand-to-hand fighting, but the news from 1st Company was less encouraging. Placing his adjutant in temporary charge of the battalion, von der Heydte and his orderly, Riese, went forward to locate 1st Company. He found them pinned down in a shallow ditch and, crawling forward on his own, von der Heydte spotted through his binoculars two British heavy machine guns, well-concealed in some shrubs beside a solitary cottage.

Back in the shallow ditch, von der Heydte sent a message instructing Schmeling and his mortar section to shell the cottage, and within minutes the British machine guns had been silenced. But the British resistance was still strong and the commanders of both 2nd and 4th companies were badly wounded as they tried to lead their men towards Chania. Then news reached von der Heydte that the battalion command post had received a direct hit, killing two and destroying a wireless set. Von der Heydte's adjutant was 'grave and remarkably pale', an indication of the ferocity of the fighting all around.

By noon, however, von der Heydte's battalion had taken most of their objectives, albeit at a heavy cost. A dressing station, established in the shade of some trees to deal with the wounded, was overflowing and von der Heydte did his best to rally the spirits of those awaiting attention from the battalion doctor. Then he saw a wounded Englishman. 'I knelt beside him and brushed his blond hair back from his forehead,' he recalled. 'One of the orderlies then saw fit to explain to him that I was the commanding officer of the battalion. With large astonished blue eyes the Englishman looked at me. "The war is over for me, sir," he said. "I hope it will be for you, too, in the not-so-distant future."'[8]

The wounded British soldier's comrades were similarly defiant as the day wore on, digging a defensive line to prevent the Germans attaining their goal of Chania. Then the defenders' artillery was augmented by the guns of the Royal Navy warships anchored in Suda Bay, and finally the British counter-attacked in late afternoon. Von der Heydte described the close-quarter fighting that ensued as 'bitter' with the British making good use of the cover. But with von der Heydte directing his men, the German paratroopers repelled the attack and the rest of 20 May passed without further serious incident.

The following day, 21 May, was relatively quiet with both sides content to snipe at one another without launching a full-scale assault. Von der Heydte had sited his battalion well, with a commanding view of the villages of Perivolia and Pyrgos to the front and the blue waters of Suda Bay to the rear. During the day, a resupply by parachute of arms and ammunition boosted the morale of von der Heydte's men, though the heavy firing they could hear coming from the direction of Maleme made them wonder how their comrades were faring.

In fact Maleme airfield fell to the Germans on 21 May and soon it was being used to reinforce the Airborne Corps with Alpine troops from the 5th Mountain Division. Together the paratroopers and the mountain troops repulsed a New Zealand counter-attack the following day, an action that proved to be a turning point in the battle for Crete. With the airstrip bringing in further German forces and supplies, and fearful of a major seaborne landing, the British began withdrawing to the eastern tip of the island to prepare for an evacuation.

On Sunday 25 May, von der Heydte's battalion was dug in on the heights south-west of Perivolia and Pyrgos, waiting to link up with the assault troops from Maleme before launching an attack against Chania. On the same day General Student argued successfully for a fresh wave of attacks on the British positions by Stuka dive-bombers (something the army opposed because they wished the aircraft to be preserved for the invasion of Russia), and on 26 May the Stukas began attacking.

So, too, did 1st Battalion, advancing on 26 May to secure Perivolia and Pyrgos, and the next day they pressed on to Chania with von der Heydte at the head of his men. They found the town deserted, the British having already evacuated and the civilians fearful of the Germans. The mayor of Chania, however, was waiting and he asked one of the battalion soldiers to be taken to his commander. Presented to von der Heydte, the mayor refused to believe that this unkempt figure before him was the paratroopers' leader. 'Well could I understand it,' reflected von der Heydte. 'Since the morning of May 19th I had not had a shave, and my clothing, which I had not changed during the past eight days, was torn to ribbons.'[9]

Von der Heydte accepted the town's surrender and, once Chania was well defended, he organized the burying of the battalion's dead, one of whom was his young orderly Willi Riese. Exact casualty figures suffered by the German airborne corps during the invasion of Crete vary but it is accepted that between 6,500 and 7,000 men were killed or wounded. The Allies lost approximately 3,500 men in the fighting. Despite the successful outcome of Operation *Mercury*, the scale of the losses so horrified Hitler that he vowed never to permit such a massed airborne assault again. 'Our losses had been caused through multiple reasons,' stated von der Heydte, who was promoted to major and decorated with the Knight's Cross of the Iron Cross for his leadership and courage during the invasion (the highest such award in the German military). 'The troops had been inexperienced in parachute warfare. For many of them the battle of Crete had been their first taste of action, and for most of them it had been their first drop against an enemy. The training of the officers had been none too thorough, and their personal bravery had not proved sufficient compensation for their lack of knowledge.'

The three years that followed the invasion of Crete were frustrating ones for von der Heydte. Having led his battalion into Russia in the autumn of

1941, he was wounded in the shoulder during the heavy fighting of the siege of Leningrad. Von der Heydte was carried to a dressing station on the banks of the river Neva, where he was examined by Dr Petritsch, the battalion medical officer, who had performed sterling work in Crete. Suddenly the dressing station took a direct hit from a Russian shell, a piece of shrapnel severing the doctor's carotid artery as he tended von der Heydte. He himself was left unscathed by the explosion.

In May 1942 von der Heydte – by now fully recovered from his shoulder wound – received word that his battalion would spearhead Operation *Hercules* – an invasion of Malta, the island that served as a vital British base for their operations in the Mediterranean. The plan was that von der Heydte and his men would jump six hours in advance of the main invasion fleet and destroy the British anti-aircraft defences. As von der Heydte began to train his men for the joint German-Italian invasion, in which they would land in gliders, General Student was summoned to see Hitler to discuss Operation *Hercules*. Student gave the Führer a comprehensive overview of his plan. In his book *Jump Into Hell*, Franz Kurowski (who served as a war correspondent in the German Army during World War II) described how Hitler listened to what Student had to say and then decided to cancel the operation because he doubted the Italian Navy had the courage to accomplish their tasks, 'and then you'll be sitting alone with your paratroopers on the island'.

Instead of dropping into Malta, von der Heydte's battalion was attached to the combat brigade commanded by Major General Hermann Ramcke and sent to North Africa. Just a few months after having fought on the Eastern Front, von der Heydte was now operating in temperatures exceeding 55 degrees Celsius.

On 30 August the battle of Alam el Halfa began, which turned out to be General Erwin Rommel's last major offensive against the British Eighth Army in the Desert War. Von der Heydte's battalion was tasked with attacking the enemy positions along the Ruweisat Ridge, but after six days of heavy fighting the Axis forces withdrew with losses of nearly 3,000 men. Von der Heydte survived the battle, winning the Italian Silver Medal for bravery, but a short while later fell ill with dysentery and therefore was absent when the British offensive began at El Alamein. Though he rejoined his battalion at the end of the year, von der Heydte continued to suffer the effects of dysentery until he was finally evacuated to the Berlin-Dahlem hospital for tropical diseases in Germany.

In February 1943 von der Heydte was transferred to the 2nd Parachute Regiment and in September of that year he was ordered to Rome to disarm the Italian forces following their armistice with the Allies. In a suburb of the Italian capital, tanks belonging to a pro-Allies Sardinian Division opened fire on von der Heydte's men, so the commanding officer sat on top of an armoured car and advanced into Rome at the head of a small convoy to draw the Italians out into an ambush. One of his men, Captain Milch, recalled what followed:

> Major Von der Heydte stopped at a marketplace and bought grapes, which we immediately ate. As we continued, we kept on seeing motorcycle messengers in Italian uniforms. Then we got to a tank obstacle … I went ahead, followed by the staff car and the armoured car. When we were not too far from the famous obelisks along the Via Ostiense, not far from the Coliseum, I saw tanks in a side street that were following our movements with their main guns. We were in a trap. In order to warn the vehicles following us, I fired at the closest tank with my rifle. A salvo from the tank's main guns was the answer. The tanks rolled out, pursued the armoured car, which was able to escape, and ran into my battery. The battery turned back all of the Italian attacks into the afternoon.[10]

By such fearless behaviour did von der Heydte successfully disarm the Italian forces in Rome and its environs by 11 September. A short while later, while on a reconnaissance flight over the city in a Fieseler Storch, von der Heydte's aircraft crashed and he was badly injured. When he returned to active service four months later, von der Heydte was appointed commander of the newly formed 6th Parachute Regiment, a unit comprised predominantly of young, raw recruits; as he had done three years earlier prior to the invasion of Crete, von der Heydte was obliged to prepare a mix of idealists, adventurers and ambitious young soldiers for the reality of war.

The regiment was based just outside Paris and throughout the spring of 1944 von der Heydte trained them thoroughly for the invasion that he knew to be imminent. At the start of June von der Heydte's regiment moved north-west into Normandy and he established his command post in Carentan, a small town of 4,000 inhabitants, situated three miles from the coast on the main road (the Route National 13) between Cherbourg in the north and Caen in the east. One battalion he stationed in Carentan, another he sent seven miles north-west to Sainte-Mère-Église, and a third was dug in around Sainte-Marie-du-Mont, four miles to the north.

Though most of the German High Command were convinced the invasion, when it came, would occur further east at Calais, von der Heydte was not convinced and conducted regular aerial reconnaissance patrols, his love of flying undiminished despite his accident of the previous year. On the evening of 5 June von der Heydte was engaged in one such reconnoitre when his headquarters received a visit from General Kurt Student, Commander-in-Chief of the German airborne field army. Student dined with von der Heydte's liaison officer and then departed for his headquarters in the city of Nancy in the east of France. 'Be alert!' he jokingly told the liaison officer as he left Carentan.

Early on the morning of 6 June, word reached von der Heydte of enemy paratroopers landing north of Carentan. He jumped on his motorcycle and raced to investigate, discovering on arrival that his men had captured more than 75 American paratroopers belonging to the 501st Parachute Infantry Regiment and 101st Airborne Division. Von der Heydte radioed his superiors that he believed the invasion was underway. Next he drove to Sainte-Marie-du-Mont and scaled the church steeple at around 0630hrs to scan the horizon through his binoculars. What he saw was unforgettable. 'All along the beach were these small boats,' he recalled nearly 50 years later. 'Hundreds of them, each disgorging thirty or forty armed men. Behind them were the warships, blasting away with their huge guns, more warships in one fleet than anyone had ever seen before.'[11]

Racing down from the church, von der Heydte headed two miles north to Brecourt Manor but the four guns of the German battery positioned in the grounds of the manor were abandoned. He hurried back to Sainte-Marie-du-Mont and instructed his men to man the battery and open fire on the beaches.

Meanwhile von der Heydte attempted to drive back the Allies as they advanced cautiously forward from the beachhead, launching an attack through Sainte-Marie-du-Mont and Turqueville. But his paratroopers encountered heavy fire from American airborne troops who had landed well ahead of the main invasion fleet and von der Heydte ordered his men to take up defensive positions and repel the Allied advance from the beaches. Fierce fighting raged for the rest of the day, and into D-Day+1, as gradually von der Heydte's men began to withdraw across the marshy ground towards Carentan.

Von der Heydte was wounded in his arm, and the damage to the nerves meant he wore it in a sling as he led the remains of his regiment towards Carentan. On the evening of 8 June the German paratroopers took up positions on the northern and eastern outskirts of the town with orders from Field-Marshal Rommel to 'defend Carentan to the last man'.

For two days von der Heydte and his men held up the American advance despite the heavy casualties they sustained. On 10 June, however, the American 29th Division arrived from Omaha Beach to join forces with the 101st Airborne and a call was made on von der Heydte to surrender. He declined, sending back a message politely asking the Americans, 'What would you do in my place?' The following day the *Wehrmachtbericht* (the German armed forces report broadcast daily on the wireless) declared that 'during the difficult fighting in the enemy beachhead and the elimination of the enemy paratrooper and air-landed forces that were dropped in the rear area, the 6th Parachute Regiment of Major von der Heydte distinguished itself tremendously'.[12]

Not that the acclaim was of much material use to the remnants of von der Heydte's regiment. That same day, 11 June, with his men down to the last of their ammunition and two of his three battalions terribly depleted, he ordered his regiment to pull back from Carentan to prepared positions further south, leaving behind one company of 50 men to hinder the American advance with heavy machine gun and mortar fire. The decision was in defiance of an order from SS Major General Werner Ostendorff to remain at Carentan until he arrived with his 17th SS Panzer Grenadier Division, to which von der Heydte's regiment had been temporarily attached. Heydte's disobedience, motivated as much by his hatred of the SS as his wish to escape entrapment, nearly resulted in his court-martial.

At dawn on 12 June the 101st Airborne attacked Carentan with Easy Company, led by Captain Richard Winters, in the vanguard. The assault, subsequently immortalized in the best-selling book *Band of Brothers*, developed into a series of bloody engagements between two elite detachments of paratroopers.

Eventually the Americans triumphed and Carentan was theirs. At first light the next day, 13 June, they prepared to push south-west towards the high ground. But before they could, von der Heydte counter-attacked, catching the Americans off-guard and causing one company of the 101st to fall back in confusion. Carentan was on the brink of being retaken by von der Heydte's shattered and depleted forces when at 1630hrs 60 American tanks appeared, accompanied by infantry from the 29th Division.

Von der Heydte withdrew his men from Carentan once and for all. Throughout the weeks that followed the 6th Parachute Regiment fought courageously among the fields and hedgerows of the Normandy countryside; in one instance, 20 of their number on bicycles and supported by one tank ambushed a battalion of American infantry.

But inexorably the Allied advance continued until, at the end of July, they broke out from the Cotentin Peninsula and wheeled west, encircling thousands of German troops. Von der Heydte and his men fought their way through the Allied encirclement at Coutances, and on 12 August the 6th Parachute Regiment was finally withdrawn from Normandy, having been involved in fighting on an almost daily basis since 6 June. Casualties had been heavy with 3,000 men either killed, wounded or missing. The survivors who entrained for Güstrow were no longer the bright-eyed idealists or adventurers of six months earlier.

By November 1944 von der Heydte had been promoted to lieutenant-colonel and awarded the oak leaves to the Knight's Cross. He was also in charge of a parachute combat school in Aalten, the Netherlands, an assignment cut short in early December. On the 9th of that month von der Heydte was summoned to see General Student and ordered to assemble an airborne battle group to participate in an imminent large-scale German offensive. Von der Heydte was not informed of where the offensive would occur, until on 15 December Field Marshal Walter Model revealed the nature of the mission.

The offensive would be in the Ardennes, the forested region on the Belgian border, along a front that ran from Monschau in the north to Echternach in the south. The aim was to punch through the Allies' front line, splitting the British and American forces, and then seizing the port of Antwerp. Ultimately, Hitler hoped that the offensive would force the Allies to the negotiating table. If the strategic objectives seemed far-fetched to von der Heydte, it was nothing compared to the timescale in which he had to prepare his men for their role – 24 hours.

Model explained to von der Heydte that on 16 December he would drop into the Ardennes with his men and seize and hold a number of roads and bridges to facilitate the rapid advance of the 6th SS Panzer Army. It was to be a nighttime drop – the first and only such jump by German paratroopers in the war – and von der Heydte's concerns over the limited intelligence supplied to him about the strength of Allied force in the region were dismissed. So too were his complaints about the lack of arms and ammunitions, the unreadiness of his men and the poor communications equipment.

Recognizing that he was being asked to lead his men on an exceptionally dangerous mission, von der Heydte decided to lead from the front. Shortly before midnight on 16 December, he and 1,200 paratroopers took off in 80 aircraft for the drop zone 50 miles behind enemy lines. In a post-war interview with author Franz Kurowski for the book *Jump Into Hell*, von der Heydte described the mission:

I was firmly convinced that in that type of operation the commander had to be the first one to jump. Not so much to make a good impression but rather to get a first impression on the ground of the terrain and the enemy situation and to assemble the forces that followed.

The scene at the drop zone was eerily beautiful. Above me, like lightning bugs, were the position markers of the aircraft and, whipping up towards me from below were the tracers of the light American anti-aircraft weapons. Beyond the black trees, like the fingers of a hand, were the probing beams of the searchlights. Then impact. The roll forwards worked. I unhooked. Initially I was alone. I ran to the designated fork in the road that was a collection point. On the road I encountered the first of my soldiers. There were only a few – far too few. There was also only a few at the collection point. What had happened to the rest?[13]

Von der Heydte only learned much later that many of the pilots who had transported the paratroopers to their DZ had lost their nerve in the face of heavy anti-aircraft fire and dropped them far too early. As dawn broke on 16 December, von der Heydte assembled his men at the fork that was seven miles north of Malmédy and counted 250 out of the original force of 1,200. 'We pulled back from the fork in the road into the woods and formed an all-round defence,' he remembered. 'The radio equipment was damaged and did not work, with the result that we could not establish contact with our own forces. I had no way at all of forwarding the most important results of our reconnaissance.'[14]

Lacking the men to carry out the original mission of seizing roads and bridges, von der Heydte sent out patrols to reconnoitre, and in one engagement with the enemy the German paratroopers retrieved the corps order (battle instructions) for the US XVIII Corps. But with no communications, and 50 miles behind enemy lines, there was no way to inform their superiors. Oblivious as to the progress of the main offensive, von der Heydte decided to head east in the hope of reaching German lines, but by now the Americans were hunting them down and they spent much of 21 December skirmishing with the enemy. Realizing that their best chance of survival was to split into small groups, von der Heydte instructed his men to head east as they saw fit. By now von der Heydte was suffering from the effects of cold and hunger as well as a fractured arm. On 24 December, unable to continue his slow trek east, von der Heydte knocked on the door of a farm near Monschau and asked the farmer to send a message to the Americans saying he wished to surrender. Three and a half years after the wounded English soldier at Crete had told von der Heydte that he hoped his war would soon be over, it was – and in the most ignominious fashion.

✦ ✦ ✦ ✦

Von der Heydte remained a prisoner of war in England until July 1947 during which time he angered many of his fellow inmates with a series of outspoken attacks on the crimes of the Nazi regime. Upon his release, von der Heydte returned to West Germany and became a professor of law at the University of Würtzburg. His war memoirs were published in 1958 to much acclaim and from 1966 to 1970 he served as a member of the Bavarian State Parliament for the Christian Social Union. All the while he retained his links to the military, rising to the rank of brigadier general in the Reserves and teaching successive generations of young men about airborne warfare.

Friedrich August Freiherr von der Heydte was still alive to witness the reunification of Germany in 1990, a joyous moment for a patriot who had emerged from the shameful years of the Third Reich with his honour intact. Now von der Heydte had also witnessed the fall of Communism in his country. He died in July 1994 aged 87, a death largely unreported in the new Germany, although the handful of men who had served under the 'Rosary Paratrooper' honoured the passing of one of the greatest airborne commanders of any nation.

ADRIAN VON FÖLKERSAM

BRANDENBURGERS

Like Friedrich von der Heydte, Adrian von Fölkersam came from blue-blooded stock and was a soldier of great courage and resourcefulness. There, however, the similarities ended. Whereas von der Heydte was a fervent anti-Nazi, Adrian von Fölkersam served in the Waffen SS and fought alongside SS Lieutenant Colonel Otto Skorzeny in his elite commando unit.

There was another difference between the two men; whereas von der Heydte despised Russia, von Fölkersam was born in St Petersburg, the son of an admiral who had served in the Tsarist Russian Navy, fighting against the Japanese in the war of 1904–05.

Adrian von Fölkersam's family fled Russia when the Revolution started and they settled in Germany. After school he completed a bachelor's degree in economics at Berlin University, and lived for a while in Vienna. Von Fölkersam was 25 when World War II started, a thin, wiry man with the air of an academic. It was his gift for languages that led him to become a Brandenburg commando.

✦ ✦ ✦ ✦

The Brandenburgers were the brainchild of Captain Theodor von Hippel, a World War I veteran who had served under General Paul von Lettow-Vorbeck in German East Africa. During the campaign against the British, the Germans had operated as guerrilla fighters with stunning success and von Hippel believed the German Army should once again employ such tactics, creating small units of highly-trained men to operate behind enemy lines.

As Ralph Bagnold would discover when he first took his idea for the Long Range Desert Group to the British high command, von Hippel also learned that senior officers within the Germany Army were dismissive of the idea of an irregular unit. Undaunted by the rejection, in the summer of 1939 von Hippel approached Admiral Wilhelm Canaris, commander of the German intelligence service, the Abwehr, and received permission to form a 900-strong force. Canaris informed von Hippel that the force would be based at Brandenburg-an-der-Havel, just an hour from Berlin and within easy reach of Canaris' HQ.

Throughout the winter of 1939/40 von Hippel recruited the men for his unit, now known as the 'Brandenburgers' because of the location of their base. Some he found within the Abwehr, others were from the Free Corps of Sudetenland, and many were bored soldiers who had missed out on the invasion of Poland.

What von Hippel sought were men who had more than just toughness. His experiences in East Africa in World War I had taught him that it was the man who could think for himself, the man of initiative, who made the most effective Special Forces soldier. He also wanted soldiers who were fluent in English and Russian, useful for when Germany looked to attack those two nations.

One of the first to join the Brandenburgers was Adrian von Fölkersam. Fluent in English and Russian, he was a lieutenant in the autumn of 1939 and though the exact details of his recruitment are imprecise, there might have been a personal connection between von Hippel and the young officer.

Von Fölkersam joined 4 Company, one of three companies based at Brandenburg with another one at Cologne and a fifth in Austria. One of the men who served under von Fölkersam at this time was Hans-Dietrich Hossfelder, a 19-year-old from Breslau in the German-held region of Silesia. 'My superior officer during this period was Adrian von Fölkersam, a wonderful officer who spoke the cleanest Russian I had ever heard,' recalled Hossfelder in an interview in 1985.[1]

Von Fölkersam, Hossfelder and the other men of the Brandenburgers underwent a rigorous training programme at Quenzgut, the Abwehr training school just outside Brandenburg. In a thickly wooded area bordering Lake Quenz, Quenzgut was where the men were drilled in sabotage, explosives, weapons, unarmed combat and parachuting. They were also schooled in how to pass themselves off as Russian army officers and members of the Soviet secret police – the NKVD – and they learned how to drive Russian and British vehicles.

'This camp was run by the Abwehr with SS instructors,' remembered Hossfelder. 'We were up at four in the morning, running ten kilometres, then coming back, have a shower, eat breakfast, attack the obstacle course, then do a ten mile rucksack run. After this it was about 1600 hours so we had dinner. We would receive political indoctrination on the tenets of National Socialism, why we were fighting the war, how great Hitler was, and why we had to swear an oath of allegiance to him. They showed us propaganda films, mostly illustrating why the Jews were our greatest enemy.'[2]

In April 1940 von Fölkersam's 4 Company, under the command of Lieutenant Wilhelm Walther, had been moved to Münstereifel in the Rhineland in readiness for the invasion of the Low Countries. When the attack started on 10 May, 4 Company was tasked with seizing a number of bridges over the Juliana Canal, the 22-mile long waterway in the south of Holland near the town of Gennep, to facilitate the advance of the 7th German Infantry Division.

Among the bridges captured by the Brandenburgers on the night of 9/10 May was the Gennep railway bridge, across which roared two motorized divisions in the hours that followed. There were failures, however; at the Buggenum railway bridge near Roermond, a unit from 4 Company disguised as Dutch railway workers arrived to inform the Dutch soldiers on guard that they were there to inspect the structure. In fact they planned to remove the explosive charges put in place by the Dutch and then overpower the guards. At first the Dutch believed their story, but when they saw the Germans tampering with the charges, they detonated the explosives, killing three Brandenburgers and wounding three more. Nonetheless, von Fölkersam's 4 Company's had contributed much to the successful invasion of the Low Countries and their reward was a letter of thanks from General Albert Wodrig, commander of the XXVI Corps, and a Knight's Cross of the Iron Cross for Lieutenant Wilhelm Walther. It was the first such decoration for a Brandenburger, but an award that in time would also be bestowed on von Fölkersam.

Months of frustration followed for the Brandenburgers after the successful conquest of Holland, Belgium and France. In late June the unit moved to Normandy in readiness for the invasion of Britain, training for a seaborne assault on Dover ahead of the main German task force. As they trained throughout the summer of 1940 they witnessed the aerial dogfights between the Luftwaffe and the Royal Air Force, a battle in which the British eventually triumphed. The invasion of England was postponed and von Fölkersam and the other commandos returned to their barracks at Brandenburg.

For the next 18 months the Brandenburgers fought in a variety of theatres, from Greece to Yugoslavia to Romania, but by the early summer of 1942 the entire unit was deployed to the mountainous Caucasus region of south-west Russia to seize the oil facilities of Maikop and Baku. With the German Army fighting on two fronts in 1942, against the Russians in the East and against Anglo-American forces in North Africa, their war machine was badly in need of oil. Hitler had told General Friedrich von Paulus, commander of Sixth Army, that the seizure of the oilfields was a priority.

In August three German divisions – the 5th SS Panzer, the 13th Panzer and the 16th Motorized Infantry – launched an all-out offensive to capture the city of Maikop in the northern Caucasus. Two units of Brandenburgers were assigned to the attack. One, led by Lieutenant Ernst Prohaska, had orders to seize and hold the bridge over the river Bjelaja so that the three divisions could race into Maikop, while von Fölkersam's unit had a far more challenging mission. Leading a 63-strong team of commandos disguised as members of the NKVD, von Fölkersam was to enter Maikop and capture the oil storage tanks before they could be blown up by the Russian defenders. It was an operation fraught with danger and one that had only two possible outcomes: success or death. To be captured wearing the uniform of the NKVD would result in torture and execution.

Lieutenant Ernst Prohaska's unit began their mission on the afternoon of 9 August; driving towards the bridge over the river Bjelaja in four captured Russian half-tracks, all were wearing Russian military uniforms over their German battledress. Passing through several Russian checkpoints with ease, the Brandenburgers arrived at the bridge to find a Soviet tanker stationed at one end with several soldiers nearby. In a carefully coordinated attack, the Germans opened fire on the soldiers, while others seized the tanker and another section searched the bridge for explosive charges. Within minutes the bridge was secured and soon the first German armour moved down it into Maikop.

By the time Prohaska's section had accomplished their task, von Fölkersam's unit was deep inside Maikop, having advanced from the direction of Alexandrovskaja on 2 August. Initially all had gone well, but then in the suburbs of the city their convoy had been stopped at a roadblock manned by some genuine members of the NKVD. In faultless Russian, von Fölkersam explained their mission – that they had been sent to destroy the oil storage tanks in the event of a German occupation of the city. He passed himself off as 'Major Turchin from Stalingrad' and was directed to the NKVD headquarters in the centre of Maikop. The general to whom von Fölkersam reported was utterly convinced by the German imposter as well as flattered that the NKVD should send a special team to assist in their hour of need.

Von Fölkersam asked for a tour of the city's defences so he could best observe where his men were needed in the case of a German attack. The general obliged and for three days the Brandenburgers reconnoitred Maikop at their leisure; then on 8 August, with the sound of the German artillery growing louder from the south, von Fölkersam briefed his men that they would execute their orders at dawn on the 9th.

Splitting into three groups, one party, under the command of Lieutenant Franz Koudele, occupied the central telegraph office, informing the workers that the city was being abandoned and they must leave at once. Koudele and his Russian-speaking men manned the telephones and informed all callers that they had received orders from Moscow that Maikop was to be evacuated.

Von Fölkersam, meanwhile, toured the city's defences, urgently telling the Russian soldiers that orders had been received for the immediate withdrawal of all troops. As the exodus gathered pace, a third party of Brandenburgers drove to the oil storage tanks and arrived just as a detachment of Russian engineers were in the process of destroying the facilities. One tank was already in flames but von Fölkersam's men ordered the engineers to leave for their own safety – they would finish the job.

The audacious mission had been achieved without a single fatality, and for his courage and leadership von Fölkersam was awarded the Knight's Cross of the Iron Cross.*

By the summer of 1943 the Brandenburgers had become a victim of their own success. No longer a small unit engaged in guerrilla warfare behind enemy lines, they had been expanded into a division and attached to the Grossdeutschland Panzer Corps. Disenchanted with what he saw as the misuse of the commando concept, von Fölkersam secured an interview with Major Otto Skorzeny, days after his brilliant operation to free Benito

---

* So was Ernst Prohaska, although his award was posthumous as he was killed later on 9 August.

Mussolini from captivity at the Campo Imperatore Hotel in the mountains of Abruzzo. 'He told me that there was great dissatisfaction in the ranks of the old Brandenburgers,' recalled Skorzeny, who was the commander of a newly formed Special Forces unit, the SS Sonderlehrgang zbV Friedenthal.[3]

Von Fölkersam told Skorzeny why he was dissatisfied and asked if he and ten other Brandenburg veterans could join his unit. 'I immediately took a great fancy to von Fölkersam, both as a man and a soldier,' said Skorzeny, 'and felt sure that in a tight corner I would certainly find him an experienced and valuable helper. I was only too pleased to assure him that I would do what I could.'[4]

It took all of Skorzeny's charm and powers of persuasion to convince Admiral Canaris to agree to the transfer of von Fölkersam and the others to the SS Sonderlehrgang zbV Friedenthal. But in November 1943 the request was granted and von Fölkersam joined the unit as Skorzeny's chief staff officer.

One of von Fölkersam's first tasks was to plan for the Allied invasion of France, expected some time in 1944. Skorzeny had been given a list of ten likely landing places for an invasion fleet along the northern French coast, and von Fölkersam was instructed to think how best they could resist the Allies should they try to establish a bridgehead in the Cherbourg (Cotentin) Peninsula. 'We suggested that we should establish small units at the points of greatest danger with a commission to attack prospective enemy headquarters and communication centres,' said Skorzeny, who submitted the plan to the German High Command but heard nothing further.

By the spring of 1944 Skorzeny's attention was drawn away from France to Yugoslavia and the problem posed by Marshal Josip Tito, the leader of the Yugoslav Partisans (estimated to be as many as 250,000) who were inflicting a growing number of losses on German forces in the mountainous regions of the country. A major assault against the Partisans was impossible; because of the war with Russia and the expected invasion of France, Germany no longer had the resources. Instead it was decided to attempt to capture Tito himself, in an audacious raid against his headquarters at Drvar in western Bosnia.

Having been given the task of organizing the mission, Skorzeny sent von Fölkersam to Banja Luka, in the north-west of Bosnia, to learn what he could of Tito's HQ from the German commander in the area. On his return, von

Fölkersam told Skorzeny that his welcome in Banja Luka had been less than hospitable and there appeared to be no desire to share intelligence. Days later Skorzeny discovered the reason for the hostility: the German corps in Banja Luka wanted to carry out the mission themselves and resented the presence of a Special Forces officer. However, Skorzeny had already decided the mission was too risky and too widely known among the general population, and his unit took no further part in what became known as Operation *Rösselsprung*, which ended in bloody failure in May 1944.

On 10 September 1944 Skorzeny was summoned from his unit's headquarters at Friedenthal, 40 miles south of the city of Erfurt, to Hitler's Eastern Front HQ at Rastenburg, otherwise known as the 'Wolf's Lair'. He arrived to find the Führer in a foul mood. With the Allies having liberated Paris the previous month, and the Red Army dominant in the east – having invaded Bulgaria and pressurized Romania into defecting from the Axis cause – the war was not going well for the Third Reich.

For three days those present at the Wolf's Lair discussed the war and listened to Hitler's furious tirades; then, at the end of the third day, Hitler asked Skorzeny to remain behind along with a cadre of senior commanders: Wilhelm Keitel, Alfred Jodl, Joachim von Ribbentrop and Heinrich Himmler. The Führer then addressed the small group, telling them that:

> We have received secret reports that the head of the Hungarian state, Admiral [Miklós] Horthy is attempting to get in touch with our enemies with a view to a separate peace.[5]

With Soviet forces massed on the east Hungarian border, Horthy was apparently eager to reach a peace accord with Stalin in order to prevent the destruction of his country. Hitler could not let this happen: not only would a Soviet occupation of Hungary endanger 70 German divisions fighting in the Balkans but it would also deprive the Nazis of Hungarian oil reserves and grain supplies. Turning to Skorzeny, Hitler said: 'You must be prepared to seize the citadel of Budapest by force, if he betrays his alliance with us. The General Staff is thinking of a *coup de main* with parachute or glider troops. The command of the whole operation in that city has been entrusted to the new corps commander, General [Ulrich] Kleeman. You are under his orders for this affair but must push ahead at once with your preparations.'[6]

Immediately Skorzeny swung into action, telephoning von Fölkersam from the Wolf's Lair at 0200hrs to stand-to a company of SS commandos; von Fölkersam himself was to meet Skorzeny at an airfield in north-east Germany in eight hours' time, from where they would then fly to Vienna and on to Budapest – travelling incognito. The pair arrived in the Hungarian capital on 12 September and toured the city so that they could 'devise a plan to alert all the [German] troops in and around the city so that they would be ready for action at any moment. It was essential that all railway stations, post offices and other transport and communication centres should always be in German hands.'[7]

Skorzeny and von Fölkersam switched their attention to the citadel, the strongly defended residence of Admiral Miklos Horthy, situated on a hill. The citadel also contained a number of government buildings and Skorzeny feared the Hungarians would hole up there if they felt threatened. 'Von Fölkersam was therefore instructed to make a most careful study of all available plans of the city and supplement his knowledge with minute inspection of the streets and buildings,' wrote Skorzeny. 'The result of his labours was full of surprises. There was a labyrinth of passages under the citadel, a nasty snag for us.'[8]

At the start of October Skorzeny ordered his company of commandos to Budapest, quartering them in barracks just outside the city. Then, having learned that Admiral Horthy's son, Niklas, was conducting secret negotiations with a representative from Marshal Tito's Partisans in Budapest, Skorzeny and von Fölkersam arranged to have the pair kidnapped at their next meeting, the morning of Sunday 15 October. 'The streets were empty at the time appointed for the rendezvous,' recalled Skorzeny. 'My company was in a side street in covered trucks. Captain von Fölkersam kept me in touch with them as obviously I could not show myself in uniform that day.'[9]

Two Gestapo officers were due to snatch Niklas Horthy and the Yugoslav negotiator but the Hungarian guards sensed something was wrong and opened fire, shooting one of the Germans in the stomach. Skorzeny watched from a car parked outside the building that Horthy and the Yugoslav were in. 'Then I heard my men running out of the side street in our direction,' he remembered. 'Von Fölkersam had taken the situation in at a glance and posted the first section at the corner of the square, while the others swept through the gardens and began firing at the house fronts.'[10]

It took von Fölkersam and his men 15 minutes to kill the Hungarian guards and carry the two targets out of the house in rolled-up carpets. Then they were on their way to an airfield bound for Germany – not as prisoners, according to Hitler, merely 'guests' of the Third Reich for the duration of the war.

Unfortunately for the Germans, the removal of Niklas Horthy failed to dissuade his father from continuing to seek terms with the Soviet Union, and that same afternoon Admiral Horthy announced on the radio that he had 'concluded a separate peace with Russia'. Skorzeny began to put into effect Operation *Panzerfaust*, the plan he and von Fölkersam had drawn up in the weeks spent reconnoitring the citadel. A cordon of troops from the 22nd SS Division encircled the citadel as other German soldiers occupied the stations, post offices and other communication centres that von Fölkersam had identified as key.

The commander of the 22nd SS Division, SS General Erich von dem Bach-Zelewski was in favour of storming the citadel and killing all inside, but Skorzeny asked to be given a chance to employ less extreme measures first. 'Von Fölkersam and I pored for hours over the plan of the Citadel which we had made,' recalled Skorzeny, 'and our ideas of the coming action began to assume definite shape.'[11]

They didn't have long, however, with von dem Bach-Zelewski allowing them only one day to try their methods before he ordered his troops to raze the citadel to the ground. At dawn on 16 October, therefore, Skorzeny launched his assault; a battalion of naval cadets approached the citadel through the gardens on the southern side while he and a platoon of his commandos, supported by two tanks, advanced towards the west of the target. Meanwhile a platoon of the 600th SS Parachute Battalion would enter the citadel through an underground passage that von Fölkersam had discovered in the plans. Held in reserve in case of fierce resistance were the rest of Skorzeny's battalion of commandos and the SS parachute battalion.

Prior to the attack von Fölkersam made some coffee for those present in Skorzeny's command post. Skorzeny recalled later the tension as the minutes ticked down to zero hour. 'In my truck I had von Fölkersam and Ostafel [another officer] as well as five NCOs who had been in the Gran Sasso show [the liberation of Mussolini]. I considered them my personal assault group. Each was armed with a machine pistol, a few hand grenades and the new bazooka. We were wondering what the Hungarian tanks in the Citadel would do.'[12]

At 0600hrs the attack began, and von Fölkersam and Skorzeny's truck roared towards the Citadel, followed by the two tanks, 'doing a good 35 to 40 kilometres to the hour'. They heard two heavy explosions from the south and then ahead saw three Hungarian tanks blocking their path. 'As we drew level the leading one tilted its gun skywards as a signal they would not fire,' recalled Skorzeny.[13]

Next they encountered a barricade of stones in front of the citadel's gate. Skorzeny's truck moved aside as one of the tanks crushed the barricade under its tracks and burst through the gate. The commandos leapt from the truck and followed on foot. 'A colonel of the guard got out his revolver to stop us but von Fölkersam knocked it out of his hand,' recalled Skorzeny. Another officer was forced to show them the way to the commandant's office and they raced up a staircase to a first floor echoing to the sound of small-arms fire. Skorzeny barged into the commandant's office and demanded his surrender. The Hungarian major-general readily agreed and the pair shook heads and each sent an officer to inform their respective troops that the citadel had been surrendered.

The storming of the citadel had been a complete success. For relatively little bloodshed (four German soldiers killed and a similar number of Hungarians), the buildings were in control of Skorzeny's men. Admiral Horthy was unharmed and in German custody.*

On 20 October von Fölkersam and Skorzeny returned to Berlin and the next day they were summoned to Adolf Hitler's bunker. While von Fölkersam

---

* Horthy remained a prisoner of the Germans until the end of the war, while Hungary continued in the Axis under a pro-German prime minister called Ferenc Szalasi.

was told to wait in the ante-room, Skorzeny had a private audience with the Führer, during which he was promoted to lieutenant-colonel and awarded the German Cross in Gold (a decoration higher than the Iron Cross First Class but below the Knight's Cross of the Iron Cross). Then Hitler and Skorzeny sat in two armchairs in the corner of the room and the Nazi leader listened to a full account of the Hungarian operation, laughing at the story of how Niklas Horthy had been removed inside a carpet.

When Skorzeny had finished his story, Hitler grew solemn and told him that he had 'perhaps the most important job in your life for you'. He explained that Germany was soon to launch a great offensive against the Allies in the West, one which he hoped would bring Britain and America to the negotiating table so that together they could fight the Soviet Union. Hitler invited Skorzeny to join him in the operations room of the bunker, where Colonel-General Heinz Guderian, the chief of the general staff, was waiting to explain the details of the offensive. In the ante-room Skorzeny introduced von Fölkersam to the Führer and Skorzeny was 'amazed when the latter reminded him of the commando operation in Russia in which [von Fölkersam] had won his Knight's Cross'.[14]

The offensive would be launched in the Ardennes, along a front that ran from Monschau in the north to Echternach in the south, the aim being to punch through the Allied front line, split the British and American forces, and then seize the port of Antwerp. To achieve its objectives, Hitler explained to Skorzeny, the offensive relied on the rapid seizure of three bridges along the river Meuse – at Huy, Amay and Engis. This was to be the role of Skorzeny and a new unit formed especially for the operation – codenamed *Greif* – called the 150th Panzer Brigade, attached to General Sepp Dietrich's 6th SS Panzer Army. Hitler then told Skorzeny that to help him achieve his mission 'you will have to wear British and American uniforms ... small detachments in enemy uniforms can cause the greatest confusion among the Allies by giving false orders and upsetting their communications'.[15]

Hitler finished his briefing by telling Skorzeny he must be ready to deploy his force by 2 December. With only five weeks to raise his commando unit, Skorzeny relied heavily on von Fölkersam; first they had to acquire Allied uniform and equipment, everything from weapons to trucks to boots. Then they had to recruit men who spoke fluent English, preferably with an

American accent. 'Von Fölkersam spent a lot of time making notes of the most pressing requirements,' recalled Skorzeny in his memoirs, as he himself concentrated on the composition of his panzer brigade. It would comprise 3,300 men in total, split into three battle groups – X, Y and Z – with two tank companies of ten tanks in each group, along with three motorized infantry battalions and a mortar section.

Throughout November Skorzeny encountered one obstacle after another in the preparation for Operation *Greif*: there was an absence of English-speaking recruits, a shortage of American uniforms and a lack of Allied vehicles. Then Skorzeny discovered that instead of the 2,000 German jet fighters promised to provide air support during the offensive, there would only be 250.

When Skorzeny and von Fölkersam reported to Hitler on 2 December, the former made clear his disappointment that the Luftwaffe had failed to provide him with aerial reconnaissance photographs of the three bridges they were to attack. Hitler was furious to learn of the omission and 'carpeted' Hermann Göring. Then the Führer turned to Skorzeny and instructed him that he was not to go on the mission himself; rather, he must remain at the command post of Dietrich's 6th SS Panzer Army and not allow himself to be captured.

Skorzeny was distraught at the order. 'Captain Von Fölkersam fully understood my dismay,' he wrote in his memoirs, 'though he regarded the Führer's word as law. "Soup's never hotter than when it's first made," he said in his dry Balt way. "Wait a bit."'[16]

On 13 December the 150th Panzer Brigade left its training base at Grafenwöhr and arrived at Münstereifel, 15 miles from the German border with Belgium, the following day. At 0500hrs on 16 December the German offensive began and Skorzeny's three battle groups headed west towards the three bridges across the Meuse. From the start the operation began to flounder. The heavy rains of the preceding weeks rendered some roads impassable, not helped by the sheer weight of traffic the commandos encountered. At the Losheim Gap, a few miles south of Münstereifel, Battle Group X lost its commander when his vehicle ran over a mine. In his place, Skorzeny appointed von Fölkersam. 'This meant the loss of my best staff officer,' reflected Skorzeny, 'but I knew that I could do him no greater service and that he would make a fine job of it.'

By the end of 16 December none of the 150th Panzer Brigade's objectives had been taken, and on the following day Skorzeny received permission to combine his three battle groups into one and attach them to the 1st SS Panzer Division; together they would strike for Malmédy,* a strategically important Belgian town 18 miles from the German border. But even that plan ran into difficulty when Battle Group Z radioed Skorzeny that they were unable to reach the rendezvous point on schedule because of the congestion on the roads.

The attack on Malmédy began at dawn on 21 December. One force of Germans launched an assault on the town itself while another attempted to secure the bridge over the river Warche. Fierce fighting raged for hours, with the Germans slowly advancing despite the heavy American artillery fire from the high ground overlooking Malmédy. Around noon as the weather lifted and visibility improved, the American artillery became even more accurate and the Germans fell back. That evening Skorzeny and his commanders attended a briefing at the headquarters of the 1st SS Panzer Division. Skorzeny arrived at the same time as von Fölkersam, and just as an American artillery shell landed on the truck carrying von Fölkersam. Skorzeny helped pull von Fölkersam from the wreckage, commenting that 'he had been remarkably lucky as a splinter the size of a short pencil had penetrated his back without reaching any vital organ'.[17]

Minutes later another salvo of shells landed and this time Skorzeny was hit, a splinter almost removing his right eye. Despite their wounds the pair remained at their posts the following day as another attempt was made to seize Malmédy. Again they were repelled and the bridge over the Warche was destroyed by American engineers.

Skorzeny knew that Operation *Greif* had failed, as had Hitler's last, desperate attempt to avoid a humiliating defeat for Germany. The offensive in the Ardennes had stalled short of the Meuse on 24 December, and the following day Skorzeny paid a visit to his old friend to wish him a Merry Christmas. 'I made a call on Von Fölkersam at his command post,' recalled Skorzeny, 'which, as usual, was right forward, barely 300 metres behind the

---

* The infamous massacre of Malmédy, involving the execution of 84 American prisoners by German SS troops on December 17, was not carried out by members of Skorzeny's unit.

front line. On my way there I was frequently flat on my face as shells of every calibre simply would not leave us alone.'

It was to be one of the last times Skorzeny saw von Fölkersam. On 28 December the 150th Panzer Brigade was withdrawn from the front line and in early January it was disbanded. Two weeks later, on 21 January, Adrian von Fölkersam was dead, shot in the head by Russian troops near Hohensalza, modern-day Inowroclaw in Poland. He was an SS-Hauptsturmführer (captain) at the time, in command of an SS-Jagdverband Ost, and it was believed he had requested a posting to the Eastern Front because his family lived close to the border with Poland.

✦ ✦ ✦ ✦

Von Fölkersam's capture of the Maikop oil depots was one of the boldest Special Forces operations of the war, more so than Skorzeny's rescue of Mussolini or Carlson's raid on Makin Island, both of which benefited from their respective countries' propaganda machines. The Maikop operation combined meticulous planning and nerveless execution, with von Fölkersam and his men fully aware that death awaited them if they failed. That he accomplished his mission was testament to his courage and resourcefulness, and the reason why he was so highly regarded by Otto Skorzeny.

Yet von Fölkersam's contribution to Special Forces soldiering has been largely overlooked, in part because no detailed records of his early operations with the Brandenburgers survived the war. In addition, von Fölkersam was not a charismatic leader in the mould of Paddy Mayne or Baron von der Heydte. Bookish in appearance, von Fölkersam combined great bravery with deep intelligence, but in character he was overshadowed by Skorzeny – a man whose force of personality attracted attention away from others equally worthy of praise. Yet as Hans-Dietrich Hossfelder recalled years later, von Fölkersam and Skorzeny deserve equal praise for their exploits in World War II. 'Both of these men were characters, but as different as night and day,' he reflected. 'Skorzeny was much taller, very boisterous, always energetic and the life of any party... Fölkersam was short, shy, very quiet and analytical to the final degree.'[18]

ORDE WINGATE
CHINDITS

In the summer of 1978 an unsightly row erupted in Britain, played out in the public eye in the newspapers and on the radio. At the centre of the furore was a man who had been dead for 34 years – Major-General Orde Wingate, founder of the Chindits, the Special Forces unit that had waged war against Japanese troops deep in the Burmese jungle during World War II. The discontent among Wingate's supporters had been rumbling away for 16 years, ever since the publication in 1962 of the third volumne of *The Official History, The War Against Japan*, an account of the campaign commissioned by the British government and paid for by the taxpayer.

In *The Official History* Wingate is more often than not condescendingly damned with faint praise for his innovative establishment of the Chindits, a Long Range Penetration brigade that, like the Special Air Service in North Africa, operated deep behind enemy lines. 'No one can deny that Wingate understood the art of guerrilla warfare,' opined *The Official History* (headed by Major-General H. Woodburn Kilby, a distinguished author and soldier), 'but … he was unwilling to cooperate with anyone not directly under his command and maintained an extraordinary degree of secrecy and furtiveness in his planning and in the conduct of his operations…Wingate had many original and sound ideas. He had the fanaticism and drive to persuade others that they should be carried out, but he had neither the knowledge, stability nor balance to make a great commander. He never proved himself to be the man of genius.'[1]

This last comment was a deliberate contradiction of what William Slim, commander of Fourteenth Army, had said of Wingate in the eulogy published shortly after his death in March 1944. 'Genius is a word that should not be easily used,' said Slim, 'but I say without hesitation that Wingate had sparks of genius in him.'[2]

The publication of *The Official History* had enraged many of Wingate's friends and former comrades within the Chindits. *Official Histories* were traditionally balanced and objective accounts of battles and campaigns, not personal attacks on generals and commanders. It was only in 1978, when the expiration of the 30-year secrecy rule permitted Wingate's supporters to browse reams of documents relating to the war in Burma, that they launched a vigorous defence of their man. Brigadier Peter Mead, a Chindit staff officer under Wingate, published a 45-page paper in which he rebutted all the aspersions cast in *The Official History.* There was a frank exchange of letters in *The Times* between those who supported the criticism made of Wingate and those who didn't. On 16 August, Brigadier Michael Calvert, DSO and Bar, a Chindit commander, wrote to the paper endorsing Wingate's reputation as a brilliant exponent of Special Forces warfare, saying 'the number of men of our race who are really irreplaceable can be counted on the fingers of one hand. Wingate is one of them'.[3] That prompted a response from Ronald Lewin, a soldier, author and broadcaster, who belittled Calvert's arguments and Wingate's reputation.

The ruckus was becoming all a little ungentlemanly, a fact which had he been alive would no doubt have amused Wingate. For whatever his strengths and weaknesses as a military commander, he was unequivocally a man who relished confrontation and never shirked from speaking his mind.

✦ ✦ ✦ ✦

Orde Wingate was born in India on 26 February 1903, the son of an officer in the Indian Staff Corps. There were military roots on the maternal side, too, but it was the Scottish Presbyterian influence of his father that most influenced Wingate's formative years. Like Evans Carlson, Wingate was subjected to mild religious indoctrination as a boy, and his sense of righteousness remained with him until his dying day. So did his fear of sin, and his belief that he failed to live up to the standards expected by God.

When Wingate was two, the family returned to Britain, setting up home in Worthing on the Sussex coast. As an adolescent he attended the prestigious Charterhouse school, where he was considered an outsider for his dislike of organized games and his odd dress sense. On leaving school Wingate enrolled at the Royal Military Academy, Woolwich, graduating in July 1923, 59th out of a class of 70. As a consequence he was commissioned into the Royal Garrison Artillery and posted to a battery stationed on Salisbury Plain.

Throughout the 1920s Wingate's military career was unremarkable. Though he learned to ride and hunt, he was always on the periphery of his regiment's social life, preferring to read and study military history than drink in the mess into the small hours. He attended various courses, including one to become proficient in Arabic, and then, in 1926, he fell in love for the first time. Just as the relationship began to get serious, however, Wingate was posted overseas to take up a secondment with the Sudan Defence Force, formed in 1925 to control the turbulent East African country.

Wingate arrived in the Sudan in early 1928 and in June that year he wrote to his father, telling him about his new life: 'It is satisfactory to find myself in command of 275 men but as this is the rain season there's little to be done unfortunately. However I'm setting seriously to work at Arabic in order to put that behind me and turn my attention to promotion exams and Staff College.'[4]

It was in the Sudan that Wingate first confessed to suffering bouts of depression, what he referred to as 'nervous melancholia', or what Winston Churchill called his 'black dog'. The attacks of depression would descend without warning and last two or three days, leaving Wingate alone and afraid. 'I could do nothing but sit by myself and hold on to my reason as best I could,' he confided to his girlfriend back in England.

When free from despairs, however, Wingate put his time in the Sudan to good use, learning much about soldiering and about soldiers. He discovered that with adequate training even the most mediocre of men could be turned into decent soldiers, while he also realized that the desert of Sudan was not the brutal, merciless environment that many British officers considered it to be; if the desert was harnessed in the right way, it was possible for small units of men to operate deep inside its interior for weeks on end.

Wingate returned to Britain in 1933, where he was promoted to captain and posted as adjutant to the 71st Field Brigade, Royal Artillery. It was a tedious appointment and Wingate chafed for something more challenging, something that would enable him to fulfil the potential that he was convinced lay within. In the summer of 1936 Wingate bearded Sir Cyril Deverell, Chief of the Imperial General Staff, when he visited the regiment to observe some manoeuvres. Wingate asked to be sent overseas to utilize his skills as a fluent Arab speaker. It was impudent on the part of Wingate, not the sort of brazen behaviour expected of a junior officer, but the gamble paid off. The following month Wingate was posted to Haifa as an intelligence officer to the British Mandate of Palestine.

Palestine at the time was riven by fighting between the Jews and the Arabs, with two British divisions trying to maintain order in the middle. Wingate arrived in Haifa as a Scottish Presbyterian with no strong views on the Palestine question, but within months he was supporting the Zionist cause. Some of Wingate's contemporaries, including the great African explorer and wartime SAS soldier Wilfred Thesiger, stated their belief that Wingate espoused the Jewish cause so readily because 'he admired their resilience in the face of the world's hostility and could relate it on a smaller scale to his own experiences'.[5]

That was only part of the explanation as to why Wingate proposed to raise a unit of counter-insurgency troops to protect Jewish settlers from terror attacks in Palestine. Imbued as he was with an intimate knowledge of biblical history, Wingate believed that the Old Testament was the incontrovertible proof that Palestine belonged to the Jewish race.

In June 1938 Wingate submitted a paper to the British High Command in which he outlined his idea for Special Night Squads, the purpose of which was to conduct 'night movements by armed forces of the Crown with the object of putting an end to terrorism in Northern Palestine'. Authorized to proceed, Wingate formed his squads as units of 12 men (ten soldiers, an NCO and an officer, all British) but in the first three months of the Night Squads' existence he also recruited more than 100 Jewish volunteers to the force.

At their base at Ein Haroad, Wingate oversaw the training, drilling the 300 men in close combat, explosives and silent patrols. Many of his men found him eccentric and driven, but they admired his thoroughness and his determination that the Night Squads would succeed.

The Night Squads operated in an area between Haifa in the south and Nahariya to the north, protecting oil pipelines from sabotage by Arab guerrillas and engaging the enemy whenever possible. The unit quickly made a difference, killing more than 70 Arab fighters in a few weeks, and Wingate was awarded a DSO for his 'consistent and arduous' conduct in raising the Night Squads and turning them into such an effective force in a short space of time.

Gradually, however, Wingate's activities aroused suspicion and eventually disapproval within the British headquarters in Jerusalem. It was considered that Wingate was fighting more for the Jewish cause than protecting British interests in Palestine. Wingate was relieved of his command and posted back to Britain, much to his disdain and the sorrow of the Jews, who had come to revere the Scottish Presbyterian as one of their own. He returned to England in the summer of 1939 to find an assessment of his work written by Wing Commander A.P. Ritchie, head of intelligence in Palestine:

> Captain Wingate possesses many exceptional qualities; however his ardent nature which gives him the power to pursue an objective enthusiastically often obscures his judgement and distorts his sense of proportion. He has a first-class brain, is exceptionally well read and has great mental energy but he is liable to employ these gifts for the furtherance of some idea which he has adopted because of its emotional appeal. While he has been in Palestine he has given his sympathy so wholeheartedly to the Jewish cause that his service to the intelligence branch has become valueless. He is an exceptional linguist, possesses great physical energy and powers of endurance and has proved himself to be a tactician of outstanding ability.

It was a prescient report by Ritchie, one that infuriated Wingate but which nonetheless could be said to have characterized Wingate's military career in the tumultuous years that lay ahead.

When Britain declared war on Germany on 3 September 1939 Wingate was serving with the 56th Light Anti-Aircraft Brigade, a mundane posting after the excitement of his work in Palestine. He spent his time during the Phoney War, the dragging winter months that followed the outbreak of war, devising methods of how best to shoot down enemy bombers, and also conjuring with the possibility of raising a Jewish army in Palestine. Following the occupation of the Low Countries by German troops by June 1940, and the evacuation of the British Expeditionary Force from Dunkirk, Wingate instead turned his mind to the feasibility of waging a guerrilla war in Britain in the event of a Nazi invasion.

By September 1940, however, the RAF had defeated the Luftwaffe in the Battle of Britain and the threat of invasion had diminished. On 18 September

Wingate was posted to Middle East Headquarters (MEHQ) in Cairo under the command of Archibald Wavell, Commander-in-Chief of Middle East Command. His task upon arriving at his new post was to wage an insurgency war in Ethiopia using local militia against the Italian forces.

Wingate embraced his new mission. As he had done in Palestine, he had found what he viewed as a noble cause to espouse, and, in Emperor Haile Selassie, Wingate had someone he respected and admired. Upon meeting Selassie for the first time on 6 November 1940, Wingate wrote: 'I told him that the liberation of Ethiopia was an indispensible part of the British war aims; that it was also of the greatest importance that the Ethiopians themselves should play a leading role in the coming campaign, and, finally, that he should take as his motto an ancient proverb found in Gese: "If I am not for myself, who will be for me?"'[6]

Wingate began raising what came to be known as 'Gideon Force' (in honour of Gideon, whose story in the Old Testament was one of Wingate's favourites). Consisting of two Ethiopian battalions and a battalion from the Sudan Defence Force, under the command of British NCOs and officers, the force planned to attack the Italians in the kingdom of Gojjam in north-west Ethiopia, while simultaneous attacks were launched by two Indian divisions in the north and three African divisions in the south.

The offensive began on 18 January 1941 and Wingate, promoted to temporary lieutenant-colonel, split Gideon Force into two as they entered Ethiopia, one half to cut the Dessye to Gondar road and harass the Northern Italian Force, the other half to wage a guerrilla war against the Italian garrisons and also seize the Nile bridge at Safartak. Before the attack commenced, Wingate instilled in his British officers the new concept of warfare upon which they were about to embark, reminding them that 'surprise is the greatest weapon of the guerrilla; that it is far easier for him to obtain surprise against the enemy than vice-versa; that to obtain value for the surprise achieved the commander must think out carefully beforehand how he will exploit the enemy's confusion'.[7]

Surprised the Italians certainly were in the weeks that followed the start of Gideon Force's Ethiopian offensive. Finding their remote forts under attack and suffering several ambushes while out on patrol, the Italians began withdrawing. Meanwhile in the south the African divisions advanced almost without resistance, occupying nearly 800 miles of territory in under three weeks.

Wingate continued to press the attacks, leading one assault on the Addis fort on 20 March that ended in hand-to-hand fighting before the Italians surrendered. By April the campaign was all but over, and at the start of May Emperor Haile Selassie entered the capital Addis Ababa to jubilant acclaim.

Hardly had the campaign in Ethiopia run its course than Wingate (who was awarded a Bar to his DSO for his conduct and leadership) was exploring other ideas to attack the enemy. In June 1941 he was in Cairo, as was David Stirling, whose own ideas of Special Forces warfare were being developed from a hospital bed. Wingate drafted his concept for a guerrilla force and presented it to Wavell. A year earlier the commander-in-chief of British forces in the Middle East had authorized Ralph Bagnold to establish the reconnaissance unit that came to be known as the Long Range Desert Group, and any innovative method of striking at the Axis forces would have been welcomed by Wavell. But Wavell was replaced by General Claude Auchinleck in July and so Wingate lost an important ally in MEHQ.

With Wavell gone and no sign of imminent action, Wingate fell into a deep trough of despair, his state of mind worsened by a severe attack of malaria. On 4 July he attempted to kill himself in the exclusive Continental Hotel in Cairo. Fortunately the officer in the adjoining room heard Wingate fall to the floor, and on investigation discovered him lying on the floor with a knife in his throat. Wingate required extensive surgery, and 14 pints of blood, at the General Scottish Hospital (where David Stirling was still a patient following his parachute accident) before he was out of danger.

Nonetheless, suicide attempts were a court-martial offence and though Wingate was not charged for his failure to end his life, he was reduced in rank to a major and shipped back to Britain to recuperate from 'acute depression'. He was given six months' leave but by the end of December 1941 Wingate had convinced a War Office medical board to pass him as fit once more for active service.

Delighted with the assessment of his health, Wingate was soon brought back down to earth when on 7 February he received his next posting – to 114 Field Regiment, Royal Artillery, in Wimborne, Dorset. But he did not have long to rage against his superiors, for on 11 February Wingate received a cable from Wavell, now Commander-in-Chief India, instructing him to travel to Rangoon to coordinate guerrilla attacks with the Chinese against Japan.

Those instructions soon changed as the Japanese conquest of south-east Asia continued. Having seized Hong Kong on 25 December 1941, the Japanese Army swept through Malaya and on to Singapore, where the British capitulated on 15 February with the surrender of 130,000 soldiers. Burma, meanwhile, had been invaded in January and the capital, Rangoon, was evacuated by the Allies on 7 March 1942.

Initially Wavell had planned for Wingate to work with the Chinese forces in India (having been prevented from returning to China by the rapid advance of the Japanese) but these soldiers were put under the command of American general Joseph Stilwell. Wingate was diverted instead to India, arriving on 19 March, and was ordered by Wavell to organize a campaign of guerrilla warfare against the Japanese in Burma.

One of the first men Wingate recruited to his nascent force was Major Mike Calvert, a 29-year-old regular army officer who had commanded a Bush Warfare School in Burma prior to the Japanese invasion, where he had taught guerrilla tactics to Allied soldiers. According to a contemporary newspaper report Calvert was 'a professional wrecker and saboteur, and the look of the artist comes into his eyes when he tells you about the bridges that he has blown … Mad Mike – flattish nose, twinkling eyes, tousled hair.'[8]

'Mad Mike', as Calvert was known to his comrades, had a personality far removed from Wingate's. Short and stocky, in contrast to the lean, gaunt physique of Wingate, Calvert was a brilliant athlete – he excelled at swimming and boxing – and he was neither religious nor a deep thinker; nonetheless he was a Cambridge graduate and more to the point he was staggeringly brave. On one point he and Wingate were of one mind – they both believed in what Calvert described as 'unconventional warfare'.

Wingate went to see Calvert at his base in Mayamo in the east of Mandalay. An instant rapport grew between the two men and Wingate outlined what he had in mind – deep penetration patrols into Burma to harass the Japanese. What Wingate needed from Calvert was his expertise on jungle fighting. Wingate had used guerrilla tactics in the Sudan, Palestine and Ethiopia but not in the fearsome terrain of south-east Asia with its mountainous jungles. Few people in the British Army knew the jungle like Calvert, who in the 1930s had served in Hong Kong with the Royal Engineers and witnessed the Japanese attacks on Shanghai and Nanking. Calvert told Wingate what he would later tell the British public in a wartime radio broadcast on the BBC: 'Burma gives far greater chances for individual initiative and responsibility to junior leaders than in any other theatre of war. A keen young soldier has greater chances there to show his powers than anywhere.'[9]

Calvert then tackled what he considered a gross misconception, that the jungle was hostile and cruel to all who entered. 'It frightens some people as a placid ocean is frightening,' said Calvert,

> because it is so large and so deep, but it is not in itself dangerous. It is like being in an aeroplane where, within reason, the higher up you are the safer you are. In the jungle, with a compass and map, there is nothing to fear … the way to behave in the jungle is as the tiger behaves – as king of the jungle. The tiger only creeps and crawls when he is stalking his prey. He is only silent when he wishes to surprise his enemy. At other times he relaxes, well camouflaged, with a wary eye open and with what one may call a battle drill ready for any emergency.[10]

Calvert took Wingate on a tour of Mayamo, demonstrating some of the techniques he had taught in his Bush Warfare school. He explained to Wingate that the best defence in the jungle is to 'seek out the enemy and attack him, and thus impose your will on him'. In addition Calvert passed on his thoughts of the average Japanese fighting man, 'a keen, hard, vigorous soldier, usually well versed in his training pamphlets, but not particularly well blessed with much imagination, common sense or knowledge of the world.

This makes him an easy person to lead up the garden path, a pastime which I, for one, thoroughly enjoy'.[11]

Inspired by his meeting with Calvert, Wingate's idea for a Special Forces unit to fight the Japanese behind their lines in Burma was committed to paper in a memorandum entitled 'Notes on Penetration Warfare – Burma Command'. He opened his memo thus:

> Modern war is war of penetration in almost all its phases. This may be of two types. Tactical or strategic. Penetration is tactical where armed forces carrying it out are directly supported by the operations of the main armies. It is strategic when no such support is possible. That is when a penetration group is living and operating 100 miles or more in front of its own armies. Of the two types Long Range Penetration pays by far the larger dividends on the forces employed. These forces operating with small columns are able, wherever a friendly population exists, to live and move under the enemies' ribs and thus to deliver fatal blows at his military organisation by attacking vital objectives which he is unable to defend from such attacks. In the past such warfare has been impossible owing to the fact that control over such columns, indispensable both for their safety and their effectual use, was not possible until the age of the easily portable wireless set. Further the supply of certain indispensable materials such as ammunition, petrol, wireless sets and spare parts is impossible until the appearance of communications aircraft.

Wavell was impressed and, as he had done two years before with Ralph Bagnold's idea for the Long Range Patrol in Italian-occupied Libya, so the commander-in-chief in India sanctioned a full-scale trial of Wingate's proposal. A training camp was established at Saugor in the Central Provinces for what was designated the 77th Indian Infantry Brigade, comprising the 13th Battalion, The King's Liverpool Regiment, the 3rd Battalion, 2nd Gurkha Rifles, the 2nd Burma Rifles and 142 Commando Company, most of whom had been resident at Calvert's Bush Warfare School. There was also a signal section, a mule transport company from the Royal Indian Army Service and eight RAF sections to provide air support.

One of the officers who joined Wingate's newly formed brigade was Denis Gudgeon, a 22-year-old from Wimbledon who had worked as a banker in Paris prior to the war. A young subaltern in the 1st Battalion, 2nd Gurkha Rifles, he found himself attached to 77th Indian Infantry Brigade without having any say in the matter. 'We'd heard about Wingate and heard he'd been successful against Italians in Abyssinia,' recalled Gudgeon many years later. 'We knew that he was a very ruthless man but also very eccentric so we were a little wary.'[12]

Though Wingate was an admirer of the Karens, Chins and Kachins who made up the Burma Rifles, he had little time for the average Gurkha soldier, whom he considered tough but slow-witted. Similarly he found most of their British officers 'ignorant of infantry tactics and inexperienced'. Gudgeon recalled that the dislike was mutual during their time at Saugor. 'I don't think many of the Gurkha officers liked him, he wasn't popular,' he said. 'He was a very ascetic man, not very tall and he had a slight stoop... You couldn't have a rapport with him, he was a very aloof man. He never said very much. He used to issue reams and reams of instructions. We were quite honestly all terrified of him.'[13]

Then there were Wingate's little eccentricities, derided by some as showmanship and others as proof he was a little touched. 'He carried a fly gun with him everywhere, which was a bit disconcerting when one was eating one's lunch,' remembered Gudgeon. 'He also carried an alarm clock with him the whole time. We used to think he was mad quite simply.'[14]

During the training at Saugor, Wingate pushed the men hard, and particularly the officers. Experience of guerrilla fighting in the Sudan and Palestine had taught him that the officers operating in small units must be fitter, tougher, and confident in everything they did if they were to retain the respect of the men. 'TETS (tactical exercises without troops) were dreaded because he would pick a hill several hundred feet high and we had to run up it,' recalled Gudgeon. 'The last officer up the hill would have to run down the hill and up again. I always managed to avoid being the last officer. And I was always terrified of being asked some detailed military rules question on these TETS as he would point his ruler at you and fix you with these beady, very clear blue eyes and my mind would go a total blank.'[15]

Wingate had hoped to have his men trained and ready for the first operation within eight weeks; he soon realized that was entirely unfeasible. Obtaining equipment and men proved more problematic than he had envisaged, and there was a further setback in August 1942 when monsoons flooded their camp and washed away equipment and the odd soldier.

Nonetheless the brigade began to take shape, with Wingate dividing it into seven columns of approximately 300 men and 100 mules, all armed with heavy machine guns, mortars, anti-tank rifles and small arms. Supplies would be dropped by air although it wouldn't be possible to evacuate any wounded.

As the training and preparation progressed, so the brigade took on its own identity. Their standard Far East battledress was dyed green and they wore bush hats. Wingate designed their shoulder patch, a yellow *Chinthe* guarding a small yellow pagoda on a blue background. The *Chinthe* – a mythical half-lion, half-dragon creature, which guarded Burmese pagodas – was later corrupted into 'Chindits'.

By the end of 1942 Wingate had been briefed by Wavell on the brigade's first mission; they were to cross into Japanese-held Burma at Imphal and penetrate 200 miles east towards Indaw, attacking the enemy's supply and communication lines, as well as laying waste to bridges, railways and depots. While Wingate's men were tying up Japanese forces in a guerrilla campaign, Wavell would launch his main three-pronged offensive towards the river Chindwin with the British 4th Corps. Further north the Chinese forces under General Stilwell would advance towards Myitkyina and the 15th Corps would push east towards Akyab in the Arakan. The aim of the offensive was to open the Burma Road, the main supply route to China, so that the full potential of the Chinese forces could be unleashed on the Japanese.

In January 1943 the 77th Indian Infantry Brigade broke camp and went by paddle-steamer and rail to Dimapur. 'We eventually arrived at Dimapur where we were met on the platform by Major Calvert, who was to be our column commander,' recalled Denis Gudgeon. 'I was immensely impressed by him. He was a very dynamic character indeed. You could tell at a glance that he'd been a professional army boxer by his flat nose and cauliflower ears.'[16] Calvert marched with the brigade the 130 miles south to Imphal.

Soon Wavell arrived at the brigade's new camp bearing bad news – the offensive was postponed because the Chinese had withdrawn cooperation at the last minute. Wingate was dismayed but not downhearted, writing subsequently: 'The brigade had been raised and trained for operations in the winter of 42/43 and the whole tempo, physical and psychological, set to that tune. Not to use [it] was to lose it.'[17] Wingate also feared that his detractors at headquarters – the 'fossilized shits', as David Stirling referred to senior officers who looked askance at irregular units – would use the postponement to try and break up his brigade.

Initially Wavell insisted that the Long Range Penetration operation must be postponed but he was won round in the end by Wingate, who pointed out that the mission would provide valuable information on the quality of the enemy soldier as well as the practicability of operating deep behind enemy lines. On 6 February Wingate's force marched out of Imphal south-east towards Tamu on the Assam–Burma border; they were to cross the river Chindwin and then embark on a series of guerrilla attacks, cutting railway lines and ambushing Japanese forces in the Shwebo region.

Wingate split his brigade into two forces, a northern force consisting of five columns and HQ, and a small southern force comprising No. 1 Column and No. 2 Column. The latter's task was to draw Japanese forces away from the main force by launching a series of diversionary raids on selected targets before making for a rendezvous point 250 miles to the east at Mongmit. On the eve of the operation – codenamed *Longcloth* – Wingate issued his Order of the Day:

> Today we stand on the threshold of battle. The time of preparation is over, and we are moving on the enemy to prove ourselves and our methods. At this moment we stand beside the soldiers of the United Nations in the front line trenches throughout the world. It is always a minority that occupies the front line. It is still a smaller minority that accepts with a good heart tasks like this that we have chosen to carry out. We need not, therefore, as we go forward into the conflict, suspect ourselves of selfish or interested motives. We have all had opportunity of withdrawing and we are here because we have chosen to be here; that is, we have chosen to bear the burden and heat of the day. Men who make this choice are above the average in courage. We need therefore have no fear for the staunchness and guts of our comrades.

The motive which has led each and all of us to devote ourselves to what lies ahead cannot conceivably have been a bad motive. Comfort and security are not sacrificed voluntarily for the sake of others by ill-disposed people. Our motive, therefore, may be taken to be the desire to serve our day and generation in the way that seems nearest to our hand. The battle is not always to the strong nor the race to the swift. Victory in war cannot be counted upon, but what can be counted upon is that we shall go forward determined to do what we can to bring this war to the end which we believe best for our friends and comrades in arms, without boastfulness or forgetting our duty, resolved to do the right so far as we can see the right.

Our aim is to make possible a government of the world in which all men can live at peace and with equal opportunity of service.

Finally, knowing the vanity of man's effort and the confusion of his purpose, let us pray that God may accept our services and direct our endeavours, so that when we shall have done all we shall see the fruit of our labours and be satisfied.

O.C. Wingate, Commander,
77th Indian Infantry Brigade.[18]

The next day, 14 February 1943, the brigade began moving across the Chindwin, each of the 1,000 soldiers weighed down by a 60lb pack. The two forces moved south and received an RAF air drop the following day before splitting. For several days the Chindits' greatest foe was the teak forests infesting the area between the rivers of the Chindwin and the Irrawaddy; they encountered no Japanese, much to the chagrin of Calvert (commanding No. 3 Column), who devised his own method of harassing the enemy, in light of their absence. 'We carried plenty of explosives with us and as we moved about we mined jungle paths if the local Burmese told us the Japs would pass that way,' he wrote in his memoirs. 'With the help of my Burma Rifles chaps we also wrote out various signs and warnings in Burmese and Japanese, "signed" them with the names of Japanese commanders and pinned them up at convenient points to add to the general confusion of the enemy.

For example some of them said "Follow this path for –", the nearest village. But any Jap who took them at their word would have ended up either a very puzzled man or a very dead one.'[19]

Apart from the odd light skirmish, it was not until the first week of March that the Chindits engaged the Japanese in any great force. On the night of 2 March the enemy ambushed one of the two southern forces and two days later one of the northern columns was attacked. In the first attack several Gurkhas panicked and fled, as did the supply mules taking with them precious rations and equipment, while the second incident was marred by poor decision-making by the column commander. No. 1 Column, lost contact with the rest of the Chindits after blowing up a railway bridge at Kyaikthin. Though the column did return to India several weeks later it was with a much depleted force after several fierce contacts with the Japanese. As a result of all these setbacks Wingate was left with four of his seven columns with which to continue the operation.

Fortunately Calvert was intent on causing mayhem, which he did with a well-coordinated attack on the village of Nankan. Having arranged with the RAF for an air strike on a Japanese camp ten miles south of Nankan, Calvert launched his attack against the railway station and two bridges on the morning of 6 March – his 30th birthday. It was, he recalled, 'an unpleasant day' for the Japanese with the two bridges destroyed, the railway line cut in 70 places and a large number of their soldiers killed – with no Chindit casualties in return. Calvert was awarded a DSO for this action.

Further north, Major Bernard Fergusson and his No. 5 Column blew up a bridge and then dynamited Bonchaung gorge, causing a massive landslide that completely blocked the vital railway line. Fergusson recalled that he woke the next morning with a feeling of 'exhilarated guilt' at what they had accomplished at Bonchaung. His elation soon turned to concern when he received a message from Wingate:

Owing no news received from No.1 Group for ten days crossing of Irrawaddy possibly hazardous … no news Four Column … leave it your own discretion whether you continue movement or make safe bivouac in Gangaw Hills to harass reconstruction railway.[20]

Fergusson was running desperately low on supplies and he estimated that the next suitable spot to receive a resupply by air was in a village 20 miles east on the other side of the Irrawaddy. They were running low on rations, though even the rations were poor; a day's ration pack weighing 2lb consisted of 12 Shakapura biscuits, 2oz of cheese, some nuts and raisins, some dates, 20 cigarettes, tea, sugar and milk. There was also some chocolate, or a packet of acid drops, depending on the whim of the ration packer.

Wearily Fergusson's column set off for the resupply drop on the other side of the Irrawaddy, hacking their way through elephant grass, just as Calvert's column was doing too. Once on the eastern bank of the Irrawaddy Calvert and Fergusson were tasked by Wingate with blowing up the Gokteik viaduct, but before the sabotage could be carried out Wingate decided to withdraw his brigade. They were almost out of RAF supply range and Wingate was also concerned that if they pressed east the brigade might be encircled by the Japanese, now hot on their trail. Wingate issued instructions for the columns to make their way back west over the Chindwin. 'The task now in front of us was a tough one,' recalled Calvert. 'We had to travel that 150 miles through some of the worst country in the world, and every inch of the way we had to keep a careful watch out for the Japs. They were becoming more and more determined to get rid of the cocky Britishers who had calmly walked into the middle of a country occupied by the Imperial Japanese Army. And they were out to teach these white men a lesson – if only they could find them.'[21]

On one occasion during the withdrawal Calvert found the Japanese first, leading his column in a devastating ambush on a force of pursuing Japanese, which left 100 of the enemy dead. Calvert's column crossed the Chindwin to safety on 15 April – exactly two months since they had traversed it in the other direction, having survived by eating snakes, lizards and any other living creature they could find. The rest of the brigade crossed in the days and weeks that followed, with Fergusson's column, ravaged by hunger, exhaustion, dehydration, lice and mosquitoes, reaching safety six days after Calvert. Fergusson had lost three of his 12 stone in weight during the operation and, when he wrote his account of Operation *Longcloth* in 1945, Fergusson turned to Shakespeare to describe the experience.

'... Perseverance, dear my Lord,
Keeps honour bright; to have done is to hang
Quite out of fashion, like a rusty nail
In monumental mockery.[22]

Wingate followed Fergusson across the Chindwin four days later, having swum the river in broad daylight with the Japanese swarming up behind. Nothing was heard from No. 7 Column until June, when they reached China, while other Chindits continued to turn up in ones, twos and small groups until as late as July.

In all, of the 3,000 Chindits who had crossed the Chindwin heading east in February 1943, 2,182 returned from the Long Range Penetration. Nearly 500 had been killed in action with the remainder having died of disease or been captured. Many of those who had survived the mission never recovered fully from the experience (one of Fergusson's men died from cerebral malaria a few days later) and only 600 returned to active service.

Dismayed though he was by the losses, Wingate was equally concerned with the fact that for all his soldiers' suffering, nothing great had been achieved. An estimated 200 Japanese soldiers had been killed (the majority by Calvert's column) and a few bridges and railway lines cut during the two months of Operation *Longcloth*. However, that didn't take into account the psychological results of the penetration. Calvert subsequently compared it to the Allied commando raid on Dieppe in August 1942 which, while ultimately a costly failure, proved invaluable in planning for Operation *Torch*, the invasions of north-west Africa in November 1942, and the Normandy landings in June 1944. Calvert wrote:

> The operation can be compared with the Dieppe operation in its successes and failures in that it paved the way both technically and in the hearts of men for the final offensive and overthrow of the enemy. Its greatest achievement was the final proof that air power in the form of air supply could ... give back to the ground forces mobility and freedom of manoeuvre without being tactically tied to ground communications.[23]

Calvert added that Wingate had learned much during the two months behind Japanese lines about equipment, medical treatment, signals and the calibre of the enemy. In addition, said Calvert, the experience had shed a light on the quality of the average Anglo-Saxon soldier who, since the fall of Hong Kong and Singapore, had been considered inferior to his Japanese foe. 'This first operation proved that the European soldier as of old can shake off the shackles of his civilized neuroses and inhibitions and live and fight as hard as any Asiatic,' wrote Calvert. 'And due to his intrinsic sounder constitution and basic health due to good feeding, better the Asiatic in overcoming hard conditions. Most Europeans do not know what their bodies can stand, and it is the mind and willpower which so often gives way first. Most soldiers never realized that they could do the things they did and hardly believe it now. One advantage of exceptionally hard training is that it proves to a man what he can do and suffer. If you have marched 30 miles in a day, 25 miles you can take in your stride.'[24]

This last point was the one seized on by the Allies, who during the Chindits' mission had been defeated by the Japanese at Akyab. Suddenly the Chindits were acclaimed as heroes and on their return to India in May were greeted by Lord Linlithgow, Viceroy of India. In radio broadcasts the BBC hailed their exploits, as did the newspapers, with the *Daily Mail* describing Wingate as 'the Clive of Burma'.[25]

Despite the blaze of publicity, Wingate locked himself away for three weeks in India and wrote a 61-page report on Operation *Longcloth*, which in his inimitable style criticized several senior officers for their perceived lack of help and general ignorance in the formation and preparation of the brigade. He was also honest in his appraisal of his force, saying that some of the soldiers had been found wanting. He concluded his report with five findings:

1. Long range penetration is an offensive weapon and should be employed as a vital part of the major plan of conquest.
2. The men should be suitably equipped and trained: Training is more important than physical hardiness. On this point more thought had to be given to basic jungle fighting including ambushes and close quarter combat.

3. RAF liaison officers must work in tandem with column commanders to coordinate supply drops and air strikes.
4. There was room for improvement in wireless operations.
5. Columns need better training in river crossing, otherwise the operation easily becomes a shemozzle.[26]

The report eventually landed on the desk of Prime Minister Winston Churchill, who read it with unbridled glee. After one defeat after another in the Far East, the British appeared to have finally found a man willing to take the fight to the Japanese, something that Churchill had been exhorting his commanders to do for months. Churchill was also a staunch supporter of irregular warfare, ever since he had witnessed the Boer commandos cause the British so many problems in the South African war of 1899–1902. His own son, Randolph, had served for a short spell in the SAS in 1942, and Churchill had been the driving force behind the formation of the British commandos in 1940.

Churchill had already replaced Wavell with General Sir Claude Auchinleck as Commander-in-Chief in India and on 24 July he waved a copy of Wingate's report at his chiefs of staff and told them that 'he is a man of genius and audacity, and has rightly been discerned by all eyes as a figure quite above the ordinary level. The expression "the Clive of Burma" has already gained currency. There is no doubt that in the welter of inefficiency and lassitude which has characterized our operations, this man, his force and his achievements stand out.'[27]

In August Wingate was summoned back to London to meet Churchill and the Prime Minister found the Chindit commander to be as promising in the flesh as he had been in his report. The next day Wingate found himself accompanying Churchill across the Atlantic to attend the Quebec Conference, where the British were expecting a frosty reception from their American allies.

President Roosevelt and his chief of staff were pressing not just for an invasion of France but for some forceful aggressive action in the Far East. Wingate had been brought to Quebec to impress the Americans and he did just that with his vision for the 'conquest of Burma north of the 23rd Parallel'. This would be done, he explained to the conference delegates, because:

Long range penetration affords greater opportunity of mystifying and misleading the enemy than any other form of warfare. It provides the ideal opportunity for the use of Airborne and Parachutist troops without risking their loss. This calls for the use of best troops available. RAF Sections operating with columns are in a position to direct our aircraft with great accuracy on targets visible and undetectable from the air. Such is the description of the vast majority of enemy targets in south east Asia. To sum up long range groups should be used as an essential part of the plan of conquest to create a situation leading to the advance of our main forces.[28]

Wingate asked for his force to be expanded to six brigades, totalling 26,500 officers and men, and he also requested no interference from staff officers in GHQ India. Permission was granted, the Americans delighted that the British had a commander altogether more pugnacious that his predecessors. In addition, the Americans put in place plans of their own to form a special air unit to support the Chindits and it was also agreed to establish an Allied Operational South-East Asia Command (distinct from Auchinleck's Indian military command) with Admiral Lord Louis Mountbatten as its supreme commander.

Auchinleck reacted with dismay when he heard the news. The formation of the new, six-brigade-strong Special Force would necessitate Wingate (promoted to temporary major-general) having carte blanche to break up many of his divisions, which were already stretched in the war against the Japanese. He was not the only senior officer to take umbrage at Wingate's rise to the point where he now had the ear of both the Prime Minister and President Roosevelt.

Back in London after the Quebec Conference, Wingate began gathering the very best equipment for his expanded force, including flamethrowers, wireless receivers, anti-tank grenade launchers, river-crossing boats and the vastly superior American K rations. He returned to India in September and wasted little time in preparing Special Force for another operation in Burma. At times, recalled one of his fellow (and supportive) officers, Wingate was 'astonishingly and wonderfully rude' in ensuring his plans were not hampered by uncooperative staff officers. Yet his uncompromising stance achieved results and the six brigades were raised and trained within five months.

Wingate, who fell ill with typhoid in late 1943, relied more than ever on the expertise of Mike Calvert in preparing the second Chindit operation. The brigades would be split into eight mobile columns each one consisting of about 400 men; their mission would be to range far and wide throughout Burma attacking targets in coordinated raids, although Wingate also insisted that they have the capability to reform as one force to launch a major offensive against one objective if need be. As a result Calvert was preoccupied in training the men for the forthcoming operation. 'One of the most important lessons rammed home in our guerrilla training was to be adaptable and unpredictable,' he wrote, 'deceiving the enemy with a feint here while attacking there, or better still a double feint while hitting a third target with everything available. Constant vigilance and deception, bluff and counter-bluff, were necessary for success in the sort of free-style fighting we went in for.'[29]

When Wingate had fully recovered his health he turned his attention to the exact nature of the forthcoming operation, already codenamed *Thursday*. There were problems with gaining Chinese approval for any major operation in Burma while the Americans – despite the general agreement at the Quebec Conference – were wary that the British war aims in south-east Asia were motivated primarily by imperial ambitions. Meanwhile General Joseph Stilwell, Mountbatten's deputy and an Anglophobe who viewed the average British soldier as an out-and-out coward, was finalizing plans to push south from the north-east and seize Myitkyina from the Japanese with his composite force of Chinese and Americans, including a new American Special Forces unit, officially named the 5307th Composite Unit, and eventually better known as Merrill's Marauders.

It wasn't until February 1944, therefore, that Wingate agreed on the exact aims of his force for Operation *Thursday*. They were threefold – namely to assist Stilwell's advance south as he endeavoured to link up with the Burma Road and re-establish an overland supply route to China by attacking the Japanese 18th Division's lines of supply and communications; to help the Yunnan Chinese offensive enter Burma; and lastly to 'inflict maximum confusion, damage and loss on the enemy forces in North Burma'.

It was agreed to insert the Chindits by air on a landing zone east of the river Irrawaddy. Mike Calvert led his men, and moved off to form a strongpoint which he called 'White City', stopping twice en route to indulge his love for blowing enemy railway bridges. These strongpoints were an idea of Wingate's to enable each brigade to remain isolated in the jungle for greater periods of time, similar to the US cavalry forts in the Indian plains 150 years earlier. Each strongpoint was well garrisoned with field artillery, anti-aircraft guns, light aircraft and a landing strip.

Once Calvert was established at 'White City', Wingate flew in to inspect the strongpoint and inform Calvert that the Japanese Fifteenth Army had launched an offensive that was now threatening Imphal and Kohima. One of the soldiers at White City was Harold Shippey from Hull, who had joined the Chindits from the Royal Scots Fusiliers. 'Wingate was a marvellous man,' he recalled in an interview many years later:

It needed a man of his ideas to produce the men for that sort of warfare. We're not jungle people but he taught us how to live and survive in the jungle. Because it was a case of not only fighting in the jungle but you had to [live] with it and realize it was not only an enemy but also a friend. He pushed us on these marches, his idea was that when you think you've had enough you only think you've had enough. If need be you can get up and do another ½ mile or 2 miles, which later on we found we had to. When you thought you'd come to the end of your tether you really haven't. This is the sort of thing that it needed, that sort of man and which he got through to us all in the finish – that if you want to survive you really had to go to the limit.[30]

Later, in the early evening of 24 March, Wingate returned to Imphal in an American B-25 Mitchell bomber flown by First Lieutenant Brian Hodges. After a brief consultation with an RAF air commodore, Wingate reboarded the plane for a short flight to Lalaghat. The aircraft never arrived at its destination and the next day a search began in an area where another

American pilot reported having seen a plane come down. The wreckage was eventually found by a three-man search team in the jungle-covered hills west of Imphal. They found a crafter 20ft wide and 8ft deep, and counted 11 bodies. Though the 'bodies were badly burned through', the search team reported that they were sure the 41-year-old Wingate was among the dead 'as his peculiar shaped topee* was found'.[31]

The death of Wingate stunned everyone at GHQ India, not least because of its mundane nature – simple engine failure on a routine flight – after everything he had experienced and survived. Mike Calvert was distraught when told the news a week later, recalling that: 'Even the men in Special Force who had seen him only once or twice at a distance felt the shock of his loss as it reverberated down the line of command. The Chindits would fight on, but they would never be quite the same again without the man who created and inspired them.'[32]

At the top of the line of command was Churchill, who received a letter from Lord Louis Mountbatten in which the Supreme Commander of Allied Forces in South-East Asia wrote: 'No one but Wingate could possibly have invented such a bold scheme, devised such an unorthodox technique, or trained and inspired his force to an almost fanatical degree of enthusiasm.'[33]

Churchill in turn wrote to President Franklin Roosevelt on 28 March to break the 'shattering news' and add: 'His death is indeed a blow to me, not only because I have made personal friends with him but because he was one of the few really dynamic and forceful leaders in the Burma war.'[34]

Lieutenant-General William Slim, commander of the British Fourteenth Army, under whose auspices the Chindits operated, appointed Brigadier William Lentaigne as Wingate's successor, a decision that was as inimical to the Chindits as the appointment of Alan Shapley as Evans Carlson's successor was to the 2nd Raider Battalion.

Lentaigne had never approved of Wingate's methods and was little respected by the likes of Calvert and Fergusson. But there were other factors at work, too, that contributed to the demise of the Chindits. Slim assigned

---

* As well as wearing a beard for much of his time in command of the Chindits, Wingate also wore a pith helmet, or topee, that he had first acquired in Africa.

them to Stilwell's operational command and the American general moved the Chindits north to help him in his offensive against Myitkyina, deploying them not as a Long Range Penetration force but as infantrymen. In June they were ordered to take the town of Mogaung, occupied by approximately 4,000 Japanese. It took the Chindits three weeks and nearly 1,000 casualties before the town was taken. 'In many ways it was the worst three weeks of the war as far as I was concerned,' reflected Calvert. 'The Chindits had not been trained or equipped for this type of fighting … we were the Chindits, the guerrillas, the mobile marauders who were at the enemy's throat one minute and away the next looking for another target … and here we were, exhausted after three months behind the enemy lines, depleted in numbers by wounds, sickness and death, and with orders from a bitchy American general to take Mogaung.'[35]

✦ ✦ ✦ ✦

When Operation *Thursday* ended at the close of August 1944, the Chindits were withdrawn to India, after five months in the field. In that time they had lost 1,034 men, with a further 2,752 wounded and many more suffering from malaria or dysentery or trench foot. Yet they had killed nearly 6,000 Japanese and sabotaged many of their railway lines and supply dumps.

This was all conveniently ignored, however, by South-East Asia Command. With Wingate dead, his detractors began doing all they could to belittle his reputation and that of his men, pointing out that as in Operation *Longcloth* in 1943 little had been achieved during Operation *Thursday* other than a high casualty rate. Calvert received no decoration for his command of the Chindits during the capture of Mogaung, even though General Stilwell recognized his gallantry with an American Silver Star. Calvert later attributed this snub to 'spite and envy'[36] on the part of Lentaigne.*

What Wingate's enemies deliberately ignored was the confusion caused in the Japanese ranks by the Chindits' guerrilla warfare, leading General Renya

---

* Calvert became brigadier of the SAS in 1945 and later served with the SAS in Malaya. He died aged 85 in 1998.

Mutaguchi, commander of the Fifteenth Army, to divert several precious battalions needed for the attack on Imphal into hunting Wingate's marauders.

One of those most responsible for the official disparaging of Wingate was Slim, who finished his life as Field Marshal the 1st Viscount Slim, 13th Governor-General of Australia. Though in the wake of Wingate's death he lauded him – 'added to the tactical daring of the guerrilla leader were a wealth of vision and a depth of imaginations that placed him far above his comrades'[37] – after the war he was openly critical, describing Special Forces units in his memoirs *Defeat Into Victory* as 'expensive, wasteful and unnecessary'. Then in 1959, having read the assessment of Wingate in the draft of *The Official History, The War Against Japan*, Slim wrote to the author to congratulate him on his work, saying: 'We are always inclined in the British Army to devise private armies and scratch forces for jobs which our ordinary formations with proper training could do and do better.'

Two years later John Masters, the Chindits' brigade major after Wingate's death and a best-selling post-war novelist, published his Burma memoirs entitled *The Road Past Mandalay*, in which he passed perhaps the most insightful judgement of all those that have been written: 'The tragedy of Wingate lies not in his early death but in the unknown and unknowable quality of what he might have achieved if he had loved instead of despising the generality of his fellow humans.'[38]

In 1962 *The Official History* was published, much to the fury of the Chindits. Derek Tulloch, who had served as Wingate's chief of staff in 1943 and 1944, was incensed and began compiling evidence to rebut the claims, though many of the official War Office files were sealed until 1978. Nonetheless Tulloch travelled to Japan where he met General Renya Mutaguchi, erstwhile commander of the Fifteenth Army in Burma. The two former adversaries talked about the campaign and Mutaguchi recalled his reaction when he had learned of Wingate's death in the spring of 1944: 'I realized what a loss this was to the British Army and said a prayer for the soul of this man in whom I had found my match.'[39]

CHARLES HUNTER
5307TH COMPOSITE UNIT

On 3 August 1944, a little over a month after Mike Calvert's Chindits had captured Mogaung, the American 5307th Composite Unit seized the nearby town of Myitkyina. 'This was most cheering news,' wrote John Masters, the Chindits' brigade major, 'and the brigade burst into a collective smile of joy and appreciation.'[1]

The victory at Myitkyina, however, had come at a fearful price for the 5307th Composite Unit. Nicknamed 'Merrill's Marauders' by the press after their commander, General Frank Merrill, the unit began operations the previous February with a fighting strength of approximately 2,750 men; six months later only 200 of that number were present to celebrate the capture of Myitkyina. That the 'Marauders' had still been able to take Myitkyina was in large part due to the leadership and example of Colonel Charles Hunter, the officer who had been with the unit since their inception a year earlier and who had assumed command after Merrill's heart attack.

Yet on the same day that Myitkyina fell, Hunter – described by Calvert as an 'admirable' soldier – was relieved of his command by General Joseph Stilwell and sent home to the United States. The Marauders were enraged by the decision, one saying of Stilwell: 'I had him in my rifle sights … no one would have known it wasn't a Jap that got the son-of-a-bitch.'[2]

Hunter was ordered to return to the United States by ship, not aircraft, so that Stilwell would have time to blacken his name, and that of the Marauders, before Hunter could reveal the truth as to why the 5307th Composite Unit had all but ceased to exist. Hunter had paid the price for his courage, not just in fighting the Japanese, but in standing up to Stilwell and holding him responsible for the failure of the Marauders. He left Burma for the long journey home carrying a letter from Merrill which ran:

Dear Chuck

I feel like hell about what you have been up against and want you to know that I have greatly appreciated and recognize all that you have done. I'm sorry that our ending is bound to be rather unpleasant for most of us. I have talked with the boss [Stilwell] and have done all I could to get many things squared away but am afraid not much except getting him to recognize that we weren't so far wrong in many things, resulted. Sincerely, Frank[3]

The origins of the 5307th Composite Unit had begun a year earlier, at the Quebec Conference of August 1943, to which Winston Churchill had brought Orde Wingate to impress the Americans. Wingate's presentation on his Long Range Penetration Patrols, along with his burning desire to beat the Japanese, did indeed electrify the Americans. General H.H. Arnold, commander of the US Army Air Force, wrote of Wingate: 'You took one look at that face, like the face of a pale Indian chieftain, topping the uniform still smelling of jungle and sweat and war and you thought "Hell, this man is serious". When he began to talk, you found out just how serious.'[4]

One upshot of the conference was a lengthy telegram issued from Washington's Operations Division (OPD) of the War Department, General Staff on 31 August 1943. It was addressed to General Joseph Stilwell, commander of the US Army Forces in South-East Asia and it was titled 'Information Pertaining to Three American Long Range-Penetration Groups'. The telegram explained to Stilwell that a

total of 2,830 officers and men organized into casual detachments will arrive in India in early November. They will all be volunteers. 950 will be battle-tested troops in jungle fighting from the South and Southwest Pacific. 1,900 will be from jungle-trained troops from the Caribbean Defense Command and the Continental United States. All will be of a high state of physical ruggedness. Above volunteers have been called for with requisite qualifications and commensurate grades and ratings to form three Independent Battalions after their arrival in the theater. They must be intensively trained in jungle warfare, animal transportation and air supply in a suitable jungle area in preparation for combat in February [1944].[5]

Stilwell was delighted with the news, even if the proposed force was a tiny fraction of the manpower he needed to recapture Burma from the Japanese and thus reopen the supply route between British-held India and China, a task that would allow the Allies to utilize the 300 Chinese divisions against Japan. On receiving the telegram outlining the arrival of the 2,830-strong American force, Stilwell wrote in his diary on 2 September: 'Only 3,000 [sic], but the entering wedge. Can we use them! And how!'[6]

Since arriving in China in March 1942 as commander of US forces in China, India and Burma, Stilwell had worked closely in 'supporting China' in the war against Japan, forming a solid working relationship with Generalissimo Chiang Kai-shek (though Stilwell referred to the Chinese commander as 'Peanut' in his diary). It was Stilwell's ultimate objective to train the mighty Chinese Army using American instructors before unleashing them against the Japanese – but that could only be done once Burma had been retaken from the Japanese.

Stilwell's nickname was 'Vinegar Joe' on account of his acidic personality and though he disliked most of humanity, he reserved a particular loathing for the British. 'The more I see of Limeys the worse I hate them,' he once said, and it was his view that the average British soldier was weak, cowardly and incapable of pushing the Japanese out of Burma.[7] So the news that 3,000 well-trained American Special Forces troops were on their way to Burma managed to raise a smile even on the lips of 'Vinegar Joe's' hard-boiled face.

Once the decision had been taken by the US War Department to raise a Special Forces unit similar to the British Chindits, moves were put rapidly in place to recruit suitable soldiers. The man tasked with overseeing the organization of the force was Colonel Charles Newton Hunter.

✦ ✦ ✦ ✦

Hunter was born in Oneida, New York, in January 1906, into a family with deep Scottish roots. From an early age Hunter wanted to be a soldier and he graduated from West Point Military Academy in 1929, where he was nicknamed 'Newt'. His West Point yearbook described him thus:

> Newt has worn the gray of the Corps with distinction, yet, we hope sometime to see him in wee kilts, and to hear him dreamily squeeze the bagpipe for our benefit. His ruddy countenance, slightly tilted nose, sandy hair, and

twinkling blue eyes carry an appeal that can pass unnoticed by no mortal lass. Fortunately for us, Newt's forefathers failed to transmit to him their most famous trait. His helpful generosity would do credit to even the Good Samaritan. Newt is a precious bundle of wit and humor, with more than his share of common sense and good fellowship. He is the type that one enjoys to have around and whom you daily learn to appreciate more and more. These characteristics are certain to gain him the best in life wherever he goes.[8]

Following his graduation from West Point, Hunter joined an infantry regiment and served three years in the Philippines and two and a half in the Canal Zone, the ribbon of United States territory in Panama including the Canal. Here he had taught soldiers the art of jungle warfare and Hunter had been marked out as a young officer with exceptional 'ability, efficiency and precision'. When America entered the war in December 1941 Hunter was recalled to the States and appointed an instructor at the infantry school at Fort Benning, Georgia.

In August 1943, after the decision had been made by the War Department to raise a Special Forces unit to serve in Burma, Hunter was the logical choice to organize the formation of such a force. Summoned to Washington, Hunter was briefed by the Operations Division on the concept of Long Range Penetration and informed of the work carried out by the British Chindits earlier in the year. Then he was told that it was the turn of the Americans to form a similar elite force to fight in Burma, where the casualty rate was projected to reach as high as 85 per cent. Hunter took the figures phlegmatically and set about raising three battalions for an imminent departure to India.

The volunteers who responded to the recruitment notices for a Special Forces unit were sent to San Francisco. One of those accepted as an officer was Charlton Ogburn, Jr, who recalled Hunter as possessing 'a mouth that was a straight line across a firm jaw, the gaze of command in a countenance that sometimes surprised you with its boyish look, a sinewy build, and a bearing that made you unaware of his being of only average height'.[9]

Ogburn, who at 30, was older than the average recruit to the unit, had come from the Signal Corps, a fact that appealed to Hunter. 'I took the occasion to summon up my courage and confess knowing next to nothing about radio,' recalled Ogburn in his memoirs *The Marauders*. 'Colonel

Hunter received this intelligence without wincing: "Then, lieutenant," he said, "you had better learn something about it."[10]

Two battalions were raised from volunteers in the United States, and a third from veteran soldiers of the Pacific campaign already stationed overseas. The unit was codenamed 'Galahad', and on 21 September the 1st and 2nd battalions sailed from San Francisco aboard the liner *Lurline* on a 42-day voyage for India.* Ogburn recalled that as he got to know some of his new comrades he was struck by a common thread that ran through them, despite the fact that they came from all corners of the United States. 'Each of them had something egging him on,' he wrote. 'In some it was the wildness of the hunting male or the nomadic instinct that is never reconciled to the settlement. In some it was a sense of what was owing a cause in which so many hundreds of thousands were having to die ... in the younger members of my platoon it was perhaps the simple high-mindedness of youth.'[11]

At New Caledonia, 12 days out from San Francisco, Colonel Hunter collected 670 soldiers of the 3rd Battalion, many of whom were veterans of the bitter fighting on Guadalcanal. A further 270 officers and men joined the 3rd Battalion when they arrived in Brisbane, so by the time the force arrived in India at the end of October they were at full strength. From Bombay, Hunter led Galahad 150 miles east to the town of Deolali where training began in earnest.

On the voyage out the men had been issued with a booklet on jungle fighting, based on the lessons learned by the Chindits. The men of Galahad already had a basic understanding of what lay ahead, and throughout November and December they were trained to be experts in junglecraft. Hunter shared the same view that soldiers must demonstrate initiative and also show versatility; in other words everyone had a basic knowledge of first aid, radio communications and mortar firing. In addition the Americans learned how to navigate, track, camouflage and fight at close quarters in the jungle. Above all, Hunter instilled in them a respect for but not a fear of the jungle, just as Mike Calvert had done with the Chindits a year earlier.

---

* Despite being officially designated the 5307th Composite Unit and later known in the press as 'Merrill's Marauders', the men referred to themselves as 'Galahad'.

Hunter procured 700 mules and, having heard of the difficulties faced by the Chindits in trying to get pack animals across a 100-yard-wide river while being chased by Japanese soldiers, he ensured he had a group of expert handlers who could get the mules over the river in the shortest time possible. At times Hunter allowed the men to relax and enjoy themselves with sport or games, but there was one rule never to be broken. 'I don't want to see anyone taking sun baths,' he told the men at Deolali. 'I don't know why it should be, but I've found that people who take sun baths are difficult to get along with.'[12]

By late December 1943 Galahad was taking shape, but further up the chain of command there were problems. Initially the idea had been that the American force would be under the command of Wingate, who intended to deploy them in central Burma in tandem with his own Chindits to attack the Japanese 18th Division's lines of supply and communications. This enraged Stilwell. He wanted Galahad to support his own offensive (using two Chinese divisions) in Burma to open up an overland supply route into China. The final decision on the matter rested with Lord Louis Mountbatten, Supreme Commander of the South-East Asian Theatre, and he acceded to Stilwell's demands, a decision that would have grim consequences for Galahad. According to Hunter, when he broke the news to Wingate he replied: 'You can tell General Stilwell that he can take his Americans and … [the language here being of even more than Old Testament plain-spokenness].'[13]

It wasn't until 1 January 1944 that Galahad was officially recognized as a regiment with Colonel Hunter its commanding officer. Ogburn recalled that by now the force had a strong sense of its own identity and this was down to the 'steadying influence' of its leader and that of the CO of the 1st Battalion, Lieutenant Colonel William Osborne. 'Each in accordance with his temperament, they gave an impression of being unworried, confident and knowing what they were about – the essentials of leadership.'[14]

Three days later, however, on 4 January, Galahad was reconstituted as the 5307th Composite Unit under the command of General Frank Merrill, a former West Point classmate of Hunter's. Merrill was two years older than Hunter and a different character entirely. Whereas Hunter was a lean, wiry, tough professional soldier, Merrill was a military engineer who had served as a military attaché in Tokyo in the late 1930s. Hunter spoke his mind, but Merrill preferred the language of diplomacy and his ability to accommodate opinions had helped him in his rapid rise through the ranks. With poor eyesight and a weak heart, Merrill was an unwise choice to command a unit about to embark on a Long Range Penetration deep into the Burmese jungle, but he was a favourite of Stilwell's. In Hunter's opinion his successor was 'rather tall, he was by no means a rugged individual, being narrow of chest and rather thin. His features were sharp but his nature ebullient, affable and confident.'[15]

Not long after the appointment of Merrill, the unit was ordered to move to Ledo in Assam by 7 February.* Hunter grumbled that the unit was 'not completely equipped or, by any stretch of the imagination, fully organized and trained'.

To compensate for the curtailment of their training in India, Hunter hatched a plan that he executed once Galahad reached their staging area of Margherita in Assam. Ahead of them lay a 150-mile route along the Ledo Road to Shingbwiyang, the airstrip and supply base from where they would embark on their first Long Range Penetration. The route, as Ogburn remembered, was 'a wilderness of mountains rising from near sea level to two 4,000ft passes'. Hunter had the three battalions of Galahad march the route in ten days. 'More than any other single part of Galahad's training, the hike down the Ledo Road, in my professional judgment, paid the highest dividends,'[16] Hunter later wrote.

Once they had arrived at Shingbwiyang the men and the mules were hardened and the few weaklings had been rooted out and returned to their unit. Fifteen miles south of Shingbwiyang was Ningam Sakan, where General Stilwell had established his HQ following the successful early advance of his Chinese force into Burma. Hunter and Merrill marched Galahad through Ningam Sakan the day after reaching Shingbwiyang in the expectation of

---

* The small town of Ledo gave its name to the road used by the Allies as the main supply route to China through Burma and was an alternative to the Japanese-built Burma Road although the original plan had been to connect the two routes.

being warmly greeted by their commander, but 'the occasion proved, unfortunately, to be one of those on which Stilwell missed the chance of an inexpensive gesture that could have repaid him in days to come'.

Stilwell did appear a couple of days later, however, to issue instructions about the forthcoming operation. Stretched out to the south was the Hukawng Valley in which were an estimated 7,000 Japanese troops of the 18th Division; Stilwell ordered Galahad to penetrate into the valley and outflank and destroy the enemy in order to leave the way open for the continued advance south of his two Chinese divisions. Outnumbered by more than two to one, the American troops also had inferior firepower, relying on light assault weapons such as bazookas and 60mm mortars.

Hunter and Merrill led the 2,750-strong Galahad out of their camp in the early hours of 24 February. Ahead of them lay an eight-day march east to allow them to then wheel around and attack the right flank of the Japanese defenders. A reconnaissance platoon was despatched first from each of the three battalions, and when they rendezvoused with the main force a few days later Hunter exuded 'paternal pride' as he listened to their reports on the dispositions of the Japanese forces.

Galahad received supply drops as they marched east, the most prized item being the 3,000-calorie one-a-day K-ration, which while better than the Chindits rations was 1,000 calories short of what Hunter had requested the previous September. For the first fortnight Galahad saw hardly any trace of the enemy but reconnaissance patrols, aided by Kachin scouts, reported that a large force of Japanese was stationed at Walawbum, a village that lay on the Kamaing Road, down which Stilwell's army intended to advance. In the approach to Walawbum in early March there were a number of brief skirmishes. In one such incident Hunter and a small unit encountered a body of Japanese soldiers as they made for a rendezvous point with the 1st Provisional Tank Group (which was unable to penetrate the jungle). In the ensuing firefight Hunter and his men accounted for two of the enemy and caused the others to flee.

The main fight for Walawbum began on 5 March with the 2nd Battalion taking the brunt of the six Japanese infantry attacks, interspersed with artillery bombardments, during a 36-hour period. Nonetheless, the battalion suffered just one fatality and five wounded while killing more than 100 of the enemy. The Japanese withdrew and Merrill assumed the fight for Walawbum was finished, but the enemy came again a few hours later, this time launching themselves against the positions held by the 3rd Battalion a little to the south-west of the 2nd Battalion. Ogburn recalled how the Japanese soldiers 'spurred on by their cries of *Susume! Susume!* [Advance!] and *Banzai!* by their leaders, had come fanning out over the grassy clearing on the other side in successive waves'.[17]

Yet despite the brave ferocity of the Japanese, they were repelled by the disciplined defence of the 3rd Battalion over three days. By 7 March Walawbum was firmly under the control of Galahad, and the failed attack had cost the enemy 800 dead.

Though only eight Americans had been killed and 37 wounded during the battle for Walawbum, the 11-day operation had diminished the unit's total strength in other ways: 136 men had been evacuated suffering from malaria, dysentery and other illnesses; 33 had suffered various injuries and ten soldiers had been removed owing to 'psychoneurosis'.

The 2,300 men who were fit to continue enjoyed a couple of days' rest and recuperation at Shikau Ga, five miles north of Walawbum, before Galahad continued south on 12 March with instructions to harass the Japanese at Jambu Bum. 'This low range of hills, with its barbaric name, formed the southern end of the Hukawng Valley,' recalled Ogburn. Contrary to the wishes of Merrill and Hunter, Stilwell had ordered that Galahad be split in two with the 1st Battalion making for the village of Shaduzup, and the 2nd and 3rd battalions tasked with seizing Nhpum Ga, 15 miles to the south-east.

The 1st Battalion set off first and 20 miles were accomplished in two days but the next 30 took two weeks as the terrain and the enemy hindered their progress. The battalion diary for 20 March was typical of the daily difficulties which Galahad had to confront:

The first battalion marched over difficult trails to Nprawa Ga where our lead platoon hit a Jap machine gun blocking the trail. We had one man killed and two wounded before the gun and crew were wiped out by mortar fire on their block.[18]

More and more men began succumbing to disease, with an outbreak of amoebic dysentery decimating the force, and there were also the hateful leeches, which Ogburn described as 'rubbery monsters, black worms with suction cups at both ends ... with the capacity of clamping on and opening a lesion without your feeling anything'.[19] Nonetheless 1st Battalion had achieved their objectives, clearing a trail through the Jambu Bum to the village of Shaduzup where a fierce engagement ended with 300 Japanese and eight Americans dead.

The other force, meanwhile, had split with 3rd Battalion securing an airstrip in the valley of Hsamsingyang and the 2nd Battalion four miles south at Nhpum Ga. Both came under sustained attack from the Japanese, with the latter besieged for 11 days. Medics, signalmen and cooks took up arms as wave after wave of Japanese assaults were beaten back. Only the dropping of fresh supplies from the air enabled the 2nd Battalion to continue its defence of Nhpum Ga, while at Galahad's command post at Hsamsingyang Hunter kept a cool head. More Japanese were rumoured to be approaching from the east, threatening an encirclement of the three battalions and alarming Captain John George of the 3rd Battalion. 'Don't you ever get scared?' he asked Hunter, whose philosophy was that it was beholden on an officer to keep his fear in a foxhole. 'Wait till you've had twins,' Hunter replied to George.[20]

The Japanese never appeared from the east and finally on 9 April, Easter Sunday, the 3rd Battalion fought its way through to reinforce their comrades and drive the enemy from Nhpum Ga. The two battalions had lost 50 men and had another 314 wounded (the Japanese lost 400 killed) in the fighting for Nhpum Ga. Also evacuated from the area was General Merrill, who had suffered a heart attack on March 28.* Hunter took over command and wrote later: 'I had no warning of Merrill's approaching illness. He had not undergone any violent exercise in the last few days to have placed a strain on his heart. I knew he was using some kind of thick purplish medicine taken with water which he told me was for dysentery.'[21]

---

* Around this time news reached Galahad of Wingate's death, an event that Ogburn said reinforced the view that the Burma campaign was riddled with 'ill chance'.

One of the first instructions issued by Hunter in the hours following the seizure of Nhpum Ga was for 500lb of chloride of lime to be dropped by air. With this he ordered his men to burn the carcasses of all the mules killed in the fighting so as to disperse the huge black cloud of flies feeding on the animals' bloated bodies.

By now the fighting strength of Galahad was approximately 1,500 and many of those men were exhausted and undernourished, desperate for the Chinese 38th Division to arrive so that they could be withdrawn to India. Then, what Ogburn remembered as a 'grotesque rumour' began to be heard among the men, to the effect that Stilwell had ordered them to capture the airfield at Myitkyina, approximately 90 miles south-east. The rumours gained credence when Hunter sent a reconnaissance patrol led by Captain William Laffin to explore the trail leading east over the 6,100ft Kumon mountain range.

Myitkyina airfield was considered vital to the Allied cause in Burma. With it in their possession they could considerably increase the supplies being ferried by air from India over the eastern end of the Himalayas to China (what was colloquially known by pilots as 'The Hump'). Yet for Stilwell and his 'stuffed baboons'[22] (Galahad's nickname for his staff officers) to task their three depleted battalions with the mission was beyond the comprehension of most of Hunter's men. They had been in the field for two months, the same length of time that the Chindits had endured during Operation *Longcloth* in 1943, and the unit was in urgent need of a lengthy rest. But there was to be none. Stilwell wrote in his diary: 'Galahad is OK. Hard fight at Nhpum. Cleaned out Japs and hooked up. No worry there.' Then he ordered them to take Myitkyina airfield.

They set out on 1 May in three columns. Hunter's was the first to depart, composed of the 1st Battalion and the Chinese 150th Infantry Regiment. Colonel Henry Kinnison commanded the second column (3rd Battalion and Chinese 88th Infantry Regiment) and the third was led by Colonel George McGee and comprised the thin ranks of the 2nd Battalion and 300 Kachin troops.

Hunter's march towards Myitkyina was subsequently described in the *New York Times* in its edition of 21 May. 'Often they followed paths known only to the Kachin tribes of the region and often climbed mountains that were so steep they were only able to make a few miles a day,' wrote Tillman Durdin, a Texan reporter who had broken the news of the Japanese massacre at Nanking in 1937. 'At times they picked their way along precipices through a rolling cloudbank where pack mules weakened and tottered and went over the side to pile up in the misty valley 1,000 feet below.'

During the agonizing march towards the target, 149 men dropped out, most through exhaustion and sickness, and one or two to snake bites. Hunter pushed on regardless until, in the late afternoon of 16 May, they were within striking distance of the airfield. Hunter decided to attack the following morning to exploit the Japanese habit of withdrawing into the surrounding woods during daylight to shelter from Allied air attack.

When the assault took place on 17 May it was executed with perfect timing, the Chinese 150th Infantry Regiment attacking the Japanese positions in the east while the 1st Battalion eliminated the airfield defences. At 1030hrs Hunter sent a message to Stilwell, saying: 'In the ring' – code for the successful seizure of the airfield.

Stilwell was ecstatic at the news, yelling 'This will burn up the Limeys'.[23] In six months his forces had advanced 500 miles into Burma and now had the key prize of Myitkyina airfield. But what he did not have was Myitkyina itself, two miles to the east. Two battalions of Chinese infantry were repulsed later on the afternoon of 17 May, and a further Chinese attack the following day also ended in failure. A third assault was ordered by Stilwell, which again was unsuccessful, and by now the Chinese had suffered 671 casualties in three attempts to oust the Japanese from Myitkyina.

Meanwhile, at his temporary command post at the airfield, Hunter was becoming increasingly exasperated with the failure to resupply his men with food and ammunition. Instead the first aircraft that touched down brought an engineer aviation company and a unit of anti-aircraft troops. Hunter soon realized that Stilwell and his 'stuffed baboons' had no plan to consolidate Galahad's position after their stunning capture of the airfield. As Ogburn reflected of Hunter's position: 'He did not know whether he was to attack the town, cross the river, or what. Indeed, he was never ordered to take Myitkyina, and when on the 18th Stilwell visited the airstrip and Hunter told him he was going to take the town, Stilwell only grunted.'[24]

General Merrill suddenly appeared on the scene but proved ineffective in stating Galahad's case; he was still poorly and Merrill wasn't a man who liked to rock the boat. Then on 19 May Merrill suffered another heart attack and was evacuated. This time Stilwell, instead of instructing Hunter to take over command, appointed Colonel John McCammon to lead Galahad. 'Why Colonel Hunter was not put in command we could never understand,' said Ogburn. 'Hunter had as much commissioned service behind him as Merrill himself, had had far more experience than Merrill with tactical units, knew intimately the tools he would be working with, and was an outstanding soldier.' The reason was simple: Stilwell didn't like Hunter and viewed his strength of character as a threat.

On 23 May the Japanese, emboldened by the failure of the American and Chinese to seize Myitkyina, launched a counter-attack with the aim of recapturing the airfield. The assault was resisted but now on average 100 men from Galahad were being evacuated each day through wounds, exhaustion and disease. Stilwell landed on the airfield on 25 May and waiting for him was Hunter, no longer able to contain his fury at the broken promises and mismanagement of a once-proud force. He handed Stilwell a statement in which he listed his grievances and accused his commanding officer of having treated Galahad 'as a visiting unit for which Theater Headquarters felt no responsibility'. As a consequence, continued Hunter, 'Galahad was now practically unfit for combat with the consequence that the sense of security afforded by its presence at Myitkyina was false.' To prove his point, Hunter brought it to Stilwell's attention that of the 3,000 men who had arrived in India a little over six months earlier, only 200 were fit enough to fight. Even Stilwell seemed to get the message, confiding to his diary: 'Galahad is just shot.'[25]

Unfortunately for Hunter there was nothing that could be done in the short term to alleviate Galahad's suffering. The Japanese were once again threatening to attack the airfield, so the 200 survivors remained at Myitkyina, reinforced by an assortment of American troops from south-east Asia. Even the two engineer battalions in the district were given crash courses in combat fighting in the event of a major Japanese offensive against the airfield. In charge of this disparate force – which included remnants of four Chinese regiments – was Hunter. With bitter irony he dubbed it 'the new Galahad', but it was nothing of the sort. The spirit of the original Galahad had been practically extinguished by a combination of sickness, Stilwell and the Japanese.

However, the Japanese attack never materialized and instead on 3 August the Americans were able to seize Myitkyina. Allied successes elsewhere in Burma (including the capture of Mogaung by the Chindits) forced the Japanese into a retreat from Imphal over the Chin Hills, the first steps on the road to eventual victory in Burma for the Allies.

Hunter's reward for the capture of Myitkyina was to be relieved of his command, the day the town fell – just two days after Stilwell had been promoted from lieutenant general to full general. Two months later Stilwell suffered a similar humiliation when he was summoned back to the States at the insistence of Generalissimo Chiang Kai-Shek, who had finally tired of the obnoxious American. By then, however, the 5307th Composite Unit had ceased to exist. Disbanded a week after they had taken Myitkyina, those who remained from the unit were incorporated into the 475th Infantry Regiment, albeit having been recognized by a Distinguished Unit Citation for Galahad's operations in Burma. The citation ended by declaring that the 'unit proved equal to its task and after a brilliant operation of 17 May 1944 seized the airfield at Myitkyina, an objective of great tactical importance in the campaign, and assisted in the capture of the town of Myitkyina on 3 August 1944'.[26]

✦ ✦ ✦ ✦

Stilwell died a little over a year after the end of war, succumbing to stomach cancer in a San Francisco hospital in October 1946. He was 63. Few who had served under him mourned his passing. Frank Merrill died nine years later, aged 52, having never fully recovered from his heart attacks suffered in Burma.

In 1962, seven years after the death of Merrill, Hollywood released a film based on the exploits of the 5307th Composite Unit in Burma; it was called *Merrill's Marauders* and Frank Merrill and Joseph Stilwell both featured prominently. Charles Hunter did not, although a man of his temperament probably didn't care much for Hollywood. After the war Hunter – who was married with three daughters (two of whom he outlived) served as deputy chief of staff of the 4th Army and was the commanding officer of Fort Sam Houston in Texas. He died in Wyoming in 1978 aged 72, largely forgotten by the general public who – thanks to the entertainment industry – believed that Frank Merrill had been the driving force behind America's Special Forces in Burma. The veterans of the 5307th Composite Unit – who never referred to themselves as 'Merrill's Marauders' – knew better. As Charles Ogburn wrote in his introduction to *The Marauders*:

Colonel Charles N Hunter had been with Galahad from the start as its ranking or second ranking officer, had commanded it during its times of greatest trial, and was more responsible than any other individual for its record of achievement.

ENDNOTES

INTRODUCTION

1. Alan Hoe, *David Stirling* (Warner Books, 1994)
2. Lecture broadcast on BBC March 1945, Mike Calvert Papers, Imperial War Museum

ANDERS LASSEN

1. Brook Richards, interview with the Imperial War Museum
2. Mike Langley, *Anders Lassen of the SAS* (New English Library, 1988)
3. Ibid
4. Ibid
5. Ibid
6. Ibid
7. Ibid
8. Stephen Hastings, *Drums of Memory* (Pen & Sword, 1994)
9. Langley, *Anders Lassen of the SAS*
10. Ibid
11. Interview with the author, July 2002
12. John Lodwick, *The Filibusters* (Methuen & Co., 1947)
13. Interview with the author
14. Langley, *Anders Lassen of the SAS*
15. Ibid

16. Ibid
17. Interview with the author
18. Ibid
19. Ibid
20. Ibid
21. Ken Smith, interview with the Imperial War Museum
22. Ibid
23. Ibid
24. Ibid
25. Langley, *Anders Lassen of the SAS*
26. Ibid
27. Ken Smith, interview with the Imperial War Museum
28. Langley, *Anders Lassen of the SAS*

DAVID STIRLING

1. Gavin Mortimer, *Stirling's Men* (Cassell, 2004)
2. Alan Hoe, *David Stirling* (Warner Books, 1994)
3. Johnny Cooper, *One of the Originals* (Pan, 1991)
4. Hoe, *David Stirling*
5. Ibid
6. Ibid
7. Public Record Office, *Special Forces in the Desert War 1940–43* (Public Record Office War Histories, 2001)
8. David Stirling, *Origins of the Special Air Service* (SAS archives)
9. Ibid
10. Ibid
11. Hamish Ross, *Paddy Mayne* (Sutton, 2003)
12. Cooper, *One of the Originals*
13. Stirling, *Origins of the Special Air Service*
14. Public Record Office, *Special Forces in the Desert War 1940–43*
15. Interview with the author, 2001
16. Interview with the author, 2003
17. Public Record Office, *Special Forces in the Desert War 1940–43*
18. Ibid
19. Hoe, *David Stirling*
20. Interview with the author, 2002

21. Interview with the author, 1998
22. Courtesy of interview with John Kane, 1997
23. John Strawson, *A History of the SAS Regiment* (Guild, 1984)
24. IInterview with the author, 2001
25. Hoe, *David Stirling*
26. Interview with the author, 2001
27. Interview with the author, 2002
28. Stirling, *Origins of the Special Air Service*
29. Interview with the author, 2001
30. Ibid
31. Interview with the author, 2002
32. Public Record Office, *Special Forces in the Desert War 1940–43*
33. Interview with the author, 2001
34. Hoe, *David Stirling*
35. Malcolm Pleydell, *Born of the Desert* (Greenhill Books, 2006)
36. Brian Dillon, interview with the Imperial War Museum
37. Hoe, *David Stirling*
38. Interview with the author, 2002
39. Ibid
40. Gavin Mortimer, *The SAS in World War II: An Illustrated History* (Osprey Publishing, 2011)
41. Hoe, *David Stirling*
42. Ibid
43. Ibid

EDSON RAFF

1. Speech given by Raff at 1997 Airborne Awards and quoted at http://www.thedropzone.org
2. Edson Raff, *We Jumped to Fight* (Eagle Books, 1944)
3. Ibid
4. Letter quoted in *We Jumped to Fight*
5. Ibid
6. Ibid
7. *Time* magazine, 12 October 1942
8. Raff, *We Jumped to Fight*
9. Ibid

10. Ibid
11. Dwight D. Eisenhower, *Crusade in Europe* (The John Hopkins University Press, 1997)
12. By kind permission of Patrick O'Donnell

EVANS CARLSON

1. John Wukovits, *American Commando* (Caliber, 2009)
2. Ibid
3. Ibid
4. Ibid
5. Ibid
6. Ibid
7. *Reader's Digest*, December 1943
8. Wukovits, *American Commando*
9. Ibid
10. General Merrill Twining, *No Bended Knee* (Presido, 1994)
11. Oscar Peatross, *Bless 'em all* (ReView Publications, 1995)

ROBERT FREDERICK

1. Howitzer Year Book, available to view at http://www.e-yearbook.com
2. Robert Adleman and George Walton, *The Devil's Brigade* (Corgi, 1968)
3. Ibid
4. Ibid
5. Ibid
6. Ibid
7. Ibid
8. Ibid
9. *Stars and Stripes*, February 1944
10. US National Archives
11. Clarke Lee, International News Service, date unknown

PADDY MAYNE

1. Gavin Mortimer, *Fields of Glory* (Andre Deutsch, 2001)
2. Ibid
3. Ibid
4. Ibid
5. Gavin Mortimer, *Stirling's Men* (Weidenfeld & Nicolson, 2004)
6. Gavin Mortimer, *The SAS in World War II: An Illustrated History* (Osprey Publishing, 2011)
7. Courtesy of an interview with John Kane, 1997
8. Interview with the author, 2002
9. Malcom Pleydell, *Born of the Desert* (Greenhill Books, 2006)
10. Interview with the author, 1998
11. Interview with the author, 2003
12. John Byrne, *The General Salutes a Soldier* (Hale, 1986)
13. Mortimer, *Fields of Glory*
14. Pleydell, *Born of the Desert*
15. Mortimer, *Stirling's Men*
16. Ibid
17. Ibid
18. Ibid
19. Ibid
20. Ibid
21. Mortimer, *The SAS in World War II: An Illustrated History*
22. Interview with the author, 2002
23. Mortimer, *The SAS in World War II: An Illustrated History*
24. Interview with the author, 2002
25. Interview with the author, 2003
26. Interview with the author, 2003
27. Interview with the author, 2002
28. *The Times*, 9 November 2009
29. Mortimer, *Stirling's Men*
30. Michael Calvert, *Fighting Mad* (Pen & Sword, 2004)
31. Mortimer, *The SAS in World War II: An Illustrated History*
32. Hamish Ross, *Paddy Mayne* (Sutton 2003)
33. *Mars and Minerva*, April 1956

RALPH BAGNOLD

1. Julian Thompson, *The War Behind Enemy Lines* (Pan, 1999)
2. Bagnold Papers, Churchill Archives, Cambridge
3. Ibid
4. Ibid
5. Ibid
6. Ralph Bagnold, *The Physics of Blown Sand and Desert Dunes* (Springer, 1971)
7. Bagnold Papers, Churchill Archives, Cambridge
8. Ibid
9. Ibid
10. Ibid
11. Ibid
12. Ibid
13. Ibid
14. Ibid
15. Thompson, *The War Behind Enemy Lines*
16. Ibid
17. Bagnold Papers, Churchill Archives, Cambridge
18. Ibid
19. Thompson, *The War Behind Enemy Lines*
20. Les Sullivan interview with the Imperial War Museum
21. Bagnold Papers, Churchill Archives, Cambridge
22. Ibid
23. Ibid
24. Les Sullivan interview with the Imperial War Museum
25. Ibid
26. David Lloyd-Owen, *The Long Range Desert Group: Providence their guide* (Harap, 1980)
27. Interview with the author, 2003
28. Public Record Office, *Special Forces in the Desert War 1940–43* (Public Record Office War Histories, 2001)
29. Bagnold Papers, Churchill Archives, Cambridge

JUNIO VALERIO BORGHESE

1. *The Times*, 3 September 1974
2. Junio Valerio Borghese, *Sea Devils* (Naval Institute Press, 1995)
3. Ibid
4. Ibid
5. Interview with Emilio Bianchi at http://www.regiamarina.net.
6. Ibid
7. Borghese, *Sea Devils*
8. Interview with Emilio Bianchi
9. Borghese, *Sea Devils*
10. Ibid
11. Interview with Emilio Bianchi
12. Ibid
13. Ibid
14. Borghese, *Sea Devils*
15. Interview with Emilio Bianchi
16. Borghese, *Sea Devils*
17. Interview with Emilio Bianchi
18. Reproduced in Borghese, *Sea Devils*
19. Ibid
20. William Schofield, *Frogmen: First Battles* (Branden Publishing, 1987)
21. Reproduced in Borghese, *Sea Devils*
22. Courtesy of www://cronologia.leonardo.it/storia/biografie/borghese.html

BARON VON DER HEYDTE

1. Samuel Mitcham Jr, *Defenders of fortress Europe: the untold story of the German officers during the Allied Invasion* (Potomac Books, 2009)
2. Baron Friedrich von der Heydte, *Return to Crete* (WDL, 1959, translation by Stanley Moss)
3. Ibid
4. Ibid
5. Ibid
6. Ibid

7. Ibid
8. Ibid
9. Ibid
10. Franz Kurowski, *Jump Into Hell* (Stackpole Press, 2010)
11. Ibid
12. Ibid
13. Ibid
14. Ibid

ADRIAN VON FÖLKERSAM

1. Interviews by Dr Heaten conducted with Hans-Dietrich Hossfelder in 1985 and 1994
2. Ibid
3. Otto Skorzeny, *Skorzeny's Special Missions* (Greenhill Books, 2006)
4. Ibid
5. Ibid
6. Ibid
7. Ibid
8. Ibid
9. Ibid
10. Ibid
11. Ibid
12. Ibid
13. Ibid
14. Ibid
15. Ibid
16. Ibid
17. Ibid
18. Interviews by Dr Heaten conducted with Hans-Dietrich Hossfelder in 1985 and 1994

ORDE WINGATE

1. Kirby and Woodburn, *The Official History, The War Against Japan, Volume III* (London HMSO, 1961)
2. Mike Calvert papers, Imperial War Museum

3. Ibid

4. Trevor Royle, *Orde Wingate* (Weidenfeld & Nicolson, 1995)

5. Ibid

6. Ibid

7. Ibid

8. Mike Calvert papers, Imperial War Museum

9. Ibid

10. Ibid

11. Ibid

12. Denis Gudgeon, Imperial War Museum Sound 2986

13. Ibid

14. Ibid

15. Ibid

16. Ibid

17. Royle, *Orde Wingate*

18. Available to view at http://www.chindits.info

19. Michael Calvert, *Fighting Mad* (Pen & Sword, 2004)

20. Bernard Fergusson, *Beyond the Chindwin* (Fontana, 1955)

21. Calvert, *Fighting Mad*

22. Fergusson, *Beyond the Chindwin*

23. Mike Calvert papers, Imperial War Museum

24. Ibid

25. Ibid

26. Draft narrative of operations of 77th Indian Infantry Brigade, CAB 106/46, National Archives

27. A.D. Harvey, *Collision of Empires: Britain in three world wars, 1793–1945* (Hambledon, 2003)

28. Royle, *Orde Wingate*

29. Calvert, *Fighting Mad*

30. Harold Shippey, Imperial War Museum Sound 12164

31. Mike Calvert papers, Imperial War Museum

32. Calvert, *Fighting Mad*

33. Mike Calvert papers, Imperial War Museum

34. Ibid

35. Calvert, *Fighting Mad*

36. Mike Calvert papers, Imperial War Museum

37. Letter from Slim to Major General Woodburn-Kirby, 1959, quoted in Trevor Royle, *Orde Wingate*

38. John Masters, *The Road Past Mandalay* (Phoenix, 2012)

39. Royle, *Orde Wingate*

CHARLES HUNTER

1. John Masters, *The Road Past Mandalay* (Phoenix, 2012)

2. Ibid

3. Charlton Ogburn, *The Marauders* (The Overlook Press, 2002)

4. Trevor Royle, *Orde Wingate* (Weidenfeld & Nicolson, 1995)

5. Ogburn, *The Marauders*

6. Masters, *The Road Past Mandalay*

7. Royle, *Orde Wingate*

8. West Point 'Howitzer' Yearbook, Class of 1929

9. Ogburn, *The Marauders*

10. Ibid

11. Ibid

12. Ibid

13. Ibid

14. Ibid

15. Charles Newton Hunter, *Galahad* (Naylor Co., 1963)

16. Ogburn, *The Marauders*

17. Ibid

18. Ibid

19. Ibid

20. Ibid

21. Hunter, *Galahad*

22. Masters, *The Road Past Mandalay*

23. Ibid

24. Ogburn, *The Marauders*

25. Masters, *The Road Past Mandalay*

26. Ogburn, *The Marauders*

GLOSSARY

88mm	a German anti-tank and anti-aircraft gun
AA	anti-aircraft
Abwehr	the German military intelligence organization
BAR	Browning Automatic Rifle
Brandenburgers	German Special Forces unit
Bren gun	Czech-derived British light machine gun with a range of 2,000 yards
C-47 aircraft	a military transport aircraft manufactured by Douglas Aircraft Company
CAA	Civil Aviation Authority
Caique	a Greek fishing boat used by the Special Boat Squadron
CO	commanding officer
DCM	Distinguished Conduct Medal, the equivalent of the DSO – second only to the VC – and awarded to NCOs and other ranks
DSO	Distinguished Service Order, the second highest British military decoration for officers
DZ	drop zone, for paratroopers and supplies

EAM	National Liberation Front, a left-wing political movement in Greece composed predominantly of Communists
EDAS	National Republican Greek League, a non-communist Greek resistance group
ELAS	Greek People's Liberation Army and the military arm of the EAM
Fallschirmjäger	German parachute regiment
Führer	German for leader, the title given to Adolf Hitler
Garand	the .30 calibre M1 Garand was the semi-automatic rifle issued to US troops
Gestapo	*Geheime Staatspolizei*, the secret police force of Nazi Germany
GHQ	General Headquarters
Gurkhas	Nepalese soldiers who have served in the British Army for nearly 200 years
Italian Gold Medal	a medal awarded to Italian junior officers and soldiers for deeds of outstanding gallantry in war
Italian Silver Medal	a medal awarded to Italian junior officers and soldiers who distinguished themselves in combat
Iron Cross	a German military decoration categorized into first and second class
Knight's Cross of the Iron Cross	superior to the Iron Cross and awarded for outstanding bravery or leadership in the face of the enemy
LCA	Landing Craft Assault, 12m-long vessel capable of carrying 35 men
Légion d'honneur	the highest decoration in France, divided into five categories
LRDG	Long Range Desert Group
MC	Military Cross

Medal of Honor	the highest military decoration awarded by the United States
MEHQ	Middle East Headquarters
NCO	non-commissioned officer
petrol bowser	a petrol tanker
'pigs'	Italian term for human torpedoes
RAF	Royal Air Force
RTU'd	Returned to Unit
SAS	Special Air Service
SBS	Special Boat Squadron
SFHQ	Special Forces Headquarters
SHAEF	Supreme Headquarters Allied Expeditionary Force
Sherman	the M4 Sherman was the most common tank of the US Army
SOE	Special Operations Executive
SRS	Special Raiding Squadron
SS	*Schutzstaffel*, the paramilitary force of Nazi Germany
SSRF	Small Scale Raiding Force
Tommy gun	Thompson sub-machine gun
VC	Victoria Cross
Vickers K	rapid-firing machine gun designed for aircraft and later used by the SAS
wadi	a dry river bed in the desert that contains water only when it rains heavily
WAAF	Women's Auxiliary Air Force
Waffen SS	the military force of the *Schutzstaffel*

BIBLIOGRAPHY

Adleman, Robert and George Walton, *The Devil's Brigade* (Corgi, 1968)

Ambrose, Stephen, *Band of Brothers* (Simon & Schuster, 1992)

Asher, Michael, *The Regiment* (Penguin, 2007)

Bagnold, Ralph, *The Physics of Blown Sand and Desert Dunes* (Springer, 1971)

Blackman, Mike, *Paddy Mayne Diary* (unpublished, 1945)

Borghese, J. Valerio, *Sea Devils* (Naval Institute Press, 1995)

Byrne, John, *The General Salutes a Soldier* (Hale, 1986)

Calvert, Michael, *Fighting Mad* (Pen & Sword, 2004)

Cooper, Johnny, *One of the Originals* (Pan, 1991)

Cowles, Virginia, *The Phantom Major* (Collins, 1958)

Devlin, Gerard M., *Paratrooper!* (St Martin's Press, 1979)

Fergusson, Bernard, *Beyond the Chindwin* (Fontana, 1955)

Gilchrist, Donald, *Castle Commando* (Oliver & Boyd, 1960)

Hastings, Stephen, *Drums of Memory* (Pen & Sword, 1994)

von der Heydte, Baron Friedrich, *Return to Crete* (WDL, 1959)

Hoe, Alan, *David Stirling* (Warner Books, 1994)

Hunter, Charles Newton, *Galahad* (Naylor Co., 1963)

James, Malcolm, *Born of the Desert* (Greenhill, 1991)

Keegan, John, *Six Armies in Normandy* (Pimlico, 1992)

Keyes, Elizabeth, *Geoffrey Keyes of the Rommel Raid* (George
      Newnes, 1956)

Kurowski, Franz, *Jump Into Hell* (Stackpole, 2010)

Langley, Mike, *Anders Lassen of the SAS* (New English Library, 1988)

BIBLIOGRAPHY

Lefevre, Eric, *The Brandenburg Division* (Histoire and Collections, 2000)

Linklater, Eric, *The Campaign in Italy* (HMSO, 1951)

Lloyd-Owen, David, *The Long Range Desert Group: Providence Their Guide* (Harap, 1980)

Lodwick, John, *The Filibusters* (Methuen & Co., 1947)

Lucas, James, *Kommando: German Special Forces of World War Two* (Arms & Armour Press, 1985)

Majdalany, Fred, *Cassino: Portrait of a Battle* (Longmans, 1957)

Masters, John, *The Road Past Mandalay* (Phoenix edition, 2012)

Mortimer, Gavin, *Fields of Glory* (Andre Deutsch, 2001)

Mortimer, Gavin, *Stirling's Men* (Weidenfeld & Nicolson, 2004)

Mortimer, Gavin, *The SAS in World War II: An Illustrated History* (Osprey Publishing, 2011)

North, John, *North West Europe* (HMSO, 1953)

Ogburn, Charlton, *The Marauders* (The Overlook Press, 2002)

Peatross, Oscar, *Bless 'em all* (ReView Publications, 1995)

Pitt, Barrie, *The Special Boat Squadron* (Century, 1983)

Pleydell, Malcolm, *Born of the Desert* (Greenhill Books, 2006)

Public Record Office, *Special Forces in the Desert War 1940–43* (Public Record Office War Histories, 2001)

Raff, Edson, *We Jumped to Fight* (Eagle Books, 1944)

Rooney, David, *Mad Mike* (Pen & Sword, 1997)

Ross, Hamish, *Paddy Mayne* (Sutton, 2003)

Royle, Trevor, *Orde Wingate* (Weidenfeld & Nicolson, 1995)

Schmidt, Heinz, *With Rommel in the Desert* (Harap, 1951)

William Schofield, *Frogmen: First Battles* (Branden Publishing, 1987)

Sharpe, Michael and Ian Westwell, *German Elite Forces* (Chartwell Books, 2007)

Skorzeny, Otto, *Skorzeny's Special Missions* (Greenhill Books, 2006)

Strawson, John, *A History of the SAS Regiment* (Guild, 1984)

Thompson, Julian, *The War Behind Enemy Lines* (Pan, 1999)

Tolland, John, *The Last 100 Days* (Bantam, 2000)

Twining, General Merrill, *No Bended Knee* (Presido, 1994)

Woodburn, Kirby S. et al. *The Official History, War Against Japan, Volume III: The Decisive Battles* (HMSO, 1961)

Wukovits, John, *American Commando* (Caliber, 2009)

ACKNOWLEDGEMENTS

First and foremost, I would like to thank all those veterans of the Special Air Service who shared with me their memories of Paddy Mayne, David Stirling and Mike Calvert. Such men are thin on the ground now and their memories are thus more precious than ever. So thank you to Albert Youngman, Mike Sadler, Bob Lowson and Jimmy Storie.

The staff at the Churchill Archives in Cambridge were most helpful in providing me with access to the formidable collection of papers in the Ralph Bagnold collection, as was Simon Offord and his team at the Documents and Sound Department of the Imperial War Museum. Similarly, thank you to the National Archives at Kew and the National Army Museum.

Cristiano D'Adamo kindly let me quote from an interview with Emilio Bianchi conducted by Andrea Piccinotti in the 1990s and which is available to see at http://www.regiamarina.net. Similarly thank you Cy Stapleton and Dr Colin Heaton for permission to quote from interviews Dr Heaten conducted with Hans-Dietrich Hossfelder in 1985 and 1994.

Emily Holmes and Kate Moore at Osprey were their customary efficient selves in the editing of the book and in securing an array of excellent photos.

I would also like to thank the following publishers for their kind permission to quote from the books mentioned: New English Library (*Anders Lassen of the SAS* by Mike Langley); Warner (*David Stirling* by Alan Hoe); Weidenfeld and Nicolson, (*Orde Wingate* by Trevor Royle); Pan (*One of the*

Originals by Johnny Cooper); Greenhill (*Born of the Desert* by Malcolm Pleydell and *Skorzeny's Special Missions* by Otto Skorzeny); Sutton (*Payne Mayne* by Hamish Ross); Stackpole (*Jump Into Hell* by Franz Kurowski); Caliber (*American Commando* by John Wukovits); Eagle Books (*We Jumped to Fight* by Edson Raff); Corgi (*The Devil's Brigade* by Robert Aldeman and George Watson); WDL (*Return to Crete by* Baron von der Heydte); Naval Institute Press (*Sea Devils* by J Valerio Borghese); The Overlook Press (*The Marauders* by Charlton Ogburn). I have tried to contact all copyright holders of material quoted. If I have overlooked any sources I apologise and if the copyright holder concerned would contact me I would happily acknowledge their generosity in future editions of *The Daring Dozen*.

INDEX

INDEX

INDEX

INDEX

Also available from Osprey Publishing as e-books
SAS Heroes by Pete Scholey and *Soldier I* by Pete Winner
and Michael Paul Kennedy

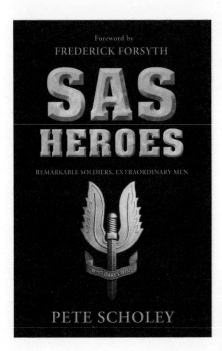

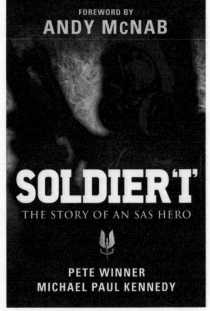